I Have a Story to Tell

R. L. Duane Duff

Surrey, British Columbia, Canada

ISBN 978-0-9810784-5-8
Printed in the United States of America

Duff Publishing
13866 60 Avenue
Surrey, BC V3X 2N1
Canada
www.duffpubishing.ca

To all those with a story to tell.

Acknowledgments

The following have assisted in some way in my efforts to locate participants for this book. I would like to thank each of them.

Daphne Andrychuk *(Alberta Medical Association, Edmonton, Alberta)*
Candy Holland *(Alberta Medical Association, Edmonton, Alberta)*
Sheila Rolfe *(Alberta Teachers Association, Edmonton, Alberta)*
Librarian *(Alberta Library, Edmonton, Alberta)*
Lois Maloney *(Mayor of Vauxhall, Alberta)*
Pam Duff *(my wife, Surrey, British Columbia)*
Robin Duff *(my brother, Victoria, British Columbia)*
Robin Scott *(Blue Springs Service Center, Blue Springs, Missouri)*
Editor and readers (Free Press, *London, Ontario)*
RCMP Headquarters *(Ottawa, Ontario)*
Christelle Bergeron *(Ministère de l'Éducation, du Loisir et du Sport de Québec, Québec)*
Rimantas Mockus *(Vilnius City Municipality, Vilnius, Lithuania)*
Tourist Office *(Vilnius, Lithuania)*
Sean Duff *(my son, Mesa de las Tablas, Coahuila, México)*
Elena Osipova *(Voice of Russia, Moscow, Russia)*
Ramona M. Morel *(Chamber of Commerce, Zurich, Switzerland)*
Bob LaPrelle *(Age of Steam Railroad Museum, Dallas, Texas)*
Librarian *(Remote Reference Service, Houston Public Library, Houston, Texas)*
David Instone-Brewer *(Tyndale House, Cambridge, United Kingdom)*

Contents

Introduction

Surrey, British Columbia, Canada

Have you a story to tell? If so, have you written it down for your family? Even if you do not think that you have one, you probably do.

This book is a collection of experiences which I have been given by friends. Actually, each chapter is like a preview to a movie. It gives a hint to what the complete story of a life has been. Only when the person writes his/her own story will the reader see the complete movie.

Although I am not a professional writer, this has been an enjoyable and an educational experience in preparing these accounts. I wrote letters (email and postal) to people, organizations, and newspapers and made telephone calls in search of about ninety people. About twenty did not respond to my invitation. Although I was disappointed, I appreciated being told by a few that they preferred not to be included and by a few that they were not able to continue because of circumstances which had arisen. Included in this book are the stories of those who did respond with a submission before it was necessary to invoke closure for this volume.

I have been very pleased with all of the submissions. They are of various lengths, based on what I was given. Each one has an educational value, regardless of length. I sent each participant a basic questionnaire and two or three specific questions different for each person. The participants were to use the questionnaire as a guide and could add to or subtract from it. A little over fifty were sent out. Some followed it more closely than others. This has made for a good variation in what each chapter contains. I tried to include as many different vocations and cultures as I was able. However, there are more participants from the area where I currently live.

One reason for my preparing this book is to have something lasting that can be passed down to our children and our grandchildren. I have already written a book of the experiences of my life for them. I hope that some of the participants will consider doing the same for their own descendants, if they have not already done so.

A second reason is that, as I have thought of my friends and acquaintances, I have felt that they might have had experiences in their lives that would be of value and interest to others. After writing these chapters, I believe that I am correct.

A third reason is that I want to acknowledge some of my friends in a book. All have done something for me. It has been an honour for me to have them participate in my project. I am indebted to every one of these fine friends. They have given me the incentive to fulfill a dream of writing that I had as a child but lost when I was in the upper grades of high school.

I would like to thank each person for making a submission and for checking his/her chapter before it was submitted for formatting and printing. I would like to thank our son Sean for his work in preparing my manuscript for the printer. I would like to thank my wife Pam for her encouragement and help in this work. Now, I hope that you will read and enjoy the chapters which follow.

1

Alvin Levitt

Wetaskiwin, Alberta, Canada

He was on lone patrol in Richmond, British Columbia, Canada. A call came in directing him to go to an area of several houses. A man about fifty years of age had gone berserk with a double-barreled shotgun. He had wounded his wife and a neighbour. As Alvin drove up, he saw the crazed man loading and shooting the shotgun around him. The police officer's main concern was to subdue him before others were injured. He determined that the man had fired two shots from the shotgun and had not reloaded. How should he stop the man? He made a quick 100-yard dash and was able to reach him before he reloaded. The officer realized that it was somewhat risky, but he felt that his action would divert the man's attention - which it did. Alvin was able to subdue him, with the man giving no resistance. He did have more shells in his coat pocket. The man later spent approximately ten years in a mental institution.

Alvin was born on a farm near Senlac, Saskatchewan, Canada - a small community in the west central part of the province, not far from the Alberta border. He started to school at Marquis School near Hayter, Alberta, a community in the east central part of the province, not far from the Saskatchewan border. All of his elementary education was obtained here. The school was named after a new strain of wheat that was developed in 1917.

A memorable elementary school experience occurred in 1942 when Marquis School, comprised of twelve pupils, won the Provost School Division Cup for softball, winning over five other teams in the division. What an achievement that was for the tiny school! Alvin continued to grade twelve at the high school in the nearby town of Provost.

After high school, he enrolled for training in the Royal Canadian Mounted Police (RCMP). At that time, part of the training was taken at Regina, Saskatchewan, and part at Rockcliffe, Ontario, near Ottawa, the national capital. At the first place, the courses were Criminal Code of Canada, court procedure, identification methods, first-aid, swimming, life-saving, and others. He obtained an Instructor's Certificate in St. John's Ambulance. At the second place, he participated in equitation breaking and training of the "Black Mounts" for the Musical Ride. During the wartime years, the Ride had been suspended. When it resumed, the first Black Mounts were trained by Alvin's class in 1947-1948.

His Squad 40 broke and conducted the preliminary training of these horses. That started the Musical Ride in 1949. The horses had been raised and mostly halter-broken at the RCMP ranch, which was then near Maple Creek, Saskatchewan. The training consisted of breaking them to ride, jump, passage, change footing while trotting, and preparing them for lance drill, saber drill, and basically to move as a unit. This training was hard for the squad of thirty-two cadets. Some had farm experience, while some had no horse experience at all. Of the thirty-two members, twenty-one graduated from the training, several were injured, some withdrew from the training, and two transferred to Marine Division. It was truly hard training.

After graduating, Alvin was posted to Nova Scotia "H" Division for two years. Postings were to detachments at Chester, Dartmouth, Halifax, Yarmouth, and Barrington Passage. He was then transferred to Manitoba "D" Division for two years. Postings were to detachments at Winnipeg, Beausejour, Piney, Tuxedo, and Portage la Prairie. In 1951, he was transferred to British Columbia "E" Division. He was still single when he arrived, but with over five years service. After two more years, he was able to get married. Postings were to Vancouver, Richmond, Bralorne, Alexis Creek, and Kamloops detachments.

One particular evening patrol he remembers when he was with the Tuxedo detachment. Tuxedo Municipality consisted mainly of patrolling the residential area streets, mostly with expensive homes, thus subject to break-ins. The detachment also covered parts of Fort Gary Municipality, 8 or 10 miles *(13 or 16 km)* to the south. There was a cement plant at Fort Gary; and near this plant was a man-made, fairly deep slough which was off the road about 100 yards *(91 m)* and not fenced. Young people often swam in this pond on warm evenings. One night, some boys, arriving to swim, noticed taillights under the water, still on. This was reported; and, upon investigation, Alvin determined that a car, for an unknown reason, had been driven into the pond; and, subsequently, two young men had drowned. A fence was later erected around the pond. The police were never able to determine the reason for the young men's action, although autopsies proved alcohol in the blood of both victims.

His most interesting years were the four which he and his family spent in the Chilcotin area of the Caribou country of interior British Columbia at a small village called Alexis Creek.

There were eleven Indian reserves in that area, with about 10,000 inhabitants. This region is situated between Bella Coola on the west coast and Williams Lake to the east. To the south, it went into the Bridge River country south of Chilco Lake near Waddington Mountain and to the north into the Nazko country west of Quesnel.

The detachment at that time consisted of two men: Alvin and a single constable. This area covered about 30,000 square miles *(77,700 km²)*, mostly range land and bush, several lakes, and some mountainous areas. That was a huge area to cover! There were only graveled and dirt roads. Many times, patrols were made via Police aircraft because of wet, impassable roads. This area was semi-isolated with no established hydro lines. It had only individual electrical generators powered with gasoline or diesel motors.

Both he and his wife Mable related well to the ranchers, provincial forestry staff, and game commission members, and also to the native population with whom they dealt. The native men quite often became intoxicated from homebrew moonshine and would fight and injure each other. However, Alvin had virtually no trouble with them whenever he had to arrest them. The police dealt most fairly and respectfully with them, and the natives respected them as law enforcement.

During extended patrols when police personnel were absent for two or three days, the corporal's wife became the "third man" and took phone calls and dealt with personal complaints, or at least recorded them. These four years were indeed trying times for all, including the four Levitt children.

By 1972, he had served in the RCMP for twenty-five years. On retirement, he was awarded a Good Conduct medal and ribbon.

Over that time, the family became used to holidays spent on the farm of Alvin's parents in Alberta. Since the children enjoyed farm life, the family decided that a farm was the place to retire. Alvin was able to purchase four 160-acre *(65-ha)* quarters of land a little to the north of the Battle River near Wainwright, Alberta. There, the children finished their schooling and learned the toils, the hazards, and the enjoyments of farm life. All graduated from Wainwright High School.

The family had range cattle, milking cows, and grain crops on their farm. The farm produced well at first when grain and cattle prices were good. It was able to pay for itself, but machinery costs kept increasing during the first twenty years. Education desires of the children became foremost in their lives, and all six children followed those avenues. After twenty years, only the parents were doing the farming, which by then, was reduced to grain production only.

Everyone enjoyed the winter sports on the farm: downhill skiing, cross-country skiing, snowmobiling, and skating. The main joys of farming were the work experiences and farm activities that they shared as a family year after year; both the hazards and the fun times. One daughter married a farm boy and lives on a farm near Senlac, Saskatchewan. The other five children have followed their education and now live the city life. Their oldest daughter is married to an Australian. Both have college teaching positions in the United Arab Emirates, a wealthy - but hot and dry - country.

Trips of significance taken include one to North Island of New Zealand; one to New South Wales and Queensland in Australia; and one to the United Arab Emirates, where all cities and most desert areas were visited.

Alvin has kept busy in his retirement. He served on the Wainwright Hospital Board for a term of eight years. He is ministering to non-resident members of his church, the Community of Christ, throughout the Province of Alberta. In his spare time, he enjoys his music hobby of playing saxophone and clarinet.

Shortly after I became a student at Manitoba Provincial Normal School in 1950, my pastor told me that there was a young RCMP officer, who was a member of our church, at the detachment on the school grounds. I went up to him in the dining hall one evening and introduced myself. Thereafter, I rode to church with him every other week when he was off-duty. Just before he was transferred from Tuxedo, he picked me up after a midweek evening service and took me back to the Normal School in his patrol car. Not long after that, we met at the gate of the school grounds. He informed me of his transfer.

The next time that I saw him was in 1973. We were sitting in our church's campground chapel during a service. We spotted each other and thought that we recognized each other. After the service, we had a visit. Since that time until I retired and left Alberta in 1985, we used to meet at church functions. We were then out of contact until I telephoned him in the summer of 2006 to invite him to participate in this book project.

2

Artena Yvonne Hutchison

Woodstock, Ontario, Canada

She arrived in the city for the first time. It was evening, after office hours. She had never been in this country before. To make matters worse, there was no food in her assigned apartment - and she was hungry! She did not know the local language or currency. Why was this Canadian - a wife and mother - here? How did she cope with her immediate problem? How did she fare during her tour of duty? Before these questions can be answered, we go back to her parents' immigration to Canada.

In May 1948, Adrianus Korevaar traveled on the ship *MS Kota Inten* from Holland to Canada to scout out this vast country and decide if this is where he wanted to live. (He was also interested in Australia.) Deciding it was, he then wrote to his girlfriend Teuntjie that he planned to stay in Canada and asked her if she would join him. Agreeing to do so, she came in July 1949 on the ship, *Volendam*. The young people were married in Norwich, Ontario, (a town south of Woodstock which still today has a large Dutch population) and settled there to begin dairy farming.

Artena was born in a local nursing home, not a hospital, with a midwife's help. She is a proud, first generation Canadian. Her parents did not know any English when they immigrated; and, because they lived within a local Dutch community, they did not learn English very quickly. They had, however, anglicized their names with Adrianus becoming Arthur (Art) and Teuntjie becoming Tina. These names formed the basis of the name Artena. They had seen the name Athena in a baby names book and had liked it. This is her answer when people ask about the nationality of her first name.

When Artena was one year old, her dad decided to stop dairy farming and moved his family to Woodstock, where he began to work at Standard Tube, a local factory. Artena completed all of her primary and high school education in Woodstock, beginning at Northdale Public School for grades kindergarten to 6, D.M. Sutherland School for grades 7-8, and finishing at Woodstock Collegiate Institute for grades 9–13.

Her parents began to speak more and more English as their children attended school. Thus, when she was young, she spoke Dutch and learned English only when her older sister started school and had to speak English. She feels that it is unfortunate that she has lost much of her ability to speak the language, but, fortunately, she can still understand it well. She loved school. This saved her from hours of housework - that good old Dutch cleanliness was certainly the rule in her family's household - and she always wanted to do well in all of her studies. However, she was very shy and did not volunteer to answer questions or to participate. Sports were her saviour as she loved any activity and could play well enough to make the school teams.

It was at high school where she met her future husband, Randy Hutchison. They began dating in grade 13. They had actually been in the same home room class in grade 11 - which neither of them remembered! Then, in grade 13, Randy began dating her best friend; but they eventually ended their relationship. However, Artena and that young lady are still very good friends. After some time, Randy and Artena began dating.

After high school, they went to university; he to the University of Guelph, and she to the University of Waterloo. Artena graduated with an Honours Bachelor of Science degree in Kinesiology. Upon graduation, they were married at Knox Presbyterian Church in Woodstock and settled in an apartment. The couple celebrated their 30th wedding anniversary in 2006.

Her first job was with the YWCA as the Physical Fitness Programme Coordinator. This was really enjoyable work because of the challenge which it provided. The programmes at the Y had dwindled to nothing; thus, her job was to build up programmes for all ages. Her salary depended on how successful she was - very motivating! She especially enjoyed the development of a Kindergym programme for 2-3 year olds and the leading of DanceFit, an aerobic fitness session, for women. Even yet, there are women who will ask her if she will consider leading another DanceFit class.

Her next job was at the local Home for the Aged, Woodingford Lodge. She took a position as a nurse aid with the hope that one of the Recreational Activity staff positions would come open. This never happened, but her time spent there gave her much experience in working with seniors and much understanding in how to work with them. Without this experience, she would not have obtained her next position with the Canadian Red Cross. It was during the five years at Woodingford that both of her daughters were born.

She applied to the Red Cross (Woodstock office) in 1985 for a supervisory position in the Home Support sector. At that time, this programme was a small, home service provided to seniors who needed help primarily with housekeeping and meals, in order for them to stay at home. There were approximately fifty part-time homemakers on staff and one other part-time office staff. She could not have imagined then that she would remain with Red Cross for almost eighteen years and have such varied opportunities to learn and to grow.

An event that resulted in a future opportunity that she would never have thought possible came about when she attended her first annual provincial meeting for Red Cross. The keynote speaker was a young man who was working as an overseas delegate in one of the African countries. Artena was very moved by his speech and thought that this kind of work must be very rewarding. Much later in her career, she found out just how rewarding it would be.

With governments beginning to provide more funds to community health care agencies, this type of service was growing very quickly, both in numbers and in the type of assistance offered to individuals. Initially the agency could hire untrained people to be a homemaker; but soon, because of the demand for assistance with bathing, anyone hired needed to receive some training as soon as being placed on staff. Soon the agency grew to eighty homemakers and two additional office staff. All agencies worked closely together to ensure that clients would receive competent and necessary care. The early 1990s were good years for community health.

Then, as with everything, changes regarding how the community health services would be administered were implemented. Because of the rising need for services, many policies and procedures were put into place; but funds never seemed to be sufficient. Pressure was always present to provide services more efficiently and more economically. By now, Artena's title was Manager of Homemaker Services and the office had two supervisors and two accounting staff.

A very big change that was brewing was the threat of unionization of the homemaking staff. Wages for community workers were (and still are) much lower than workers in such other areas as nursing homes. Thus, with the promise of better wages and less shift, most areas voted in favour of being unionized. Now began the work of developing the initial contract and developing relationships with union representatives. This particular union had not been in health care previously and came in very hard-nosed and aggressive with their demands. They soon discovered that, when the government only pays the agency, especially a not-for-profit one, a flat fee for service, it is impossible to increase wages. In addition, when clients need assistance morning and evening for personal care, it is very difficult to reduce shift. However, everyone forged ahead to make it work as well as possible. Artena missed the freedom of trying to work out problems individually with staff as it now it had to be done according to the contract.

Red Cross, in an effort to be more cost efficient and remain competitive with other agencies, asked if she would be willing to take on the manager duties of the Stratford office when that manager would retire in a couple of months. Although worried somewhat about workload, she agreed to try it. Fortunately, all went quite well, even though Oxford and Perth Counties operated quite differently. One might think that there would be some standardization between sites; however, that was not the case. Despite that, the two offices continued to grow and be very busy. Government funding was not keeping pace with the demand on services, thus wages for staff remained stagnant (only in the spring of 2006, did the government finally announce some increase in wages for homemakers – to start at $12 per hour). As a result, recruitment of homemaking staff became (and still is) very difficult.

Once again, to remain competitive, Red Cross asked if she would consider being responsible for yet another office – this time, the one in St. Thomas. Now she was quite sure that this workload would be impossible, yet she agreed to try it for six months. If she could have used the drive time in the office, it might have worked. However, on some days, meetings would require her to be at two different offices in one day; and, a couple of times, she even had to be in all three sites! Talk about time management! In reality, all would have been manageable if the three sites operated similarly; but, because of varied demands of the Community Care Access Centres, it took longer and longer days to complete everything. At this point, Artena began to think about looking for different work. She did not want to become so stressed that she would become ill. She did realize that she was lacking balance in her life. Definitely, she was not spending much time with her husband and her daughters. Thus, the decision to leave was made.

She provided plenty of notice to her employer. It was during this notice period that a job posting was listed describing an overseas position wanting someone with community health care experience. When she read this, her heart jumped because she knew that she wanted this experience. She went home and hesitantly mentioned it to Randy and the girls. To her surprise, they were very excited and encouraged her to apply – a dream come true! Of course, she did not yet have the job. Because the international office had been trying to fill this position for some time, things moved very quickly. Artena applied in April, and was on her way at the end of May. In a matter of weeks, she was interviewed, offered the job, packed, obtained the appropriate medical and needles, and said goodbye to her husband, her daughters, and the rest of the family. Then she went to Ottawa for briefing.

The position was for a Home Care Coordinator in the former Federal Republic of Yugoslavia (now Serbia-Montenegro) for a six-month posting. She would be required to assist the local Red Cross offices in setting up a programme to assist their elderly, and do this with very limited funds (meaning no paid staff). Prior to going to Yugoslavia, she went to Geneva, Switzerland, (location of the International Red Cross and Red Crescent Head Office) for two weeks of training and orientation. Then she was sent to Budapest, Hungary, (location of the Regional Office for Eastern Europe Programmes) for further orientation. Although she was a bit lonesome, she was too busy to become homesick.

Finally, at the end of June, she arrived in Belgrade, as was mentioned at the start of the chapter. The driver who met her spoke little English, drove her into Belgrade, and left her at her place of accommodation. He also indicated that he would take her to work in the morning. She was naïve in expecting to find food in the apartment; but there was no food and she had none with her. How would she be able to locate food if she does not know the language and the currency? Now she had a whole new appreciation for her immigrant parents who could not speak English on their arrival in Canada!

Instead of panicking, she began to reason. In her

possession were some euros and, down the street from the apartment, she had seen a store. Therefore, out she hurried to the store, hoping that the owner might know some English. She was wrong again! She showed the lady her euros and pointed to the bananas and milk. The clerk nodded her head and an exchange took place. Now, Artena could eat! Later, she calculated that the amount was right. She returned to her apartment, called home, and cried her eyes out! What was she doing here? Very soon, she received telephone calls from her sisters and her mother - everyone reassuring her. Their encouragement made her feel better. Maybe, she really made the right choice in coming. She fell exhausted into her strange bed and actually slept.

The next morning, her driver returned and took her to the Red Cross office. Another disappointment met her there! The local staff was very aloof toward her. She learned much later that they were not in favour of having a so-called "expert" come in and "tell" them what to do. She met all the other delegates, all from different countries - a very interesting experience. She was also told that there was no room for her in this office until September and she would be based in another city, Novi Sad, for the first two months. Now she was really feeling "unwanted"! However, things have a way of turning out - Novi Sad is a lovely city. She hired a wonderful person as her assistant - who is still a very good friend. There was another Canadian delegate in Novi Sad who was working for American Red Cross. Artena had no place to stay in that town as no apartment had been leased yet. The other Canadian promised to find something by the time she would arrive in Novi Sad - and he did. It was adjacent to a market (noisy at 5 a.m.) that had the most heavenly fresh produce that she would buy daily for her meals. Novi Sad had been heavily bombed by NATO airplanes, with the bridges over the Danube River receiving the worst hits. People, understandably, were very angry - mostly with Americans - about this as their water and electricity supplies were still affected. It affected Artena greatly to hear about their experiences of the bombings and to see the destruction.

Finally, she began to work on her project. That was so exciting! The local staff in Novi Sad welcomed her and exhibited a friendly attitude toward her. As language was a problem, she received approval to hire an assistant who would translate for her and would make calls to set up appointments for areas to visit. Also, she had a desk to use; but she had to wait for a computer. That was not a problem - she decided to go out and do the visits with the various Red Cross branches and assess each for programme potential. Each visit took a long time as everything said needed to be translated back and forth. Her assistant caught on very quickly, and, after a few visits, she knew exactly what information was needed to do a proper assessment.

The other important task was to confirm funders for this programme. Besides some Canadian donations, they were fortunate in having money donated from Sweden and Norway. Lastly, they had to develop their course of implementation for the programme and the training that the workers would receive. This occupied the summer months.

Outside of work, Artena spent time becoming acquainted with the area. She walked everywhere that she could and was able to find her way around quite well. She feels that she must have looked Serbian as well because people would stop and ask her for the time or for directions. She received two special treats during the summer - both her sister and her older daughter came to visit her. That was really wonderful!

When September arrived, it was time to return to Belgrade. She was somewhat apprehensive, remembering the frosty reception before. She located a beautiful apartment in the centre of Belgrade, not far from work. This time, there was some office repositioning to make room for a desk for her. The local staff still was not friendly, but she carried on with her work. She called a meeting with everyone, in which she made it clear that she was not the expert - they were. They knew the people and their needs; they knew what would work and what would not; and, without their knowledge, the staff would accomplish nothing. That seemed to help considerably.

Artena met with the funders and the Regional Health delegate. Everyone was excited about the potential of this programme - now to make it all functional. With much hard work on everyone's part, they had ten areas trained and running after six months. The amazing part was that all of the workers volunteered their time. Duties required were divided into two groupings. Personal care, meals, and working with difficult clients were for the adult volunteers. Housekeeping, errands, making simple meals could be accomplished by youth volunteers. The number of involved youth was amazing.

It was so successful, Artena was asked to extend her stay until April. After talking with her husband, it was agreed that she would extend as long as she could go home for two weeks at Christmas.

In January, the staff performed the whole process over and selected another twenty-five areas in which to implement the programme. That kept everyone busy; but, once again, the staff successfully met its goals with everyone's tremendous cooperation. Because of this success, all branches (total of ninety throughout Serbia/Montenegro) wanted to implement the programme. Thus, Artena was asked to extend again. By now, she had much confidence in the local staff - more than they had in themselves. Therefore, instead of staying, she suggested that they take on the next phase and she would come back in the fall to see how they were doing and to set up an evaluation tool. This was accepted and she looked forward to returning to Canada. However, before doing so, she accepted an invitation to visit a Finnish friend whom she had met in Serbia. Thus, she spent an amazing week in Finland and took a boat cruise to Sweden. She thoroughly enjoyed the polar swims followed by the sauna!

In October, Artena returned to Belgrade. By now, it was like going to her second home, and she was excited to find out about the programme's progress. This time, there was an opportunity to visit Montenegro, which has a beautiful coastline and some fantastic historical sites. She also was asked to go to Sarajevo, Bosnia, to evaluate their programme. She had thought the destruction in Serbia was bad, but it was nothing in comparison to that in Bosnia. However, work was underway to restore the capital. She found the areas were very quaint, in spite of the damage.

The programme in Serbia/Montenegro continued to be successful despite reduced funding from international funders. This proved that the programme would not fail if international help should cease. Everyone hoped that eventually the local governments would provide some funding so that workers could be paid. Now, her work there was truly finished and, knowing that she would be leaving permanently, it was very difficult. The work which they had accomplished together made such a difference to the people, and everything which they did was so appreciated by those receiving help from the volunteers. In fact, coming back to Canada was difficult - listening to people here complaining about the littlest things. This attitude was very annoying to her.

She had the opportunity to visit other countries and cities for her vacations. These included London, Prague, Cyprus, Istanbul, and Latvia (one of the delegates invited Artena to her wedding). Of these, Istanbul was the most intriguing. She even visited a Turkish bath and "stepped" into Asia. What an experience her vacations were!

In total, she spent two and one-half years going back and forth between Canada and Serbia. She had one final assignment, which was to go to Bratislava, Slovakia, to assess programme potential with the Red Cross there. She learned much from these travels - people everywhere are basically good; Canadians do not know what a good life that we have; and all things happen for a reason, and usually they turn out well. It taught her to be thankful for even the smallest things and always to stay optimistic.

Now, she is working as a facilitator with Fanshawe College Employment, an agency which offers programmes for individuals who are job seeking. It is part time (and fairly stress free), which is perfect as Randy is now retired. Ironically, she used their services when she began to job search! Working with a small group of co-workers in a pleasant environment is certainly the way to wind down one's work life. It gives her time to spend the summer "up north" at their cottage situated on the Pickerel River – the best place on Earth! She does not know what the future holds for her, but she does know that whatever she will do has to have "value" and be of help to others.

My wife Pam was offered a position as a homemaker at the Woodstock office of the Canadian Red Cross in the same year that Artena became manager there. Pam stayed for a little over a year, at which time the United States Immigration Service approved our family's move to the State of Missouri. Pam always spoke highly of Artena. One of our sons, Sean, and I did some volunteer work at the office when we had a few free days. From our family's association with Artena, we can understand why she has had success in her various areas of work. The Canadian Red Cross and those she has helped have been blessed by their association with her.

3

William E. Paul

Franktown, Colorado, United States

Can a boy who starts out "on the wrong side of the street" become a successful minister in adulthood? As a twelve-year-old, Bill joined the Boy Scouts. Since the troop was affiliated with a church, all members were required to attend Sunday school. One class session was enough for Bill! However, he was allowed to remain in the Scouts. He did enjoy sports, especially baseball, and even talked with the famous Honus Wagner.

In his home, he did not know about the Bible or praying. However, he was familiar with arguing, profanity, and the use of beer and whiskey there. He did not know about religious thoughts or experiences. He watched children walking to Sunday school and wondered what they did in the churches. As a teenager, he struck up a friendship with older young men. Smoking, drinking, and going to dances became routine. He became a part of the "zoot suit" craze. On one occasion, some boys enticed him to be involved with setting a man on fire. This placed him in trouble with the police. However, when Bill and his dad appeared at the station a few days later, there was no record of a charge. He learned that someone had prayed for him. This memory stayed with him.

What future would this young man have? He was headed the wrong way. It did not improve when he was in the U.S. Navy. Could he be rescued? Can you see him as a dedicated minister for fifty years? It may be difficult to imagine, but he crossed the threshold to a new life. It was a beautiful Christian girl named Bethel who turned him around.

Bill was born at home in Alliance, Ohio, about 65 miles *(105 km)* southeast of Cleveland, Ohio, USA. He was the second of two children born to parents who had immigrated to the United States from Austria-Hungary in the early 1900s.

He began his formal education at South Seneca School, in Alliance, where he was a very popular and capable student. In his eight years in this school, he received very good grades, even with little studying. He often became the envy of friends and fellow students because of being exempt from taking final examinations. In his final year, he served as editor of the Seneca *Flash*, the school newspaper, and was voted most popular boy and most likely to succeed, as well as being class president. However, Bill found Alliance High School and Youngstown South High School much more difficult.

Bill served in the United States Navy amphibious force in the Pacific Theatre during World War II, first on the USS Electra, and then on landing craft support vessels. One day, while out to sea, he decided to read from his small, Navy-issue, pocket New Testament. Not being familiar with the Bible, his first impression was that it was unintelligible, so tossed it into the bottom of his sea bag, where it remained for over a year. He was impressed, however, by a friend aboard ship who would not go to bars and dance halls when on leave as the other sailors did. He wondered if this person might be a genuine Christian.

While in Japan, on occupation service, he was concerned about there being an official Army brothel in Kobe, and was bothered by the sight of the devastation in Hiroshima, which he was able to tour fifty-three days after the atomic bomb was dropped on it. Over the years, he was a patient in both Naval and Veteran Administration hospitals. Because of a lifelong incurable skin condition and eyesight problems, Bill spent some fifteen months in hospitals during the balance of his life.

While still in the navy, one day while stationed in Portland, Oregon, a sailor friend, Bennie Hummel, asked Bill to go on a blind date with the sister of the girl with whom he had a date. After being shown a photograph of the beautiful girl, he readily accepted the invitation. This turned out to be the event that had the greatest impact on his future. The two sailors rode by Greyhound bus for about 20 miles *(32 km)* east of Portland, and then walked a short distance on a dark, paved road until arriving at a small frame house. After being introduced to his date, Bill was instructed to take a box of picnic snacks to a Model A sedan in the yard, where they were joined by several other young people. After a short drive, the car stopped at a church building. Bill was shocked as that was quite an unexpected place to go on a blind date! In the back room of the church, he saw other people, and soon discovered that he was in a midweek Bible study and prayer service - a new experience for him. Although determined to make the best of it, he was still surprised when everyone knelt and prayed - out loud!

Following the church service, the young people returned to the car and drove to a sandy beach along the Sandy River, near the Columbia River. Here, a wiener and marshmallow roast commenced. Bill noted that there was no beer or sex, both of which were common preferences of many sailors. After awhile, Bill and his date, Bethel, strolled a short distance away and enjoyed a pleasant visit during which they were able to learn much about each other.

Bill became quite interested in Bethel and contacted her a week later. However, Bethel was not really interested in this sailor who was not a Christian. They dated occasionally, but Bethel wanted them to be friends - and nothing more. Nevertheless, in time, this blind date led to Bill's becoming a Christian and to their eventual marriage. He has never regretted that blind date, although, at the time, he felt quite uncomfortable in such religious surroundings.

After his discharge from active duty during World War II, and with considerable encouragement from his wife Bethel, Bill obtained his ministerial education at Midwestern School of Evangelism, in Ottumwa, Iowa, (Bachelor of Sacred Literature in 1955, Bachelor of Theology in 1977, and Master of Sacred Literature in 1978). This became his principal vocation for the next fifty years. His ministry included serving as an instructor in the Church of Christ Bible Training School in western Nebraska and in Rocky Mountain College of Christ in Colorado; editor of *Impact,* his church publication; a radio ministry on KWIV in Douglas, Wyoming; and the editor of *Bible Collectors' World*. He ministered to several Churches of Christ in the United States as well as participating in short mission trips to the Bahamas and Jamaica.

On one occasion, Bill was called on to conduct the funeral service of a 38-year-old minister friend in the Bahamas. The church building was packed for the service, and then was followed by a long motorcade to the tent-covered burial site. The large crowd in attendance, including several ministers, attested to the fact that the deceased man had been well-loved.

The next day, Bill was asked to conduct another funeral

service, this time for the eight-month-old baby of a poor African woman. There were only three other persons present, including the mother. During the service, Bill noticed that the body had been chilled only, not embalmed, thus drawing flies. The little casket was placed into the trunk of a relative's car and driven to a large, rocky field. After the small grave was located, it was discovered to be too small. So, with the aid of sticks, Bill and the others did their best to enlarge it. After a reading of Scripture and the delivering of the committal, everyone covered the grave with dirt. As a finale, Bill placed a nearby wild flower over it. What a contrast this was from the service of the previous day!

One night when Bill and Bethel were ministering in Florida and were away at a Bible study, their two oldest boys were wrestling on their bed. Suddenly, one leg of the bed broke through the termite-eaten floorboard of their rented, old frame house. Not wanting their parents to know about this, the boys hit upon a plan. One of them crawled under the house in the dark, dragging pieces of concrete blocks and bricks to place under the spot where the bed had pierced the floorboards, while the other held a flashlight. The mission was accomplished successfully. They did not encounter any diamondback rattlesnake, cottonmouth water moccasin, copperhead, or coral snake, which the family had been warned could be nearby, especially at night. The boys' parents eventually found out about this - several years later!

It is a rare and valuable opportunity when one can attend a church service of a people of another culture. But such was the case for Bill and some colleagues who were attending a Bible collectors' conference in Ohio. The region has the largest group of Old Order Amish people in the world.

They are known for leading a very simplistic and primitive life by general American standards. Yet, there is something marvelous about them that holds their visitors in awe.

First, there are the buggies - no cars. Then, there is the lack of electricity and other modern conveniences in the homes. Married men wear beards; while all men and boys wear black suits held by hooks - not buttons. All women and girls wear bonnets and long black dresses. The meeting-place is in a large out-building on one of the farms - not in a church building.

Upon arrival at the farm, all the men meet in a clean barn and greet each other simply. Then they file into their meeting building where the women are seated on benches on one side, while the men take their places on benches on the other side. The service begins with a lengthy period of singing without a leader, but is accomplished in orderly fashion. Then there are long prayers, with all rising, and then kneeling at their bench. There is also preaching - short and longer talks by different men. No one, not even the children, appeared to fidget during the long service. Unless a visitor were familiar with either High German or Pennsylvania Dutch, no words are understood.

After the service, everyone files out of the building to visit on the grounds, followed by a fellowship meal served in the building with food prepared the day before. The experience was fascinating and refreshing for Bill with the simplicity and plainness of the people. It made a deep and lasting impression on him.

In 1999, Bill and Bethel were away from their home on a well-earned vacation - the longest in their lives - that took them to the homes of family members in Colorado and

Florida. Upon arriving home, relaxed and happy at the end of their trip, they were about to have a bombshell drop on them! Little could they have realized what awaited them as they drove up to their home in Seattle. Why were the lights on in their condo? Why was there loud blaring music emanating from it? Who were those strange people in the kitchen preparing food to eat?

Bill demanded to know why these strangers were there and how they came in, and then emphatically ordered them to leave. As the three people made their hasty exit, Bill and Bethel assessed the damage. Electronic equipment was missing. The refrigerator was almost empty. Unmade beds contained cigarette burns, which also appeared on the living room carpet. Their car was parked out front - not in the garage where it had been left. It reeked of tobacco smoke and was filled with clothes and junk. Keys to the car and to the condo were gone. Drug paraphernalia and syringes were discovered in drawers over the following days. What a mess everything was!

The police investigated but never found the intruders! They had more pressing cases to solve. The one good ending to this tragic affair was the help that was received from the insurance company, who replaced all damaged or stolen items with new ones. The church people also provided help financially - anonymously - which was much appreciated.

Bill had begun a Bible collection with some twenty or thirty books in the early years of his ministry, which grew to over six hundred in later years. In the mid 1960s, he learned of the periodical *The Bible Collector* - later *Bible Collectors' World*. His interest was enhanced after meeting another collector, Donald Heese. In 1991, he was contacted by the president of

International Society of Bible Collectors, asking him to be editor of the Society's official journal *Bible Collectors' World.* After deciding that it would be a good retirement activity with the minimal time required to edit the quarterly, he accepted and was installed as editor.

In 1993, after reading through the *American Standard Version* again, he decided to write out its New Testament as a means of receiving additional benefit. Since he encountered some difficult passages, he proceeded to reword those parts for his own devotional needs, and so that others would be able to understand the meaning of the original. He used numerous Bible versions and several reference works to accomplish this work. Much encouragement and help were received from his wife Bethel and from Dr. Robert G. Bratcher, translator of *Today's English Version*. The first draft was completed in 1994, twenty-one months after he had commenced. He had three purposes in doing this work: to gain a better personal understanding of the Scriptures; to leave a legacy for their children and grandchildren; and to provide something of value for those with Bible translation interests. In 1995, the limited edition of *The New Testament: An Understandable Version* was delivered to him by the printer.

While his literary career involved editing journals and writing numerous books, booklets, and magazine articles from 1955 until the present, what stands out as the most significant is the work that Bill did in producing this translation of the New Testament.

Any person who has had some measure of success in their life's work will feel that there is something that could have been accomplished better. This is true for Bill. Because of his involvement in church work, including traveling, teaching in Bible colleges, and conducting gospel meetings, camps, and workshops over the course of a fifty-year ministry, together with having a constant battle with health issues and receiving only a minimal income, he felt he was not able to spend as much time with his family as he would have liked. Vacations, family outings, and doing things with his wife and children were too few and far between. As a result, those quality time experiences, when precious family memories are made, did not occur as frequently as he would have liked.

Several persons have had a significant influence on Bill's life and ministry over the years. One in particular was the late Donald G. Hunt, of Ottumwa, Iowa. He was one of Bill's Bible college professors from whom he learned much about the Bible, dedicated ministry, and diligent study habits. He used some of those teachings as objectives to follow throughout his own life. He often heard Professor Hunt preach in gospel meetings and rallies. Hunt had invited Bill to write for his publication, *Voice of Evangelism,* in the early years of his ministry, thus providing him opportunities to improve his literary skills. It also opened doors for speaking in numerous churches, camps, rallies, and workshops around the country. Their interaction in person, along with an ongoing correspondence, provided much encouragement to Bill as he sensed Professor Hunt's continual confidence in his capabilities.

Bill also did much writing, especially in his retirement years. Some of his numerous books are the following:

- *Development of the English Bible*
- *Memorable Moments in the Lives of a Loving Couple*
- *A New Testament Study of the Eldership*
- *Bethel: A Place Where God Dwells*

- *Fascinating Stories About the Bible*
- *News and Notes About Bible Versions*
- *A Christian View of Armed Warfare*
- *They Go About Two by Two*
- *English Language Bible Translators*
- *A Compilation of Bible Translations on Acts 2:38*

Besides Bill's wife Bethel being instrumental in his becoming a Christian, she was also very supportive of him in both good times and difficult times. So it was a blow to him when she suffered her first major stroke in 1997. Now, it was his turn to offer support to her in the best way that he could. He is her sole caregiver.

In whatever responsibility that he has had over the years since he made his commitment to the Lord's service, he has been completely dedicated. He worked despite his life-long skin problem, his weak eyesight, his long hours, his limited financial resources, and the several controversies into which he was drawn.

His philosophy of life can be summed up in the Bible passage of Matthew 6:33, which says, "Seek ye first the kingdom of God and his righteousness, and all these things [material blessings] will be added unto you."

When I was collecting Bible versions as a hobby, I came across *The New Testament: An Understandable Version.* Since a copy was not in my collection and I had never heard of it, I contacted the translator, Bill Paul, who was then living in Seattle, Washington. We have been in contact several times since then. I would like to thank Bill for giving me permission to use an online version of his autobiography, *Starting from Scratch: The Story of My Life*, from which I have gleaned much of the information for this chapter. However, Bill also provided some additional information through our correspondence during its preparation. I read his autobiography completely and enjoyed it. Although it was written mainly for his family and close friends, there are experiences and insights that can be appreciated by anyone, regardless of one's religious faith. It can be read at http://www.faithlegacy.info/pdf/PaulAutobiography.pdf.

4

Blanche Friderichsen

Edmonton, Alberta, Canada

It is fit for a queen! That is a common saying in speaking of something that is good. However, three young sisters were not fit for a queen - or so they felt. In 1953, they sailed from Canada to England to be in London at the time of the coronation of Queen Elizabeth II. Having camped in Trafalgar Square, in London, overnight, they were assured of an ideal spot for watching the parade in the morning. What a thrilling experience! They even managed to obtain invitations to the Garden Party at Buckingham Palace. But, alas! One look at the required dress code indicated that the knapsacks of these budget travelers would not be able to produce what would meet the criterion for the gala event. Thus, after more than fifty years, one of the sisters - Blanche - still has the invitation, which is now a precious souvenir.

Blanche was born in Saskatoon, Saskatchewan, Canada. Following a year in kindergarten, she attended Haultain Public School in that city for eight years. Each morning, the children lined up in front of the "boys" or "girls" entrance and marched into school to a Philip Sousa tune played on the hallway gramophone. Miss Victoria Miners, the principal, stood tall, looking at each of the children over her pince-nez. Blanche thought that she was wonderful! It was a thrill when she was asked by Miss Miners to make a scrapbook of her clippings of the 1939 visit of King George VI and Queen

Elizabeth to Saskatoon – like the one Blanche had made for herself. That summer Miss Miners visited China, and, as a thank you, brought back a hand painted bracelet, which Blanche still cherishes.

High school at Nutana Collegiate, passed quickly without any memorable incident. However, during her final year, Blanche worked in a nearby branch of the public library after school and on Saturdays as a page for the grandiose sum of ten cents an hour.

After high school, Blanche enrolled at the University of Saskatchewan, in Saskatoon, and earned her Bachelor of Arts degree. While at the university, she worked in the University Library, in hours arranged around her classes. Night was not a preferred shift because the bats that lived in the limestone building would become active. For some reason, those mammals liked to swoop down the corridor toward the library. At such times, Blanche had no interest in being a zoology enthusiast. She was much relieved when a colleague or student exhibited the bravery needed to persuade the bats to leave the premises and search for their meals elsewhere. There is usually a practical joker in any class. One must have thought that Blanche should develop an appreciation for these useful animals. On opening the suggestion box one day, she was horrified. Right there before her wide open eyes was a motionless specimen of the Order Chiroptera that would fly no more!

Her experience in working in a public library and the university library and her good grades opened the way for a scholarship at the University of Toronto. Now, she knew the field for her future career. It was a typical library class of the day with the girls outnumbering the boys by thirty to five.

During her time in library school, she felt that she would like to work with children. Thus, when the position opened, she became the first children's librarian at the Strathcona Branch of the Edmonton Public Library.

However, she was not ready to settle down. She needed more travel time. It has often been said that one should travel when young as it might be more difficult in later years. About this time, there was much interest in the upcoming coronation of Queen Elizabeth II. Her experience is described above.

While she was overseas, she might as well do some extra traveling. For the next two years, she hitchhiked through the British Isles and continental Europe. Yes, this young lady hitchhiked! It was much safer to do so in those days than it is today. She took temporary jobs during the time to finance her living expenses. In London, she was a secretary. In Sidcup, Kent, she worked in real estate. In Bromley, Kent, she initiated children's services in the public library. Finally, in Oslo, Norway, she was a chambermaid at the University of Oslo student residence summer hotel. She was obtaining valuable experience in a range of endeavours.

Although she returned to Edmonton in 1955, she still had the urge to travel. She spent some time at the University of Toronto Library in acquisitions and at McGill University in cataloguing. She returned to Edmonton and went to work for a struggling lawyer – who later became a noted QC (Queen's Counsel). Shortly after this, she received a call from Edmonton Public Library. She was made an offer which she felt that she could not refuse. It was in the adult circulation department.

Then, a most significant event in her life occurred. She met a tall, handsome fellow from Denmark who shared her zest for travel! When she and Andreas (Andy) Friderichsen married in 1956, the scene was set for a life of travel adventures. Many trips to Europe followed. Fifty cruises to most parts of the world, ranging in length from five to seventy-two days, were taken. In addition, they traveled in the United States and Canada. They even tried white-water rafting, hot air ballooning, and house boating. What fond memories these two must hold!

Life was not all travel and learning. There were enjoyable jobs at home - Andy in audio-visual sales and Blanche in library. A change in focus came for Blanche. After she had given an address at a career day, the Superintendent of Schools of the County of Strathcona said that he needed a Library Coordinator for the twenty-one schools in his jurisdiction. Being interested, she applied for the position, with the provision that she could make arrangements to work toward a Bachelor of Education at the University of Alberta. The timing for the move was ideal!

At that time, teacher-librarians were in demand and school libraries were deemed to be important. However, many school administrators and classroom teachers did not comprehend the amount of time, effort, and knowledge required to manage a school library.

During her nine years in Strathcona, teacher-librarians were hired for larger schools and library clerks for the smaller ones. A central library service was established, from where catalogued books, AV resources, supplies, and furniture for the new school libraries were ordered. Curriculum-related programmes were introduced. Blanche visited all schools regularly, taught library skills, and held story hours in the smaller schools. She recalls the memorable moment when a grade 4 boy eagerly said to her, "Now I know how to use the

Dewey Chemical Situation!" Such moments are so precious.

When an opportunity arises, one must take advantage of it. That is what Blanche did in 1966 when the Department of Education created the position of library consultant. Again, she entered a position on the ground floor. She had her Bachelor of Arts degree and was finishing her Bachelor of Education degree. In her new job, she traveled from Wandering River in northern Alberta to Milk River in southern Alberta. She saw an astounding assortment of rooms and areas called "libraries". She led in the creating of guidelines which most districts endeavoured to meet.

The University of Alberta added courses for teacher-librarians and teachers. Blanche had the opportunity to teach a few of the summer school courses. An interest in everything related to school libraries escalated until the late 1970s. At that time, a special library grant from the Department of Education, with guidelines for spending, did not achieve its intended purpose. One of the Deputy Ministers boasted that it was not necessary for him to use a library until his doctoral dissertation. Can you believe that? How little did he know! Blanche felt sorry for his attitude and sensed that it contributed in some degree to the mounting lack of priority to school library services.

Educational priorities changed with reduced funding in the 1980s. This was a catastrophe. Most teacher-librarians and clerks were dedicated and passionate. Those who were kept on tried to maintain their prior level of service, but it was not possible! Teacher-librarians saw their library time reduced and their classroom time increased.

Her twenty-one years with the Department of Education provided Blanche with opportunities to meet school library personnel throughout the world. Over the years, she

- helped to develop an in-service course for the Alberta Public Library custodians;
- was a member of a school library committee for Statistics Canada;
- served as an assessor to select a state librarian at the University of Seattle, in Washington State;
- received honours from the Library Network Technology Council and the Learning Resources Council of the Alberta Teachers Association;
- completed her Master of Education degree.

English is her principal language, although she can read some French. Her philosophy is "Qué será, será." She has had five entries in *Readers' Digest,* the latest in the July 2006 issue.

I met Blanche in the late 1960s at school library meetings. We were members of the provincial executive of the Alberta School Library Council and members of the provincial Educational Media committee. She visited my libraries when I was teacher-librarian at David Thompson High School and later at Vauxhall High School. She provided valuable assistance to me when I was president of the Southern Alberta Regional School Library Association. She was welcomed and liked by school librarians across the province in her role as Department of Education school library consultant. It was regretted not only by her but also by all school librarians as we saw the decline of our role in the schools of Alberta. Blanche served her profession well.

5

Brian Masschaele

St. Thomas, Ontario, Canada

You want to learn some history of the area where you live - your farm, your town, your county, early settlers, to mention only a few. Where do you go for information? The first place that comes to mind may be your public library. However, you may need to be more specific. Probably the best - but not necessarily the only - place is the archives of your county or municipality.

The person who can best help you is the archivist. However, you must know what you want and be prepared to do some in-depth searching. Be aware that the archivist - wherever the archives - is a busy person. He/She is trying to provide the most resources that he/she can for everyone and can devote only a limited time to any researcher. Brian Masschaele, Elgin County (Ontario, Canada) archivist, urges patrons to be patient and take the time necessary to locate the needed information. Many answers to questions are very complex, and too many researchers are impatient when searching. Only so many resources can be placed online.

Brian was born in Simcoe, Ontario, Canada, a town a few miles north of Lake Erie. His first language is English, but he has some knowledge of French. He would like to be more fluent in a second language, particularly French.

His first school was St. Michael's School, Walsh, not far from Simcoe. His Grade 13 graduation from Port Dover

Composite School was probably the best time of his life as he received several academic scholarship offers and also was awarded the Rotary Shield for exemplary character and conduct among his peers. He took advantage of his opportunities and obtained his Bachelor of Arts from the University of Western Ontario, in London, and his Master of Arts from the University of Manitoba, in suburban Winnipeg.

He may have prepared to be an archivist in university, but it was in his internship that he really began to learn about the profession. What was a rural Ontario boy doing working in the massive National Archives of Canada in Ottawa, the national capital? After the stars had cleared from his eyes, he settled down to the practicality of fulfilling his internship and learning to be a quality county archivist. His time as an archivist at the Simcoe County Archives was very formative in terms of developing necessary skills to succeed in the profession and also in terms of learning about a model facility and programme.

He had more to learn. His time as Archives Advisor for the Province of Ontario was a golden opportunity for him, personally and professionally, as he spent over four years traveling the province, providing advice on managing archives and records. He visited most of the province, including a few native communities that were accessible only by airplane. This was enjoyable work! He remains in contact with many of the people whom he met. The time spent in this position went far in preserving recorded heritage. He accomplished much, not only for himself, but also for the province and its citizens.

Like most people, he has experienced his fair share of personal disappointments and failed relationships. However, he has overcome them so that, ultimately, everything has worked out for him. That is probably because he believes that hard work is always rewarded.

Brian gives much credit to a former teacher, Dr. Tom Nesmith, archival studies professor in the History Department at the University of Manitoba. He imbued Brian with a passion for archives and the history of Canada. The professor had an effective teaching style and inspired him to be a better student, including giving support on his thesis pertaining to records of the federal cabinet during the Second World War. Brian was very pleased with his own work on this topic and he has seen that it has benefited many people since. Tom has become a close friend, a colleague, and a mentor since university days. What a wonderful tribute to his professor! It is no wonder that he enjoys his work as an archivist.

Brian also pays high tribute his mother and father. His mother is still alive, but his father passed away in March 2006. Neither had a formal education but saw fit to give each of their five children that opportunity. The family operated a tobacco farm, on which his parents worked very hard for their children. Today, all have university degrees and are highly successful in their careers, including a high school teacher (Tom), an educational consultant and former teacher (Diane), a medieval history professor (Jim), an owner/operator of a retirement home products company (Steve), and an archivist (Brian). In the case of his parents, they have realized the efforts of their hard work and their dedication to their children.

He is extremely proud of having started a new archival programme from the ground up. He was hired by the County of Elgin in 2001 to develop the Elgin County Archives in St. Thomas, Ontario. His mandate included development of a facility and policies, arranging acquisitions, and hiring additional staff. The archives opened in November 2002 and have been a great success. The facility continues to grow. Brian is very happy to have had the opportunity and support to develop the programme. To see the online website, type in "Elgin County Archives" in a search engine (e.g., Google).

Obtaining quality materials for inclusion in the archival collection has never been a problem. The facility and staff are of high quality; and, as a result, the public trusts them with their records. He continues to be amazed at the quality of collections that they have acquired for a relatively small and rural area. It makes him wonder what happens to these records in many other parts of Canada where such an option may not exist.

Probably his most meaningful trip occurred when his father took him to West Flanders, Belgium. That is where father had grown up. This experience provided Brian with tremendous insight into his ancestry.

Brian enjoys playing hockey, which he did on a competitive level as a child and on a recreational basis in adult life. He is waiting for the Montreal Canadiens to win their next Stanley Cup. He also enjoys playing and watching baseball, including listening to broadcasts of the Detroit Tigers' games on radio. His other hobbies include brewing (from his Belgian ancestry) and volunteering at the local community museums.

Near the end of 1997, I contacted all the municipalities in Elgin County for lists of reeves, mayors, and wardens. The information that they sent me was arranged and placed onto our family website. Brian happened to see it and pointed out something that needed to be updated. Since that time, he has, every year, sent me an update of the changes in the county.

This has been very helpful to me. On another occasion, he performed some research on some of my ancestors who had settled in Malahide Township of Elgin County. In Brian, the county has a quality man to direct their archives.

6

Carlos Osvaldo Barbarito

Muñiz, San Miguel, BA, Argentina

Una y otra vez procuré,
sin fortuna, obtener descendencia:
de una sílaba perdida,
de un tallo enroscado en otro tallo,
de una pluma llevada por la brisa.
Poco hubo, apenas esto,
una casi inaudible respiración
al otro lado del muro,
un nido pequeño, desarreglado y vacío
entre raíces desparramadas sobre la tierra.

Time and again I tried,
without success, to obtain descendants:
of a lost syllable,
of a stem wound around another stem,
of a feather carried by the breeze.
It yielded little, scarcely this,
an almost inaudible breathing
on the other side of the wall,
a small nest, untidy and empty
between roots scattered over the earth.

These are the words of Carlos Barbarito, a well-known contemporary poet of Argentina. Javier Petit de Meurville comments, "Carlos Barbarito has the grace (the gift?) of believing in language. Through such belief, the experiences that wound or seduce him are transformed into the poised music of language."

Carlos was born in Pergamino, in the northern part of the Province of Buenos Aires, in Argentina. He attended primary school at Number 6, Juan Alberdi Baptist, in Pergamino. After this, he attended secondary school in the National School of Commerce, in Pergamino. Following graduation, he studied library science in the I.S.F.D.Y.T. Number 42, of Bella Vista, Buenos Aires.

He liked the primary school because he spent time with his friends of the neighbourhood. However, he hated secondary school very much. Boredom was felt in both of them. He read in his home for many hours since he already knew what the teachers taught. In addition, no one spoke of the Beatles or of space flights. He wondered why they were not mentioned.

His first language is Spanish, but he reads and writes some in English. He was exempted from military service when it was compulsory. His profession is librarian, but his main activity is being a writer. The poet Alejandro González Gattone influenced him.

For about fifteen years, Carlos was employed in the Judicial, where he worked in the probate (inheritance). He knew that in those worlds there were not people, but proceedings, papers that make reference to people.

He has taken several memorable trips. One was through Europe in 1981 and 1982. His favourite region to visit is the

Patagonia, in southern Argentina. A great experience occurred the first time that he saw the sea. Anyone who lives inland can echo this sentiment.

Carlos prefers the music of Keith Jarret to the Gregorian songs; old maps; photography; cinema; and painting. His philosophy of life is to live. Yes, to live, not merely to exist! He is following this through his interests, his writings, and his travels.

Muñíz, a part of San Miguel, Buenos Aires, Argentina, is home to Carlos. It is a small city, a residential community having many trees. In the plaza, among the other trees is an araucaria (monkey puzzle tree). Now, the city is becoming a place where restaurants, pubs, and other commercial enterprises have developed. There is also an old train station.

His country, Argentina, seldom recognizes poets. Carlos says, "I am almost invisible." However, his ability has been recognized through several prizes and distinctions:

- Gran Premio Libertad
- Pemio Bienal de Crítica de Arte Jorge Feinsilber
- Premio César Tiempo
- Premio Concurso Régimen de Fomento a la Producción Literaria Nacional y Estímulo a la Industrial Editorial, Fondo Nacional de las Artes
- Premio Fundación Alejandro González Gattone
- Premio Francisco López Merino
- Premio Fundación Argentina para la Poesía
- Premio Raúl Gustavo Aguirre Sociedad Argentina de Escritores
- Premio Tierras Planas
- Premio Hespérides
- Premio Iparragirre Saria, España

- Menciones de Honor Carlos Alberto Débole y Leopoldo Marechal
- Mención Plural, México

He believes that his greatest accomplishment is his poems. This list of prizes bears witness of that.

I met Carlos through email. We had placed a section on Latin American authors on our website. My Argentina listing included Carlos. He saw the site and wrote to me in appreciation. We corresponded a few times in Spanish, and then stopped for about two years. Then I contacted him to be a participant in this book project. He quickly accepted my invitation. On checking the internet, I have found that, in Latin America, there are some good reviews of his work.

7
Charles "Chuck" Sperry

Siguatepeque, Honduras

Crackle! Crackle! What was that sound that Regina heard as she was hanging out laundry at her home in Honduras? She turned to look toward the woods behind the house. There was a forest fire on the nearby mountain!

Since the wind was blowing toward the house, she knew that the fire would reach it in a few hours. What should she do? Should she move the truck close to the house? Should she and the children close the house and escape to the town? It was her decision to make since her husband Chuck was not at home at the time. She decided that the best thing to do was to pray for help. Thus, she gathered the children and they had prayer together. Then, they sang the hymn "God Will Take Care of You" and offered another prayer.

Because of the recent construction of the house, there were many rocks and bare earth around it so that the building would be safe. Yet, the smoke would create a problem. She walked to the property line and leaned over the barbed wire fence. Here she prayed for a change in wind direction.

She walked back to the house. Before she entered, she noticed that the wind had changed its direction. She looked up toward the sky and smiled, went into the house, and closed the door. Now, with confidence, she told the children that everything was all right. A few hours later, she brought in the laundry. She praised the Lord for His goodness!

Chuck was born in Independence, Missouri, United States. He obtained his early schooling here. Following high school, he attended university and obtained a Bachelor of Arts in Languages and International Business.

When he was young at home, a missionary family with twelve children lived with his own family on their farm for a time. This family had a profound impact on Chuck, resulting in his becoming a missionary himself. He has served as a missionary for the Lord in Mexico, Guatemala, Belize, Honduras, France, Israel, and Taiwan. His first language is English; but he is also fluent in Spanish, French, and Hebrew.

When Chuck was attending Brigham Young University in Utah, he had an experience which determined which church that he would be a member. Following is a condensed version of his story.

He had attended the university for one year when he had an experience that persuaded him that the Mormon (Latter-day Saint) Church was true. He feels that, on the day of his baptism, he was saved by the Holy Spirit from being baptized into that church and became a new creature in Jesus Christ.

A Mormon friend told him that it did not really matter in what church that Chuck would be a member as long as he believed in the Book of Mormon. However, Chuck refuted this because there were many doctrinal differences between the LDS Church and the RLDS (Reorganized Latter Day Saint) Church. It was agreed that they would fast and pray for each other until God revealed to them which church was right. The fasting lasted for a month.

Towards the end of the month, Chuck had an experience in which a spirit testified to him that the Mormon Church was true. This surprised and confused him because of all the contradictions between Mormon doctrine and the Scriptures. However, the two young men continued to pray and fast. Because of this experience, Chuck stopped asking the Lord to show them that the RLDS Church was true. He began instead to pray and ask the Lord to show him which church was true.

A week later, he was attending one of the Mormon sacrament meetings. During this meeting, he had another experience. The same spirit came to him and told him again that the Mormon Church was true. He began to pray silently, asking the Lord if this was His Spirit. The feeling became stronger as he prayed more. He had become convinced that the Mormon Church was true and told his friend that he wanted to be baptized.

Chuck had his baptismal interview with a seventy (missionary) and was approved for baptism. He asked the seventy if he would perform the baptism. He accepted. The baptism was scheduled, but he told the seventy that he wanted to have a confirming testimony before entering the water. He received this a week later.

Again, he was in a sacrament meeting praying silently when, all of a sudden, the same spirit came to him in great power and told him that the Mormon Church was true. However, Chuck still had one burning question. How could the Mormon Church be true when there were so many Scriptural contradictions with the doctrine? His French professor told him that if the Mormon Church were true, it would mean that the RLDS Church did not have authority; and, if it did not, he could not have been baptized by the Holy Spirit. If he had not been baptized by the Holy Spirit, he could not understand the real meanings of the Scriptures because it is the Holy Spirit that gives people true understanding of the Scriptures. Chuck accepted this explanation because it seemed to be logical.

On the day that he was to be baptized, he returned to BYU, in Provo, from a visit in Salt Lake City to prepare for it. On arrival, he was told by the dorm mother that his father and another man were waiting for him in his room. He asked a friend who had served his mission in Independence, where Chuck's home was, to accompany him in talking with his dad and the other minister, both representing the RLDS Church. Together they went to the room and found his father, Charlie Sperry, and Bill Whenham there waiting for him. He greeted them and asked them if they would be willing to have another person present for the talk. They agreed. The young men's purpose was to help the older men accept the doctrine of the Mormon Church and theirs was to help Chuck and his friend recognize the fallacies in Mormon doctrine. After a prayer, they established guidelines for their discussion. Everything had to be based on the Scriptures that were common to both churches. The discussion lasted for four hours.

During this time, Charlie and Bill had two visions. As the discussion progressed, the young men tried to refute what they were being told, but they could not prevail. Chuck and his friend had their experiences. As time was running out before the hour of the baptism, Charlie prayed that there would be a postponement. His prayers were answered, but Chuck did not want to tell his dad that someone had informed him of this during the discussion. Since Chuck's friend Joseph had another appointment, they agreed to meet again the next day.

In the meantime, Chuck had a spiritual experience in which the heavens were opened and he was, in his words, "born again." The next day, his friend Joseph did not want to talk about the Scriptures, but preferred to rely on his experiences. Afterwards, Chuck saw the same attitude in the seventy's family. Chuck was ready to return to Independence with Bill and Charlie. In a church service a couple of weeks later, Chuck received his confirmation that he had made the right choice.

Chuck relates two later testimonies when he was a missionary.

In a small village high in the mountains of Honduras, Central America, a man drove slowly over rough, almost non-existent roads to his place of birth, San Nicolás, Intibuca, Honduras. He has made this three-hour trip many times for over three years in order to share the gospel with his family. His hopes were sure, but it had been a slow process.

The road has been repaired. It now takes only one and one-half hours to travel to San Nicolás - a total of 17 miles *(27 km)*. Chuck and the congregation of Siguatepeque were invited to a baptism in August 2001. They traveled in a little yellow bus. Twenty-two people - brothers, sisters, nephews, and cousins - were being baptized in a local river. The man is Socorro Vasquez. He, Chuck Sperry, and Gerardo Tinoco assisted these people with the ordinance of baptism. This was an important event for them.

There were singing, prayer, and even tears. A woman covered her face as she entered the river because of her fear of water; but her desire to be baptized was greater than her fear. Then a problem arose! The bottom of the baptismal site was very slick. While Chuck was immersing the first man, he suddenly found out that the man also was petrified of the water. He would not allow his head to go under it. Suddenly, he bumped into Chuck and knocked him off the ledge into a deep hole! Chuck had to swim out of it and perform the baptism again. He talked with the man, attempting to assure him that everything would be all right. The baptism was repeated. Again, the man resisted letting his head go under the water. As a last resort, Chuck pushed him under the water and then lifted him out of it. Afterwards, he, Socorro, Gerardo, and Chuck had a good laugh about it.

Shortly, everyone headed for their vehicles. There were forty-four people in that eighteen-passenger bus. Socorro had twenty in the bed of his Toyota truck and eight more in the cab. They hugged and said goodbye after they had returned to the village. Despite the fear of water and the crowded vehicles, it was a successful and memorable day for all.

Traveling in Mexico and Central America is normally safe if you take routine precautions. Driving a car through winding, mountain roads at night is definitely discouraged. Public transit is the proper way to go then. What if circumstances are such that night driving must be done? Chuck, Regina, and their family had an experience that they will never forget.

It was about 6:00 p.m., with about one and one-half hours of sunlight left, when they drove out of Guatemala City. Their destination was Escuintla, a smaller city to the south, toward the Pacific coast. Unfortunately, the person reading the map made an error which was not discovered until they reached Chimaltenango, a city to the west. Since there was still daylight, they headed south through Antigua toward Escuintla, where they planned to spend the night.

When they arrived at the highway near Escuintla, there was no place to stay. They did not want to go into the town itself because it is nearly impossible to manipulate the narrow streets with a Ford extended cab pickup. It is even worse when towing a small trailer. At about 8:30 p.m., and not having found a place to spend the night, they decided to stay at the next town regardless of what they found. That turned out to be a questionable decision.

Just before 9:00 p.m., three vehicles traveling at high speed caught up with the Sperry vehicle. Two passed and then slowed down. Chuck successfully passed one truck, but could not pass the other one. Therefore, reacting quickly, he accelerated his truck to over 95 mph *(153 km/h)*. As they neared the top of a hill, Chuck eased off a bit. The second truck took advantage of this and pulled along side of his. Then a passenger started shooting! Chuck rammed the other vehicle. Regina yelled for the children to fall to the floor. At least seven bullets entered the truck.

Then, another man commenced shooting. Regina was hit on one hand and on her arm near her elbow. Three bones were broken and her elbow was shattered! A bullet which went through the driver's seat hit one of the boys on the leg. Another bullet struck another son in the back. Chuck suffered slight injury as a bullet hit him on the arm and a fragment glanced off his head. Other bullets came close.

Chuck continued to ram one of the cars until it disappeared and drove another one off the road. Then he raced about 3 miles *(5 km)* until he reached a Shell gasoline station, pulling up behind two semis. He asked for someone to call the police. However, there was no telephone or cell phone that was working. The two older children, who had trained for emergency preparedness with the Scouts organization, began to treat their mother in an effort to stem the loss of blood.

Eventually, one of the truckers had his cell phone in operation. He was able to contact the police. The assailants watched, but were afraid to attack now. Despite the injuries, the family was blessed in not being killed.

In about twenty minutes, motorcycle police arrived. They did not want to escort the family to a hospital, but wanted to wait for the firemen. Chuck eventually persuaded them to do as he had requested because of Regina's serious condition. After arrival at Hospital Nación in Mazatenango in about an hour, she was stabilized and all of the family were x-rayed. Work was done to remove any bullets. The police placed guards within the hospital and near the truck lest there be a hit squad sent to the scene.

The next morning, Chuck contacted the American Embassy in Guatemala City. The local police responded well to the quick action by the American officials. The police commissioner took Chuck back to the Shell station to examine the site. A witness there was able to identify one of the vehicles used in the assault.

Regina was released from hospital four days later so that she and the younger children could return to the United States by air. Neil Simmons and Kreg Levengood, ministers of the church, arrived in Mazatenango to help. The family and these men were taken to Guatemala City by ambulance with a police escort. The American Embassy provided security at their hotel in that city.

Under police escort, Chuck and the oldest son left for Xela (Quetzaltenango), where their truck was being repaired. After that, they would drive the truck back to Missouri. While the repair job was being carried out, Chuck was able to perform successful missionary work in a home.

Both Chuck's family and medical personnel who treated them - in Guatemala and in Missouri - saw that a miracle had taken place to save the lives of the family. Despite the horrible experience, Chuck saw that it gave him the opportunity to provide ministry where he would not have done so otherwise. The family testifies to the divine protection that they received during this experience.

Chuck feels that his greatest accomplishment in his ministry has been the bringing of an atheist couple to a saving belief and relationship with Jesus Christ. The area in which he would like to have been more successful is in being a better preacher.

He takes time for several hobbies. These include reading, hiking, running, martial arts, playing guitar, and building computers.

Honduras is the second poorest country in the Americas. In the community where they live, there are two dry seasons, during which they obtain water for about twelve hours once a week. For the rest of the time, it is necessary for them to draw water from a concrete holding tank which they have on the side of their house. Sometimes, small frogs and freshwater crabs come through the waterline. Of course, they filter the water for this reason. Most of their neighbors now have latrines or toilets. They have had electricity where they live since 2002. However, it fails on the average of two or three times per week. The basic food staples are beans, rice, and tortillas. Usually once or twice a day, there will be a chicken or beef served with the meal.

About 90% of the population in Honduras is mestizo. There also are small minorities of African, Asian, Arab, and indigenous Indians. Officially, 98% of the population is Roman

Catholic; but the reality is that about 30% of the population is Evangelical. While Spanish is the predominant language, some English is spoken along the northern coast and is prevalent on the Caribbean islands. Several indigenous Indian languages and Garifuna (a mixture of Afro-indigenous languages) are also spoken.

Our family met Chuck and Regina at a church shortly after we moved to Independence, Missouri. We became friends and visited in each other's home. Soon after we arrived, Sean and I were asked by friends in Florida to go to their home to provide ministry for them and a few friends. We accepted the invitation and took Chuck with us. We also made contact with some people of our church on our trip both ways. This included unexpected ministry with an alcoholic man at a motel in northern Alabama. At a later date, Sean and Chuck provided ministry to a group in Kansas. The last time when we saw Chuck was at the international airport in Houston, Texas. He was returning from Honduras and Pam, Janet, and I were returning from Monterrey, Mexico. Missionaries of any religion lead exciting - even dangerous - lives; but, when they see good results in their work, they feel that it is worth it.

8
Clifford Raymond Elle

Beaver Mines, Alberta, Canada

Cliff had many positive experiences in school. However, there was one that certainly was not. He was in either grade 6 or 7 when, one morning on his arrival at his rural school, he was met at the door by the teacher. Something was wrong! The teacher immediately charged that young Clifford had said something negative about him and that the boy needed to apologize before being allowed into the building. What had he said? The poor little fellow tried to remember what negative comment he had uttered about his teacher. He drew a blank. To add to the quandary, the inquisition carried on for about fifteen minutes. How embarrassing it was to stand there while other students passed by him as they entered the school, being aware of what was transpiring!

If that were not bad enough, the boy was told that he must make the apology in front of the class. In order to draw closure to the event, Cliff agreed. Then, standing in front of his classmates, he told the teacher that he apologized. Now, the day's work could begin. On his arrival home, he informed his parents of the event. Not wanting to take any action which might have unpleasant consequences, they advised their son to forget the incident. What a difference the outcome of this was from how a similar situation would have played out today! He still has no idea what he might have said that upset his teacher.

Cliff was born at home on a farm near Richmound, Saskatchewan, Canada. He started school in the neighbouring small community of Golden Prairie. His father was a poor farmer. When Cliff was in grade 4, the family moved to another small community, called Horsham, which was close by. Here, his father became a grain buyer. The three communities are near the Saskatchewan–Alberta border, to the northeast of the city of Medicine Hat, Alberta.

On graduating from grade twelve in 1959, he enrolled at the university in Regina. Since he was not as successful as he would have liked after one year, he moved to the University of Calgary, in Alberta. With one full year completed there, he commenced his teaching career in a small two-room country school 34 miles *(55 km)* southeast of Medicine Hat. After many summer school courses and some evening courses, he graduated in 1968 with a Bachelor of Education degree from the Univerisity of Calgary. Then, for two years, he taught grades 4 through 9 at Cypress View, also south of Medicine Hat. Following that, he taught junior and senior high school at Hilda - which is approximately 52 miles *(84 km)* to the northeast of that city - for three years. From there, he moved to Seven Persons - 12 miles *(19 km)* west of Medicine Hat - for one year. He had been the principal of each of these schools, except for one year. The next two years were spent as the Supervisor of Instruction for the Medicine Hat Rural School Division. Then he accepted a position with Taber School Division, a little farther to the west, for two years as the Assistant Superintendent.

In 1971, after spending the previous three summers attending the University of Oregon, in Eugene, Oregon, where he obtained a Master of Education degree, he became the

Superintendent of Schools in the community of Foremost for the County of Forty Mile. This jurisdiction lay to the southeast of Taber. Their three girls, born in Hilda, had now started school and his wife Anne was a "stay-at-home mom." The family stayed in Foremost for eleven years, and then moved on to Vulcan for nine years, where Cliff was the Superintendent of Schools for the County of Vulcan, located between Lethbridge and Calgary.

In 1991, they moved to Beaver Mines, near Pincher Creek, in the southwest corner of Alberta. Here, Cliff became the Superintendent for the Pincher Creek School Division. When the school jurisdictions in Alberta went through a process of amalgamation in 1994, Cliff became the Superintendent for the newly-formed Livingstone Range School Division. After many years in the classroom and in administration, he took early retirement in 1996.

He remembers one experience which he had as a school superintendent that demonstrated to him that one is better off trying to resolve a problem in person instead of by telephone or by letter. He received a call from an angry parent about 3:00 one afternoon. The man swore at Cliff and called him a g**d*** liar. This outburst placed the superintendent at a loss for words. Finally, he asked if he could go out to the man's farm to discuss the matter. This was agreeable. Cliff phoned Anne and told her what he was doing. She suggested that he take someone with him or, at least, be careful. When he arrived at the farm, the greeting was a grunt and an invitation into the house. After about thirty minutes, the problem was solved; and Cliff was invited to stay for supper. What a relief!

Cliff realizes that many people have impacted his life in a positive way and in different aspects of it. However, one man stands out - Raymond Clark, his mentor in his early years as a school superintendent.

Raymond, who was Cliff's senior by about thirty years, was a school trustee and also the chairman of the board. It is important for the superintendent and the board chairman to work well together. After a short period of time of "testing each other," the two men developed a real respect for each another. The chairman was very honest and trustworthy. The young superintendent could bounce problems and issues off him. He would listen intently and then tell Cliff what he would do in that specific situation. He always respected Cliff's decision, even when it was contrary to the advice he had given. Cliff appreciated the fact that he ran a very good meeting, being a good chairman. There were times when he had to reprimand a fellow board member for unprofessional comments or behaviour. It was usually accepted in the respectful manner in which it was given.

Raymond was a leader among trustees. He served as the president of the Alberta School Trustees Association, but was best known for his role as chairman of the Southern Alberta School Authorities Association. SASAA was set up to negotiate teachers' salaries on behalf of the school boards. He was "hated" by most of the rural teachers in southern Alberta. He enjoyed the adversarial nature of negotiations. Because he was a very competitive person, bargaining was his "cup of tea."

Cliff learned from him that, even though you are in an adversarial relationship, you must always be fair. You always give your competitor a chance to go back to "his people" with something - so that he can look like a winner. Even when you are in very serious negotiations with someone, always remember never to say or do something that would hinder your ability to work together in the future.

Raymond Clark had a very positive impact on Cliff and on education in Southern Alberta. As a former teacher in SASAA, I knew of Mr. Clark's reputation. However, our teacher negotiators considered him a tough, but fair, negotiator and respected him.

Since 1987, Cliff, his wife Anne, and two of their daughters have owned and operated up to three Sylvan Learning Centres. Two were in Calgary and one was in Lethbridge. The two in Calgary were sold in 2002. After he retired, Cliff helped out in the operations. The one in Lethbridge is being run by their daughter Karen, with some assistance from Anne. The centre, at which parents pay for service, offers help to students in Reading and Mathematics after school and on Saturdays. Students are successful because the instruction is individualized.

Cliff feels that public education in Alberta and Canada today is in a very bad way. Society has changed so much over the past forty years. Families are very different because of both parents in many families working, of the high divorce rate, of many single-parent families, and of a generally more permissive society. These factors make it extremely difficult for teachers to teach.

I asked Cliff to tell about the Chinook winds, which are very common in the area where he and Anne live. Here is how he describes them.

"Pincher Creek is situated in Southwestern Alberta. We experience the famous Chinook winds. As the winds come in from the west coast laden with moisture, they rise to cross the mountains and deposit the moisture on the west side of the mountains. They then become a dry warm wind coming down the mountains blowing over Southern Alberta. During cold winters, they are very welcome. The temperature can rise from -15ºF *(-26ºC)* to +15ºF *(-9ºC)* in a matter of an hour or two. You can go to bed when it is very cold outside. Half through the night you hear the wind blowing outside and the water is running off the roof. During the summer the Chinook is a very hot, dry wind; and it dries out the soil and can cause drought conditions."

I might add that, when the Chinook Arch, a formation between the cloud cover and the sky in the southwest, we know that these winds are coming. Seeing it and experiencing what Cliff has described for the first time will hold the witness in awe.

He is currently involved in the Rotary Club and the Chamber of Commerce. Retirement is great! The family also did some grain farming on weekends and during summer holidays.

Our family had moved to Vauxhall, in the Taber School Division, about two years before Cliff became Assistant Superintendent there. He was well-liked by our staff. We were sorry to see him leave as we saw his potential as a Superintendent. From what I have read on the internet, on speaking with him, and in his submission to me, I feel that we had been right about his potential.

In 1971, there was the need to have a clerical assistant hired for the school library where I worked. When two ladies applied, Cliff interviewed them in their respective homes. Then he came to me with his impressions. One could type, but the other could not. He seemed to favour the latter, but left me to decide. Although I needed a typist, I chose the one that did not type. As it turned out, the one who could type moved out of the town in a year or two. The other one remained as my aide for nine years, performing a good job in her role. Except when I had a student earning credits by working for me on two occasions, I did the typing. Both Cliff's recommendation and my selection turned out well. When I telephoned Cliff to invite him to participate in this book and told him who I am and where I had been the school librarian, he remembered me.

9

Dennis Hawn

Surrey, British Columbia, Canada

He is a white-haired man just over fifty years of age. By his own admission, he is overweight. He can be seen in his apartment block, on a sidewalk, or in the local mall on his power wheelchair. He asserts that he is a survivor! What has he survived? How has he been able to survive? This is the story of a man who would not give up when faced with adversity. It has not been easy by any means. He is a symbol of hope for those who have similar situations.

Dennis was born in St. Joseph's Hospital in Comox, British Columbia, Canada. On birth, it was learned that he had a congenital defect called *spina bifida,* caused by an incomplete closure (an opening) of one or more vertebral arches of the spine, resulting in the malfunction of the spinal cord. In the case of Dennis, he was born with a hole in his back, immediately above his tail bone. He was bleeding to death! The statistics indicate that only 2% of babies with this condition survive. Dennis was one of that minority. He survived!

Attending school presented challenges. He was an outcast in his class. He was also the biggest student in each grade throughout his time in school. At the age of twelve, Dennis spent much time in hospital for orthopedic surgery. This procedure is not without risk. He survived!

After about grade 5, Dennis discovered how bullies operate. He was a sitting-duck for their pea-shooting target practice. He could not avoid their missiles - and they knew it. Bullies - children, youth, and adults - are everywhere to attack the vulnerable.

He did have good times though. He hiked through the forests near his home at Fanny Bay on Vancouver Island, in British Columbia. This was accomplished on crutches. He showed that he was capable of taking a boat by himself to go fishing. Most people were frightened by his bravery and composure. They saw only a boy on crutches. They did not see a boy who had a desire and a willingness to do something that he liked and knew he could do. Rowing was a pastime that gave him much enjoyment. His boat was not an ultra-light rowing shell for competition. It was a 10-foot *(3 m)*, 132-pound *(60 kg)* practical boat that was built at home. More fun was supplied by 3-foot *(1 m)* waves, but they were not essential. Lying in the bottom of his boat in complete solitude and drifting along in the water provided relaxation on many summer days. He was not yet a teenager!

Because of the economic situation in the mid 1960s, Dennis left his favourite places on Vancouver Island, moving to where his dad found work, near White Rock, a border city to the south of Vancouver. Moving did not give him a favourable impression. Nevertheless, he learned what was available for recreation in this new setting. He could no longer go boating when the tide was high. In its place, he went camping at the most deserted and primitive places that he and his friends could find. He could adapt to a new situation. Despite the crutches, he was able to keep up with the other boys. He could even move backwards with his crutches. He survived!

When Dennis was in his mid twenties, he faced another

challenge. He met what he considered to be a fantastic woman. She seemed to accept him for what he was and to want to help him overcome a rut into which he had fallen. Since she was married, it seemed as though it should have been a safe relationship. He discovered that this was not the case. What she really wanted was someone who was so desperate for love that he would let her do whatever she wanted. She used Dennis to provide her with the unconditional support that she needed to leave her husband. When Dennis' dad died, this woman invited Dennis to move into her home with her.

Within three years, it became very evident that this woman, who had been abused by her mother and spoiled by her father, was very insecure. She had been diagnosed with progressive multiple sclerosis of the brain stem. Dennis stayed with her while she went through the diagnosis and a very poor form of adaptation. She was in denial over her ailment. She felt that Dennis was weird and that, if he were behaving like a "real person" or a "functional human", she would overcome her problems and return to normal. This, of course, was not going to happen.

Dennis says that he endured much because he was either too stubborn or too stupid to quit. By this time, she was in a wheelchair and he had to do everything for her. In her estimation, he did not do anything properly. Frequently, he had to pick up her evening meal from the floor because he was eating too quickly, thus making her self-conscious. Another quirk was that she required him to board up the windows because it was too bright outside. He survived - but barely!

He did have a respite from the abuse of this woman - but it was in a hospital. Here, he recuperated from the overuse of tranquillizers. This little hint that paradise was lost went largely unnoticed except when the inconvenience to her was too much. Then, Dennis would be reminded that he was the "crazy" one. He considers it amazing how that works.

Dennis stayed with that situation for ten years. He had felt that it would be a failure on his part if he would leave her. He later read an article in a magazine of a study that had been carried out. The study found that women fear dead bodies more than anything else. However, what men fear most is failure. He cannot speak for women, but he does agree with the finding for men. That was his fear!

Eventually, he woke up. That was nearly ten years ago. He has a new circle of friends. However, he still has a certain amount of hesitation or panic when he thinks about a new close relationship. There are scars - mental scars - that do not show. He does not know if those will ever heal, but he says that he will survive.

At age forty-five, he went back to school and earned a diploma in automation and robots. While at school, he met two very positive people who provided a good effect on his life. One was a wise counselor who gave him the title of "survivor" and then taught him how to embrace it and grow from it. Another was an instructor who believed in Dennis and encouraged him at all times.

He uses the knowledge gained in school to teach computer literacy for the Parks and Recreation Branch of the City of Surrey, a suburb of Vancouver. He is also branching out into amateur radio and the local Emergency Social Services programme. He not only survives, but he lives to help others.

Dennis has had an interest in amateur radio for at least

thirty years. When he was at college, he learned that one of the other instructors was a volunteer examiner who could give him the required examination. Dennis recognized the opportunity and took advantage of it. He now has the call sign VE7DGH.

Since he lives in a small apartment, he does not have the option of a large, spectacular antenna array. However, he does have two short range radios. He has joined the local emergency communications network. In case of the inevitable earthquake in the Vancouver area, he is prepared to assist local officials in several capacities.

He survives, for now, as always, one day at a time and one crisis at a time. He can laugh and joke as he watches the coming of the end of the world as we know it. Most importantly, he survives! How many of us would survive and even find some enjoyment in doing so? How many of us would give up trying and, instead, expect family, friends, or government agencies to do everything for us?

I met Dennis one day when my wife and I went on a bus tour with residents of the complex where Dennis lives. Dennis and I sat across from each other on the bus and visited until we reached our destination. Since then, I have seen Dennis at various times at the complex and at the mall. He always stops for a little visit. I see him as a man who has ability in various fields and who uses it wherever he can instead of sitting back and doing nothing.

10
Don Summers

Surrey, British Columbia, Canada

He could not believe it! He was looking at the water bill for Green Timbers from the City of Surrey, British Columbia. For one month's use of water, the charge was $12,000. How could that be? The nurseries on site were closed down. The only demand for water was for drinking and for toilets. It did not seem possible that seven people would need that much for a whole year, let alone one month.

Don's heart was pounding as he and his staff sought the site where there was flooding. They searched through the buildings, around the seedling compounds, over the creeks and ditches - all over the site. They even jumped on the pavement in the parking lots where they knew that the water mains traveled underneath. Don phoned the city's water department and asked them about it. However, they insisted that their method of data recording was foolproof.

Everyone returned to work. While they kept on watching for floods, they monitored the city's water meter for two weeks and could detect only a small flow into the site. Even after presenting the evidence to the water department, it took another month of wrangling with them, using Green Timber's representative in Victoria, the provincial capital, to have the issue resolved.

Can you guess what the problem turned out to be? Their water meter reader had missed a decimal point in the readout.

Who says that decimal points are insignificant little dots?

Don was born in Vancouver, British Columbia, Canada. The first school which he attended was Sir Sanford Fleming Elementary School, in South Vancouver. Tackling the physical sciences in high school was a huge chore for him, but it taught him that if you really want to do something, you can do it. He needed those courses to achieve a degree in biology - something which he desired very much.

His post-secondary education was obtained at Simon Fraser University, in Burnaby, a suburb of Vancouver. From this institution he earned a Bachelor of Science degree, a Master of Pest Management degree, and a certificate in Business Writing, Public Relations, and Marketing Communication.

Don, whose only language is English, has served in the Naval Reserve - at HMCS Discovery, in Stanley Park, Vancouver.

Although his principal vocation was an extension biologist and manager, he has been a hospital janitor and a cleaner for newly constructed buildings for several years each. He also worked in a pulp mill for a couple of years, and is currently a professional writer in Surrey, British Columbia, another suburb of Vancouver. He has had a number of menial jobs, but he has also managed programmes with million-dollar budgets. What he has learned is that if you trust people to do a good job for you, they will.

When he worked for the Forest Service, he made numerous memorable trips from Victoria up-island and over to the south half of the British Columbia from Ft. St. John to the United States border. He met and talked with many local people and was able to experience some of their lives. Those trips around the province taught him that there are many ways to make a living, and that there are more important things in life than the position you hold or the amount of money you earn.

On one occasion, he was one in a party which had some research trials going on in Salmon Arm, in south-central British Columbia. Their home base was Victoria, the provincial capital. In the spring, they had laid out the trials and taken their initial measurement. They were on their way back in the summer to check the results.

They traveled by ferry across the Strait of Georgia to Tsawassen, just south of Vancouver, and were on their way down the causeway when Don asked his technician, "Did you bring the spring data and maps along?" Hmm, the answer was a sheepish "No." As there could be no turning back at that point, they continued on their trip. When they arrived at the worksite in Salmon Arm, it was necessary for them to figure everything out again. Fortunately, they had used much flagging tape on the trial trees and had noted the initial data that they had collected on the tape. That taught Don the value of redundancy in everything, which he did as a scientist from then on.

Working as a biologist with the British Columbia Forest Service meant that he traveled throughout the province many times. The main roads to many places became very boring after traveling on them time and time again. Eventually, he and his colleagues learned to take alternate routes, either paved roads or Forest Service roads. What can he say? British Columbians have a beautiful province, and he has spent much of his life exploring it. He seldom thinks about traveling elsewhere. He has not finished learning about his home province yet.

Don uses two terms in regard to his work: R&D and extension. I asked him to define them for the benefit of readers who might not be familiar with them. "R&D" means research and development. "Extension" basically means connecting the people who do the research with those who use that research in their work.

An example of extension might be a forest geneticist connecting with people who produce seed, or a tree physiologist connecting with some nursery workers. It might involve arranging training, translating technical jargon, writing information articles that explain how research might be used, or other situations. In the United States, extension is frequently used to describe adult education for those working in forestry, agriculture, horticulture, and other such fields.

Don had the honour of managing the Extension Services site at Green Timbers Urban Forest, in Surrey, for thirteen years. He was in charge of the R&D facility, the program, and the talented staff that made it a success. He managed to negotiate successfully with provincial authorities in Victoria over the years and to provide the resources which the staff needed, while encouraging them to invent their own programmes. They all succeeded. He and his staff were known all over Canada, the northwestern United States, and many parts of Europe and Asia. The group was held up as a model for extension for several years. This, indeed, was a great achievement!

He has no regrets regarding his work over the years, and he is happy with the success that he has had. If he had been more successful in the conventional sense, he would have missed many interesting experiences. His philosophy of life is to learn, earn, contribute, and have fun. Too many people tend to concentrate on only one or two of those attributes.

He had an opportunity to work with Jenji Konishi. This man was a forester, the manager of Seed Production for the Forest Service in the 1980s, and he hired Don to work there. He was a firm, but kind and thoughtful, boss. If you went to him with a half-baked idea, he would turn you down flat. However, if you showed that you had thought things through, he would listen. He was an inspiration in how to manage staff, deal with conflict, and find common ground between disparate points of view. Don says that he learned much from him.

I asked Don to tell about the beginning and the purpose of the nursery at Green Timbers and why was it terminated.

The nursery began in the 1930s as a way to quell the anger of residents who had seen the last remaining forest in the area cut down. The timing was perfect because there was a growing recognition that the forests which had been cut down around the province must be re-stocked. Natural regeneration was not doing the job.

On Shelbourne St. in Victoria, there was a small research nursery that just happened to have some stock to transplant over at Green Timbers. That gave Green Timbers a roaring start, and the momentum continued into the 21st century.

The Green Timbers Reforestation Centre was a success and ended up being the provincial center for forest nursery R&D and extension. It produced three to five million seedlings a year for reforestation. Interestingly, it was also a centre of community involvement right from the start. The province was able to involve the local politicians in the 1930s by having them plant the commemorative plantation when it opened.

The site is still attracting politicians and the community to this day.

However, all good projects eventually come to an end. The provincial government started to take a hands-off approach to the forest industry in the late 1980s. It privatized most of the forest nurseries which they had and retained only three: Green Timbers Nursery and Surrey Nursery in Surrey, and Skimikin Nursery in Salmon Arm.

For several years, the government helped the nursery industry to establish itself though R&D and extension programmes operating from Green Timbers and supplied their small business programme with trees from the remaining nurseries. By the 2000s, they felt that the industry could stand on its own. That coincided with a new government's efforts to downsize the provincial Forest Service. Thus, the remaining three nurseries and the R&D centre at Green Timbers were privatized or shut down.

Don's hobbies are computing - exploring 'Web 2.0' - and photography. He is returning to the latter after many years of being inactive.

I met Don when I telephoned his office at the time that I was doing research on the Green Timbers Arboretum for our website. I spoke with him once again when I telephoned the membership of the Green Timbers Heritage Society. Shortly after the latter, we met each other in person at an Arbor Day event at Green Timbers. Since that time, both of us have served on the board of the Green Timbers Heritage Society. With his wealth of experience, Don is a valued member of the board.

11
Elena Frolovskaya

Moscow, Russia

A mother taught her young daughter numerous proverbs and sayings which she, now as an adult, remembers clearly. She testifies to the truth in them through her own experiences. Here are a few of them.

- A friend in need is a friend indeed.
- Two minds are better than one.
- Give credit when credit is due.
- Place business before pleasure.
- An eel cannot be hidden in a sack.
- A word is like a sparrow - you cannot catch it once it has flown.
- You cannot die before your death.
- A burden of one's choice is not felt.
- Don't play with fire!

There is one that may sound odd, but it is so true. "You cannot die before your death." Regardless of our circumstances, we have life and should make the most of it. This chapter is about a woman who portrays the beauty that can be in one's life.

Elena (pronounced something like "Yellenna" with the stress on the second vowel) was born in Moscow, the capital of Russia, shortly after the end of World War II. She believes that was a hard time for people all over the world. She is most grateful to her dear parents who did everything possible - and impossible - to make her life happy. As a child, she was very happy indeed. Her surname is Frolovskaya, her husband's family name.

She was nearing seven years old when she started to school. Because many of her classmates were one year older, she was required to pass an examination because the examiners did not want to accept her because of her age. She was very pleased with her success in doing so and waited excitedly for her first day of school. On September 1, she awoke early and announced that she was not going to school. Her parents were greatly surprised. Why would she say that? She had passed the examination. She answered, "I cannot go to school because I know nothing!" Her mother kindly assured her that it was all right and that soon she would learn many things at school. She learned that her mother was absolutely right, just as she always was.

At school, Elena was the monitor for many years and was also active in helping schoolmates and pupils of junior classes with their studies. Probably that gave her the idea that she should become a teacher. She completed school at the age of sixteen, and was awarded a silver medal for her good grades.

At the age of seventeen, she entered the pedagogical faculty of the Moscow Linguistic University. After five years of study, she emerged with two professions - interpreter and teacher of English and German. She was one in a group of graduates sent to Egypt to work as interpreters.

Elena enjoyed her two years of working in Egypt very much. During this time, she took the opportunity to see this ancient country from inside. She visited every museum and every interesting place in Cairo. She traveled to Alexandria,

Luxor, the Valley of the Kings, Memphis, Saqqara, Aswan, Suez, and many other historical sites. Of particular interest were the Great Pyramids in Giza! She visited them "dozens of times." She even entered the Great Pyramid of Khufu! Although she attempted to climb it, it was too high to go far. The Sphinx also impressed her greatly. It is the largest sculpture in the world - 80 metres *(262 ft)* long and 20 metres *(66 ft)* high - and "hand-made!"

These visits provided unforgettable impressions! She kept her camera busy recording "hundreds and hundreds" of photographs, which help her to maintain a good memory of her stay there - the greatest experience in her life.

After her return to Moscow from Egypt, she joined the English Section of Radio Moscow, which a year later became part of the recently organized World Service in English. For two years, she was a producing editor. Her assignment was to arrange the recording of programmes in English and to prepare materials for live broadcasts. It was a very interesting position, but having to work shifts was not convenient for her.

Thus, in 1980, she transferred to the Letters Department, where she has been working since. In that same year, she met her future husband, Alexander, who worked in the African Service of the same radio station. They have been married since 1982, and have two daughters - Olga and Anna.

Elena really likes her work. She enjoys corresponding daily with dozens of people from all over the world. She says that she and they are very different but, at the same time, they have much in common. All desire to find the essence of life.

Her colleagues are very professional journalists and broadcasters - and great enthusiasts, too. It was a privilege for her to have worked for so many years with Joe Adamov, the legend of Russian broadcasting. Anyone who has listened to the Voice of Russia will agree with her. He is missed by colleagues and listeners alike.

Elena has time for several hobbies. She likes to travel. She has visited Hungary and Romania. During the time of the U.S.S.R., she visited Armenia, Azerbaijan, Georgia, Lithuania, and Ukraine.

Photography is a hobby that she has enjoyed for over forty years. It was her father who interested her in this wonderful pastime. When she was only twelve years old, he gave her his camera and said, "Go out and take some pictures. Do it as you feel like doing." Out she went and took pictures. That night, she and her father developed the film together in the dark bathroom, and then they printed some pictures. Oh, how bad they were! At that time, her father gave her advice on how to avoid typical mistakes. This young girl learned well and still follows the rules which he provided. Today, she enjoys walking about Moscow with her camera and taking pictures.

Elena has been collecting recipes for thirty years. Her dream is to publish a cookbook for her daughters and her friends. When her daughters were four or five years old, she decided that she must teach them to cook. They began with helping her to prepare salads. At the age of twelve, they could make a cake. At the age of fifteen, they were good at cooking some meat and chicken dishes. By the age of twenty, they could prepare dinner for a small party. This achievement by the girls has made their mother proud of them.

She likes to crochet, but has very little free time for this hobby; to sing, but only when nobody can hear her; and to watch films based on Agatha Christie's books. She gathers information about Princes Diana of the United Kingdom. Since her school years, she has been interested in UFOs and has read numerous books about them, in both Russian and English.

Her family has a small county house with a little garden where they go on weekends in the summer and for their vacation. Elena has a fascination for growing flowers. I asked her to describe this place, known in Russia as a *dacha*. Here is how she describes it.

"I enjoy going to our *dacha* on weekends in spring and summer, and I also spend my vacation there. I usually have my summer leave in July. I live in the centre of Moscow, in one of the streets of Sadovoye Koltso (Garden Ring) - one of the noisiest and most polluted places in our city, with practically no trees despite its name; so you can guess that throughout the year my only dream is to go to the country for a breath of fresh air. My dream comes true from early May, when it is time to go to *dacha*, till the end of September, when the weather becomes cold for staying there overnight because we have no heating there.

"Our *dacha* is a small two-storey wooden house where we can live in warm weather. We have three small rooms and a kitchen on the ground floor and a room and a little hall on the first floor - quite enough for the family and guests. In our flat in Moscow there are two rooms and a kitchen.

"Originally, the owner was my father; but, after his death, it belongs to me. Back in 1970, my father got a small plot of land 50 kilometres *(31 miles)* from Moscow for free. It was one of 40 plots in the forest one and a half kilometres *(1 mi)* from the railway station. By the way, it takes me an hour to get there by train and then a 20-minute walk from the station to the house.

"I remember very well how my parents and I were

discussing the plan of our future house and the garden – in which part of the garden would we have the house built, what size it would be, how many rooms would it have, what plants we were going to grow, and so on and so forth. It was so exciting that I remember it till now.

"Our plot of land is 30 metres *(98 ft)* long and 20 metres *(66 ft)* wide, which is 600 square metres *(3/20 acres)*. The house – 6 metres *(20 ft)* long and 6 metres *(20 ft)* wide, which is 36 square metres *(388 sq ft)*, on the ground floor, and 18 square metres *(194 sq ft)* on the first floor.

"When I come to my *dacha*, I forget all about my problems. All my troubles seem to be so far away when I enter my garden with the flowers blooming, vegetables growing, butterflies and bees flying, birds singing, and the sun shining brightly! I am happy there always, even in rainy weather.

"I enjoy growing cucumbers, pumpkins, squash, greenery, garlic, and onions. I have many flowers and a green lawn. I have five apple trees and two pear trees. I can see the results of my activity immediately. I sow the seeds – and they grow! I trim the tree – and it looks beautiful! I plant flowers – and they bloom! My neighbors follow my activity and encourage me.

"I have wonderful neighbors, very good people, who are sure to help each other in need. Actually, we all have known each other for over thirty-five years. We are more than friends – we are a family.

"*Dacha* is the place where you can realize your talents as a designer or an architect or a gardener. *Dacha* is the place where you can put your energy – there is so much you can do in the garden and around the house. By the way, even when you are tired, you have a good rest! *Dacha* is the place where you can grow fruit and vegetables and save money on buying them. Besides you will always know what you grow have no chemicals. (We cannot be sure about what we buy). *Dacha* is the place where you can have a good rest. Actually, you need not do anything about the garden except cutting grass twice a month.

"I also like my *dacha* for the opportunity to get up early in the morning and to go out to the forest to pick berries or mushrooms. Do you know the taste of the mushroom soup with forest mushrooms in it? It's unforgettable!

"Also, I like it very much when my whole family comes to my *dacha* on weekends and we have a dinner in the garden, making salads with our own vegetables, cooking meat on hot coals "*shasklyk*", and boiling water for tea in a *samovar* - things impossible in town."

I asked Elena to tell a little about the city where she lives. She suggests that, if you ever go to Moscow, try to walk, especially round about the centre of the city.

Moscow is an ancient city, founded by Prince Yuri Dolgoruky in 1147. Be sure to see the Kremlin. It was designed by Italian architects - but there is nothing more Russian than this great fortress and the buildings inside, which were erected by Russian workers in the 14th to 16th centuries. Outside one of the walls of the Kremlin are Red Square and St. Basil Cathedral. Elena often goes there, because she has a feeling that she belongs there. Incidentally, "red" is not the exact translation into English. Several centuries ago, the Russian word used to mean "beautiful" and not the red colour as nowadays.

In Moscow, there are many old buildings with "a history" behind each. She likes to locate information about various houses in guide books first and then to go and see them. During each walk, she learns something new, although she has been studying places of interest in Moscow for some twenty years. It sounds as though she would make a good tour guide - one who knows the places and enjoys seeing them.

When Elena feels sad or when things seem to go wrong, she opens her Bible and reads it slowly aloud. She is not baptized, but reading the Bible calms her. She always keeps another book nearby. It is a selection of verses by Anna Akhmatova, a 20th century Russian poet.

Elena is a happy person. Why? In the morning, she goes to work with pleasure and, in the evening, she goes home with pleasure. Why? She has a wonderful family. Why? She has many friends. Why? She lives in the 21st century. Her slogan of life is "Live and let live!"

There are many people who have much but cannot cope with sadness and cannot enjoy life as Elena does. She is a good example for them to follow.

Here is the official statement about the Voice of Russia, where Elena works.

The Voice of Russia is a state radio company that has been broadcasting for foreign audiences since October 29, 1929. It is funded by the federal government and has a chairman and an editorial board that bring together chiefs of its broadcasting services.

The Voice of Russia Charter has been endorsed by the government. The Voice of Russia radio company has a writing staff of professionally independent journalists.

The Voice of Russia aims to brief the international community on developments in Russia, to present a true-to-life picture of what is happening in this country, and to help audiences abroad to get a better understanding of Russia.

As of date, it broadcasts in Russian and 31 foreign languages. Its 340 features introduce listeners to various sides of Russian life. People in more than 160 countries use conventional and electronic means of communication to keep in touch with the station.

There have been about 64 million visits to the Voice of Russia site on the Internet since its opening in July, 1996. People in 120 nations have visited that site. The Voice of Russia presents Real Audio broadcasts in Russian, English, German, Spanish, French and Japanese.

The Voice of Russia has collected an extensive data base on its audiences. Documentation on as many as 1,000 international projects of the Center of Sociological Studies can be found in its research archive.

Its own and foreign-based investigators feel 100 million people listen to Voice of Russia broadcasts. Most of them are socially active people of 31 to 55 years of age. They are white-collar workers (22-25%, depending on the country), college students, school teachers, and college professors (20-25%), intellectuals (10-18%), technicians and engineers (10-14%), and retired workers (20-40%). They tune in to Voice of Russia broadcasts 2 to 3 or more times a week. It is the Russian view of Russian developments that attracts up to 80 percent of the listeners. Sixty percent of the listeners are curious about life in today's Russia, and 50 percent are keen on Russian culture, history, and traditions.

The Voice of Russia has its own news agency, *Efir Digest* (Broadcast Digest), which comes out with daily roundups of broadcasts of other radio stations.

The Voice of Russia TV shop started working on its Russian- and English-language features in 1990. It has produced about 100 cultural and historical films.

The Voice of Russia maintains a partnership relation with a number of leading radio stations, which enables it to act as a reliable intermediary in attempts to sell publicity and other commercial materials to foreign media editions and streamline a specialized programme exchange.

The Voice of Russia is famous for the exclusive character of its newsreel presentation. It is considered the least biased and most democratically-oriented source of information on Russian developments. People in many countries see it as the only provider of reliable and up-to-date information on developments in this country.

Over the years when I had access to shortwave bands, I had listened to VOR occasionally. Eventually, I came across a programme entitled "Moscow Mailbag," in which listeners send in questions to be answered by the host, the late Joe Adamov. I sent in a question and Elena sent a friendly response to my message. Joe Adamov answered my question. From time to time, I would send in a question. Through my doing so, we came to know Elena better. Occasionally, she would send a seasonal greeting card, which we much appreciated. From the information that she sent me for this chapter, I can see that her many contacts around the world, too, receive friendly responses in her emails. VOR is blessed with having Elena as a valued employee. The management's willingness to allow her to continue to work after her official retirement date shows that they recognize that she is a good ambassador for Russia.

12

Ellen Edwards

New Westminster, British Columbia, Canada

It's a baby girl! The supervisor of a group of young men planting the Fraser Highway hedge in the Green Timbers area hailed John Tompson. Someone at Saint Mary's Hospital in nearby New Westminster, British Columbia, Canada, had telephoned him the news. On hearing that message, John dropped everything and ran to his old Model A Ford. He sped off toward the new Pattullo Bridge over the Fraser River, stopping only long enough to pay the toll. As mothers in those days were required to stay in hospital on two weeks' bed rest, she was very weak when John took her home. As it was winter, he carried both mother and baby all the way down a very long driveway to a cabin which he had built by Bear Creek. He quickly built up a warm fire, and all were happy in their cosy home.

This little home was in the Green Timbers / Newton area of Surrey, British Columbia. It even had electricity because nineteen-year-old John had built a waterwheel on the creek. This produced electric lights for his house, his father's house, his shop, and his barn.

Within the next ten years, three other children were born into the family. By then, John had built the house that can be seen today at the corner of 144th Street and Hawkstream Drive, in Surrey. Quite the engineering feat it was to pull this house off its foundations, down by Bear Creek, to the new road called Archibald, named after a pioneer in the area.

Ellen commenced her formal education at the one-room Green Timbers School in Surrey. It had opened about twenty years earlier when there were ten students, enough to merit a school. It was heated by a pot-bellied stove. Her teachers, Miss Evans and Miss Davies, were her inspiration to become a teacher later. Because her father had taught her to read and to do arithmetic before she started to school, she was ahead of the grade 1 class and was immediately assigned to grade 2. Enjoying reading, she helped other students who could not.

As she would often finish her grade 3 work first, the teacher would ask her to help two boys with their reading. They would go to the back of the classroom, where she would help them sound out the letters. Now she knew that she would be a teacher. Many years later, in grade 12, as part of the Future Teacher's Club, she returned to the Green Timbers School (the big new one) and marked papers for the grade 6 class. That experience reinforced her goals.

Ellen obtained a Bachelor of Education degree from the University of British Columbia, in Vancouver. She took three years full time study, interspersed with teaching four years and several summer schools between school seasons.

Her only language is English, as is her ancestry. She studied the reading and writing of French for many years, but not the conversational.

Her basic profession is schoolteacher. However, she built on that base and combined the aptitudes for management positions later on in her career. Her work life was continuously in British Columbia, Canada. She feels that teaching is a most rewarding career, and from it she has many memories. She taught in various schools, usually with mixed grades. One year at Harrison Mills, there were grades 1-5 in one room. That was a most enjoyable challenge! Their Christmas programme was the community highlight of the year! Her favourite classroom was in Castlegar - Twin Rivers, a grade 5 class with many Doukhobor children, during the year of the Big Trek to Kent. It was a very good mix of bright and slow students. A chess club was started with them.

Ellen taught grade 1 while her daughter was very young. Her sitter's husband would bring the child into the Mission school ground on his motorcycle, and the two of them would peek through the window.

This was the time when headphones and tapes were becoming popular. Thus, her classroom had three educational interest areas for the children to choose after their reading questions were completed: Artistic, Scientific, and Listening.

At Port Mann School, during the time the Port Mann Bridge was being built, she would permit the children to stand and watch the old Samson sternwheeler paddle by on the Fraser River. That is what they remember of the two years when she was there.

At Fleetwood School, she realized that all children cannot be taught in the same way to read. She yearned to learn how to help one little boy. It did not work with colourful books about trains. Both teacher and pupil needed more skills. It was at that school - grade 5 class - when they experienced the traumatic afternoon in which President Kennedy was assassinated. The children thought it was the end of the world and they wanted to stay close to Ellen.

As a teacher, she would like to have known better how to coach students who could not read. During the 1960s, the profession did not know about learning disabilities. Even after the turn of the century, there are still problems with that. That was her greatest disappointment in her professional life.

For thirty years after leaving teaching, she was involved with employment counseling and the training of career, vocational rehabilitation, and job search professionals, and other important social services. These government positions were at the New Westminster Manpower office, and then at the Regional office for British Columbia and Yukon in Vancouver. At the time, it was known as Canada Employment and Immigration Commission. She became the federal wage subsidy programmes coordinator for the region, and then wrote her own job description as training coordinator for the professionals hired to work in the numerous community contracts toward employment of youth and special needs people.

Recognition of her work was given to Ellen in 1989, when she was awarded the first national Quality of Service Award from Canada Employment and Immigration, a department of the Federal Government of Canada. For eighteen years, her work involved coordinating employment programmes for youth and special needs clientele, and training the employment counselors throughout British Columbia and Yukon Territory.

As a new employment counselor and always sensitive to training needs, she planned tours of industry and social service agencies, and organized seminars on labour market and counseling skills, for all at her workplace. The manager gave her a new position titled Agency Relations Coordinator, and she wrote the job description!

She is known as one of the stakeholders in defining competencies and setting guidelines for the career development sector practitioners in Canada (www.career-dev-guidelines.org). The cross-Canada team is still working on fine-tuning the standards to provide professional certification.

Since 1991, she has been self-employed and has developed an educational association, providing seminars and courses for those working with the full range of unemployed clientele (youth, older workers, immigrants, and people with disabilities). Her two-desk office was upstairs in her home in the Queen's Park area of New Westminster. From 1991 to 1995, while developing the business, she returned to teaching on an on-call basis, for special needs children in School District Surrey, and really enjoyed it.

Retirement from full time work comes for all. For Ellen, she made the decision at the end of 2005. "Her" educational association was transferred over to the Board of Directors and the new coordinators. After a training seminar, they joined in a party, and midst many wonderful accolades, she said farewell. The organization now had about 1,000 people involved with regular professional development days in four parts of the province. Her name is known across Canada regarding the setting of standards within the career development professional sector. Despite retirement, she is still involved in some committees.

Special friends and family members feted her retirement at the Pen Café, in New Westminster, shortly afterwards. The theme was "Release into the community after forty-five years of hard labour!" The guests all wore black and white, and the décor was most creative. A friend made a striped cap for her. As she threw it off, they all shouted, "Released!" She was ready. She does not regret retiring, but has applied for on-call teaching positions, a return to the first career.

Ellen's most memorable trip was an unexpected one to Ireland. Her cousin, Mary Butler, invited her to go with her to a Butler reunion. This worldwide family descended from the Butlers who were administrators of Ireland for the King of England. The visitors would tour their wonderful castles and mansions. The only thing that she knew about Ireland was that it is very green and that the Book of Kells resides in Trinity College Library in Dublin. The book was the one thing that she really wanted to see, but she expected to be so busy that she would be unable to do so. Mary was making the arrangements, and wrote apologizing that she could find only a very small dormitory; and, unfortunately, it was on campus at Trinity College. Also, she advised, the tour would not start until three days after her arrival in Dublin. How perfect that was! It was no hardship for Ellen!

You can imagine what she did. She visited the library every day, and learned more about the Book of Kells each time. It was housed in a locked glass display case and the Librarian of Antiquities turned the pages of the book so that a different page could be seen each day. The magnificent Book of Kells is dated about 800 CE, and written and illustrated by the monks of Ireland. There is debate as to whether they were from monasteries in Iona, Northumbria, or Kells, where it was located. The Internet article says, "Richly decorated, the Book of Kells is a masterpiece of Celtic art, and exemplifies the ecclesiastical, mystical, and artistic imagination of this early culture."

Giraldus Cambrensis, a 13th century scholar, wrote, "Look closely at it and you will penetrate the innermost secrets of art; you will find embellishments of such intricacy, such a wealth of knots and interlacing links that you might believe it was the work of an angel rather than a human being." This has inspired Ellen to have a room in her home decorated with Book of Kells designs.

Hobbies are a part of Ellen's life. Grandchildren are a major item in her "hobby" list. She enjoys keeping company with them and entertaining them. She takes them on adventures, to picnics, and to parks. They paint pictures and display them, and they make cookies. They sleep on the porch, make birdhouses, make animal farm fences out of bits of wood, and always have eggs for breakfast.

Photography is a favourite activity. Thus, each grandchild has a photo album on which to work when at her home. She records her ancestral home areas when visiting England, and special church and family events. Gardening is another hobby, but it is quite necessary in the upkeep of a home. Leadership in associations of interest has always been part of her life. One day, she will take out her gift of an easel and return to painting landscapes.

Her philosophy of life centres on love. It can accomplish much. Let the love of God flow through you and out to everyone you know.

A person who had a positive effect on Ellen was Miss Fumerton, a young lady who was the minister at the new church in Cloverdale, now a part of Surrey. She encouraged and utilized the talents of all fifty people in the little church. The values there meant that everyone used their abilities for the Lord. If one played an instrument, that person played in the orchestra for every service. If one could sing solos, that person was called upon to do so. Everyone shared the workload. At nine years of age, Ellen's potential for leadership was realized, and she started by leading the choruses. Soon she was helping in the Sunday school, and later with the youth group. That was an important start in her life – to a life of leadership.

Because of her knowledge of the Green Timbers area since childhood, I asked her to tell of the changes that she has seen in the area over her lifetime. Following is her description.

"When I was a child, our family would drive by the small trees in our Model A, or '49 Chevy or '52 Chevy, on the way to Fraser Highway. They were mostly all the same height, and every year grew taller. Dad (John Tompson) would tell us about how he and the other local young men hired by the Green Timbers Nursery, stumbled over stumps and fallen branches and brambles to dig holes to plant new seedlings, after the big logging (Kings Mill) was over. They were advised how many to plant in a certain area, and it seemed that the area could hold many more seedlings than they planted. But it worked out just right, as the trees grew quickly and taller and took more space, and soon made a wonderful forest for wild animals and birds and native plants like salmon berries. We had a lot of deer around in the 40s and 50s, but the bears (of the Bear Creek) disappeared when the forest disappeared in the 30s. While we picked thimble berries and salmon berries in the forest, we would hear woodpeckers pecking, squirrels chattering, and birds chirping.

"When I was fifteen, for the fall months I would ride my bicycle every Saturday morning up to the house of the owner of the gas station that was at the corner of Nichol (140th) and Fraser Highway. Mrs. Orrock was my guitar teacher and taught me several chords and how to use the capo, and then I could play even more! And then I had to play guitar at church! That was okay because I could mark the chords on the hymns in the hymn book, so I knew when to change them! And – I got to sit beside my boyfriend, which I couldn't do, otherwise.

"The Green Timbers area consisted of families spread out every five or ten or twenty acres *(2, 4, 8 ha)*. There were not that many people living in the two miles *(3 km)* from my home at Hunt (80th) up Archibald (144th). As we drove or walked or cycled on the gravel road, we could name all the families, including the bee man who had barking German Shepherds tied to the bee hives. Janson's Grocery Store was right across from the Green Timbers' School (and sold jawbreakers - 3 for 1¢), and Janson's big dairy farm was many acres at 144th and 88th. There was a strawberry farm, and several small farms. Most people had a few chickens and a cow and a big vegetable garden and a fruit tree or three. It was in the days of self-sufficiency. Every mother canned fruit and vegetables, and every man raised a calf for meat, which was stored in the Freezer Locker in Whalley.

"Now we see subdivisions on every property. There are no acreages left. Houses, houses. Mostly large. No small homes with tall fir trees at the front. No woodsheds and barns. No horse or cow at the fence. No chicken houses to clean, or eggs to gather. But the area looks prosperous, with tidy gardens and lots of people coming and going. When I was a girl in the area, Kennedy Road (88th Ave.) didn't go past Janson's farm. We had to walk through a trail to Fleetwood School for our one school outing, and I remember we were given Dixie cups with a tiny wooden spoon. The highlight of our year! Now 88th Avenue is a major four-lane thoroughfare, wider than Fraser Highway. Green Timbers Forest was to be a Forest in perpetuity. That is what my father always said. The Minister of Forests had promised this in his speech at the Inaugural Plantation as the dignitaries, standing on clean boards, planted the trees that are there today. (Dad, Harry Baker and other young men prepared all this while working in the mud, so as not to mess up those boards!)

"Well, the Governments did not live up to the promise too well. We have a Hydro line through the Forest, and also 96th and 100th Avenues cut through it. Then came the disturbing discovery that a great area was cleared for a stadium or something. The old-timers and the present Green Timbers neighbours rallied together and said 'NO!' Therefore, about twenty years ago, we formed the Green Timbers Heritage Society, agreed upon a lake for the cleared area, with access to the woods. We work closely with all governments and have their continuous support, to maintain and protect the Green Timbers Forest. It is an ongoing negotiation.

"The Forest today is proud and tall, natural, and mature. The Society has cut trails and built bridges so everyone can enjoy the Forest. We have provided educational Arbor Days and signs and tours, to urge everyone to protect this part of our country."

I met Ellen when my wife Pam and I joined the Board of Directors of the Green Timbers Heritage Society. She has a friendly smile and a kind word for everyone. She tends to any responsibility given to her quickly and efficiently. She can be seen at any event involving Green Timbers Urban Forest. If the event is something that children can enjoy, her grandchildren can be seen with her. I hope that any visitors to the Vancouver area of British Columbia will take time to visit the Green Timbers Urban Forest in Surrey that Ellen has remembered so well.

13
Erkan Kiraz

Alikahya–Izmit, Turkey

It was 3:04 in the early hours of August 17, 1999, when the tremor hit his city. It was devastating! Erkan, his wife Hanife, and their two young daughters, ages five and two, survived. The people living in the affected cities of Izmit, Sakarya, Duzce, and Istanbul, in the Marmara Region of western Turkey were in deep sleep when it happened. Under the extreme heat of this terrible August, most people were wearing only pants or were completely naked.

In an instant, the daily life of peace and prosperity was changed into a time of despair. The apartment block of eight floors where the family lived was destroyed. As a result, they and others like them lived in the streets and in open areas for months. Then, they moved to a tent town, where they stayed for more months. They waited in a town of prefabricated houses on the nearby plains and hills while permanent mass housing was completed. The earthquake and its effects were very traumatizing on the Turkish people of the area.

Erkan was born in Derince, Izmit-Kocaeli City, Turkey. Izmit is an industrial city in today's Turkey. However, its history goes back 3,000 years through Thracian times, Bithynian Kingdom, Roman Empire, and Ottoman Empire. In ancient times, the city was called Nicomedia, and was the capital city of the Eastern Roman Empire. The name was derived from King Nicomed of the Bithynian Kingdom.

Through the years, the name Nicomedia was transformed into today's Izmit.

Erkan began his education at Cumhuriyet Primary School and finalized it at Pirireis Primary School of Derince Town in Izmit City. After seven years, he graduated from Izmit High School for Imams and Preachers. Then, he entered the Graduation Final Examinations of the Derince High School, Izmit City.

He had to work during the day and study at night in the midst of everyday ideological conflicts among students having left, right, socialist, and communist ideologies. This brought about daily street violence and murderous clashes.

His first language is Turkish. However, he has a working knowledge of English, German, and French. Erkan would like to mention three persons whom he honours for what they have done for him in helping him to learn other languages. Naci Arici, his Arabic teacher, provided him with much advice in his learning of French and German. Mr. Kemal provided much assistance in improving his English. Muhammed Aslam Zahit, from Karachi, Pakistan, with much patience, taught him much about English writing and grammar through his many letters.

Erkan served as a 2nd Lieutenant in the Turkish army during 1979–1980. He started as Commander 2nd Lieutenant Officer Candidate Trainee at Egridir Isparta City. He continued with the same designation at Tuzla Istanbul. His next assignment was as Infantry 2nd Lieutenant Officer at Istanbul, and then was reassigned as Artillery English Translator 2nd Lieutenant Officer in Istanbul, and finally at the Joint Turkish-American Nuclear Batallion Detachment at Corlu, Tekirdag City.

His principal occupation is that of an import–export specialist in Turkey. He has also been a marketing expert, an advertisement collection expert, and an English translator - also in Turkey.

When he graduated from Higher School of Marketing of Kocaeli, there was no opportunity to use his new skills. However, he did not sit back and do nothing. He set targets for himself by which he could most easily attain his career in the shortest time. He was successful, but he is amazed now with how he was able to accomplish his goal.

He feels that his greatest accomplishment has been in building his life from scratch on his own without any outside help. He gives much credit for his success in his current career of Import–Export Specialist at TMMT [Toyota Manufacturing Turkey] for more than fourteen years to his reading and his learning attitudes

The areas where he would like to have been more successful are in regard to his documentary photography and his travel essays writing. Given his positive learning attitudes and his willingness to face challenges, he will be able to fulfill his desire to do well in these areas.

Travel is an activity which he enjoys. A backpacking trip from Bulgaria, Older Yugoslavia, Austria, Germany, Liechtenstein, and France is among his most memorable. Using that method of travel, one learns about a country's geography and its customs in a much different way than by motoring or by using public transit. Another one was a trip in which he flew to Poland. His most memorable cities on these two trips were Vaduz, Liechtenstein; Krakow and Warsaw, Poland.

Besides traveling, Erkan has numerous other interests.

He enjoys reading books on economics and politics. He likes to learn new languages, having a command of three as previously mentioned. He is not bothered by challenges in adopting changes in daily life. Among those are the computer, the Internet, and the digital world. If all these were not enough, he takes documentary pictures, writes travel essays, and keeps memoirs. He certainly is accumulating information which, some day, could be a book or several books for his descendants and for the general public.

His philosophy of life is that one should work without expectation of any instant return and use its profit return for one's long lifespan infinitely. He has exemplified this in his life when he started with nothing and, over the years, has built up his successful career.

Through documentary pictures and travel essays, he has met many people, either in person or by correspondence. He appreciates his friends, whether they be national or international. He mentions some of the prominent ones. They include the following: Savas Karakas; Mesrob II Mutafyan, Holy Patriarch of Turkish Armenians; Barthelemeos, Holy Patriarch of Turkish Phanar Orthodox Patriarchy; Professor Dr. Atilla Cetin from University of Sakarya; Dr. Yusuf Cam, from Commerce University of Istanbul; Professor Dr. Hikmet Ozdemir, from Armenian Research Center for Turkish History Society; and Duane Duff and Patrick Little, from Canada.

I asked Erkan to tell a little about the Muslim faith in his country. Islam means peace in essence. For him, the best and adoptable practice of Islam was carried out only by the Ottoman Empire by allowing every race, nationality, and religion within its territories. To obtain a better understanding of the essence of this faith, he suggests that one should examine the Ottoman Empire's Social and Religious Life History.

I wanted a Turkish translation of one of the pages in the section on railroad museums on our website. Therefore, I wrote to a Turkish museum and asked if someone would do this for me. The translation was undertaken by Erkan. I have noticed that visitors to that part of our website check that page. Later, someone wrote to me in Turkish about railways. I forwarded the letter to Erkan, who translated it for me into English. Then, he translated my response back into Turkish. I appreciated it very much.

I have seen many pictures that Erkan has taken. He has a wide range of subjects, but I particularly like his nature pictures. He seems to enjoy this pastime very much.

14

Frederick Harley McCurdy

Cambridge, Ontario, Canada

Have you ever wondered what it was like behind the scenes of a sports' telecast in the 1950s? Friday night was fight night in New York City. The Canadian Broadcasting Corporation (CBC) carried the telecasts for Canadian viewers. Fred, who worked for MacLarens Advertising, had the task of supervising the commercial portions of the programme following the fights. The programme was sponsored by Buckingham Cigarettes, with Herb May as the commercial announcer and Jim Coleman as the sportscaster/interviewer. Do you boxing fans detect a possible problem? Yes, there was a real problem. Those at CBC never knew how long the show would run. It could be five minutes - or fifty, depending on who knocked out whom, and when.

Add an ingredient. This night, Jim Coleman was scheduled to interview Jack Kent Cooke. Who was he? He was the owner and operator of Toronto's most successful radio station, CKEY. He also owned and operated the Toronto Maple Leafs Baseball Team, a member of the International League. Personnel rehearsed Mr. Cooke for the programme - including time out for commercials. Everyone awaited the end of the fight. However, the boxers did not know that the interview of the radio and baseball magnate was waiting, too. There was no knockout!

Instead of the usual fifteen or twenty minutes, the fight

ran long, leaving a bare three minutes for the programme. In such a circumstance as that, the procedure was to run without sponsors - therefore, there would be no commercials. Mr. Cooke did not understand this, and could not believe there were no commercials, since his radio success at CKEY was based heavily on commercials.

Air time! Jim introduced his guest, and, after a short preamble, asked Mr. Cooke a question, whereupon Mr Cooke looked a little puzzled and asked, "Where is the commercial?" Jim, without blinking an eye said: "There is no commercial. This is the CBC. Thanks for being with us, Mr. Cooke." That was the end of the show!

MacLarens and Fred McCurdy did not hear the end of that for a long, long time. It was years before Mr. Cooke consented to appear again on the CBC.

Fred was born in Tillsonburg Memorial Hospital and grew up in Corinth, a small cross-roads community west of Tillsonburg, east of Aylmer, in Elgin County, Ontario, Canada. He is the product of a schoolmaster's son and a cheese maker's daughter. He suggests that this is why he likes squeaky-fresh curds - or nippy old cheddar cheese with a fresh-from-the-oven apple pie!

Two-and-a-half years later - just as he was becoming used to his surroundings, a brother came to live with Fred and his parents. After that addition, his mother told everyone, "That was it; she had everything zippered up. Case closed." That comment left her young son with a curious feeling about the opposite sex and a somewhat murky impression of producing babies.

Family life proceeded very normally during the years of the depression of the 1930s. Fred's dad, Harley, succeeded his grandfather as cheese maker, and he began his formal education at Corinth Public School.

Not long after, Harley left his job, suffering from a serious mental depression. He stayed inside at home, and was really very ill. To help him to come out of it, Fred's parents opened a small store from a front-facing storage room in the house where they lived.

In addition to the store, they installed gasoline pumps. Old-timers will remember the kind - the ones with the ten-gallon *(45-litre)* glass holding tank at the top. Fred thinks that he pumped about a million gallon-feet of gasoline into those tanks. Eventually, pumps as we know them today came into being, eliminating all of that pumping.

The store included a brand new Coca-cola soda pop cooler - the kind with the lift-top and half filled with ice-cold water. Fred had the responsibility of seeing that the cooler was filled with pop - which included Stubby orange, Vernor's ginger ale, Wishing Well cream soda, and Dad's old-fashioned root beer! Of course, there were always Coke and Pepsi - all at a nickel a bottle and two cents more for take-out. They purchased the cooler for nothing down and a dollar a week until it was paid off.

Within a couple of years, World War II began. Harley went to work in Ingersoll - a town about 15 miles *(24 km)* from home - at the Morrow Screw and Nut factory, where he worked in the heat-treating department, toughening up screws and fasteners that were required in the war effort. Since he worked the night shift, he could not tend store with Fred's mother, Ruby, during the day because he had to catch as much sleep as possible before leaving for work in the evening.

As the elder son, Fred's responsibilities increased and included the unpacking of the weekly grocery order, delivered in cartons by truck from the wholesaler in London, Ontario. The family had a circulating heater in those days, and he remembers well piling fire wood and shovelling coal from the bin in the basement to fuel the heater so that they could keep warm in winter!

Since Canada was at war, there was rationing with which to contend as well. Butter, sugar, preserves, meat, and gasoline were some of the items that were rationed. His dad would often collect coupons from those who did not need them as much, and use them for those who were really short-handed. To this day, friends still say thanks for such help during difficult times. For example, during the tobacco harvest season, from June through September, farmers would often exhaust their bank credit. The McCurdys were able to provide supplies and food to keep them going. It all helped.

In 1942, they installed frozen foods storage lockers, complete with a hanging room and butchering table. Farmers would come in, hang their animals; and then, several days later, they would come in and butcher them, wrap the meat, and freeze it in the storage locker, which they could rent for a year. The fee was $5 for a small box, and $10 for a large one. Eventually, home freezers became popular and replaced lockers.

The food lockers, the gas pumps, and the groceries provided a growing business. Harley worked in Ingersoll, and Ruby ran the business and the house. Fred made out very well. At age ten, he was allowed to work during the tobacco season on his uncle's farm - driving horse-drawn boats of tobacco leaves to the kilns from the fields - for a dollar a day.

He earned enough money to purchase a bicycle that first season, and used it to carry his brother Bob on the crossbar to school, which was a mile and a quarter *(2 km)* from the store – and on gravelled road, too!

With helping at the store and going to school, he still had time for some recreation. In the winter, it would be an evening skating on the local pond. In the summer, it would be playing any kind of game with a baseball out on the road, during quiet times in the store. I had the pleasure of joining him on numerous of such occasions since I lived close by. Swimming was often a midnight dip in Lake Erie – just a short drive to Port Burwell, after the store had closed.

When Fred was in high school, his mother developed an incurable cancer, forcing his dad to quit his job. Shortly thereafter, Harley became a widower having the responsibility of caring for a business and two teenage sons. At that time, he suffered a relapse and fell again into depression.

Fred's responsibilities at home and in the store took their toll on his schooling; but he managed to graduate from high school in 1948. His dad's health improved to the point of a second marriage to a wonderful woman and great helpmate.

Just as he was graduating, a new radio station began broadcasting in St. Thomas, the county seat; and he thought that broadcasting might be in his future. In an initial interview, the gist of which was, "Go and get some experience, then come back and we'll talk." They pointed him to a new school in Toronto that was teaching "everything one needed to know about broadcasting" – an institution with a very high sounding name, "The Academy of Radio Arts".

Aside from its intriguing name, the school had a certain quality. Its founder and principal instructor was Lorne Green, who later became a star of the television series *Bonanza*. In addition, the school had many excellent teachers: Lister Sinclair, who taught the art of writing for radio and television; Mavor Moore, who taught acting; Johnny Wayne and Frank Schuster, who talked about comedy on the air. The students learned speech, speaking technique, and television production. It was lots of fun! The whole course was crammed into six short months!

Probably the favourite session for the students was the lecturing by Lorne Green in the announcing class. They were kept laughing by his feisty stories, bloopers, and behind-the-scenes tales of harried announcers, producers, and actors. I have wondered about the disappearance of Lorne Green from the CBC and later emergence with *Bonanza*. It was a very hot August evening in the Jarvis Street studios of the CBC when "The Voice of Doom" met his "Waterloo".

Air-conditioning hardly existed anywhere, especially in the little 6-foot by 6-foot *(1.8 m by 1.8 m)* announcing booths where the National News was read each evening. The military confrontation between German General Rommel and British General Viscount Montgomery was being waged in the North African desert. The German Army was pushing the British Eighth Army back toward El-Alamein, in Egypt. The Allies were short of men, materials, and equipment, ammunition, and guns - basically, almost everything.

On this particular day, Montgomery was beginning a successful counter-attack because his supplies of men, materials, and equipment to transport them had recently arrived. Tanks and huge armoured ten-ton trucks allowed Montgomery to launch his own attack and ultimately drive the Axis forces 2,000 miles *(3,220 km)* back across the desert.

There you have the situation. Lorne Green, in his twenties, but already known as "The Voice of Doom" for his readings of the National News bulletins, came into the studios this extremely hot and humid August evening wearing only shorts and t-shirt. He picked up his copy, doffed the shirt because he knew it would be insufferably hot in the announce booth, entered, turned on the light, and prepared to read his newscast.

Lorne, as he told it, was already dripping with perspiration when he closed the booth doors. It was both sound-proof and stifling hot. As he sat down to read, he stripped off his shorts and sat in his underwear since it was cooler that way. Perspiration dripped from his eyebrows, ran down his neck, dribbled onto the bulletins that were to be read. He received his cue from the operator and began to read.

"Tonight, Montgomery and his Eighth Army troops launched a powerful offensive against the Nazi forces of General Rommel. Troops, guns and ammunition were carried across the desert by huge new trucks. (A pause to wipe the sweat off face and eyes.) These ten-tin ... ten-ton tricks ... uh, let's start again. These tin-ten tru ... THE BIGGEST DA** TRUCKS IN THE WORLD!"

No more would "The Voice of Doom" grace the airwaves reading the National News of the CBC. What CBC lost that night, Hollywood gained some time later.

After graduating from Lorne Green's college, Fred moved to CHLO St.Thomas, not far from his home. The station was officially known as "The Voice of the Golden Acres." However, the employees had a less reverent name for it.

While at CHLO, Fred met and, two years later, married a

wonderful lady named Audrey from Chilliwack, British Columbia. Soon after that, the couple moved to the Fraser Valley to work at the local radio station, in Chilliwack. They soon moved down the Fraser Valley to New Westminster on the coast for a year-and-a-half. Here, Fred was copy chief at CKNW, the leading western music station in the Vancouver area.

The couple returned to Ontario where ailing parents were a primary concern. Fred obtained a position with MacLaren Advertising in Toronto. He remembers the day when he was hired very well. Waiting patiently for a 5:00 p.m. interview on the eighteenth floor of the building, he was able to look out the southwest corner of the building to see a fleet of small boats floating together towards shore at the Exhibition Grounds. Later, on the way home, he heard on the car radio that Marilyn Bell had just landed there from her swim across Lake Ontario. That was a major sports story as this young girl was the first person to accomplish the feat.

Fred recalls another MacLaren and CBC incident, with 45-minutes of air time to fill. It was an interview with a young and promising boxer from Toronto, by the name of George Chuvalo. Fred had not met George before this evening; and, aside from having a huge body frame, his most outstanding feature was his hands. They were "gi-normous". It did not take imagination to understand the damage those hands could do against a skull or, worse, to the stomach inside or outside the ring! The only other person whom Fred had seen with hands like those belonged to the famous former goaltender of the Toronto Maple Leaf hockey team, Johnny Bower.

Unfortunately at the time, George was more than a little nervous and found that he could not talk with his hands. The forty-five-minute time slot was filled with question after question by Jim Coleman and answered in monosyllabic "yeses" and "nossirs!" The producers filled that programme with as many commercials as possible.

George has since lost his nervousness, and now covers Canada giving talks to school children about the dangers of alcohol and other addictions. In 1966, George lost to Muhammed Ali in a fifteen-round decision. In 1972, he lost to the champion on a decision in twelve rounds.

Although Fred had good times at MacLarens, he eventually began looking for something different. It was during his stay there that he met Wes McGregor, a dour Scottish type who was instrumental in establishing Direct Mail as a legitimate and viable method of communicating directly with those people considered best prospects for a product. Fred liked it because one would know very quickly whether the message was successful - or not - in creating a sale.

An advantage was that one could move quickly in reaction to changes - which were a constant - in the marketplace. Today, the term used is "Direct Marketing", involving direct response techniques for space ads, for radio, for magazines, and for television. It was Direct Mail in the 1960s; and, if you really did not like it coming to your door, you called it Junk Mail.

Interestingly enough, the Junk Mail designation was dreamed up by newspapers and magazines fighting for every advertising dollar that they could obtain. Yet, these companies used Direct Mail to acquire subscribers; and they were a major force within the Direct Mail industry. It was called Direct Marketing in the 1970s and early 1980s and is called Response Marketing today, to involve the use of all media, including the internet, to obtain a sale without going through the normal channels of distribution.

In 1967, the family, which now included three children, moved from Etobicoke, a suburb of Toronto, to Cornwall, a city along the St. Lawrence River upstream from Montreal, to work for Sovereign Seat Cover, a manufacturer of automobile seat covers. The company used clear plastic, synthetic rayons and nylons, and blended materials in their product to protect car upholstery. Sovereign employed over 400 people cutting, sewing, and creating seat covers for practically every model and type of car.

In addition, Sovereign marketed a new product associated with drivers of cars, a pair of car coats, which were short jackets that hung loosely just below the buttocks. It kept one warm while driving, without the bulk and weight of a full-length coat.

During his time in Cornwall, sales virtually doubled. In the beginning, seat covers were the major product. They were about 5% of sales later on. Auto manufacturers developed stain-resistant and heavy-duty upholstery, making seat covers redundant. Sovereign's aim was to develop new products to replace them.

The next move was to Cambridge, a city to the west of Toronto, where Fred worked for Whitman Golden Limited, a distributor of *Little Golden Books* and the Disney books for boys and girls. The company's products also included a complete line of *Betty Crocker Cookbooks* for housewives, an essential part of every recipe library.

His responsibility was to build a base for a direct marketing department using the children's books, and a new Betty Crocker Recipe Card Library, newly introduced in

Canada. This library consisted of several hundred Crocker recipes, each one on a 3-inch by 4-inch *(8 cm by 10 cm)* card. On one side was a full-colour picture; while on the reverse was a complete recipe for the dish. Cards were categorized and sold in decks of 25-30 cards each. These decks were filed in a handy plastic countertop container, which came with the initial shipment of cards. When customers received the shipments of three decks at a time, they were offered other merchandise which they could buy.

Eventually, Fred returned to Toronto, to work with Telemedia Publishing Co., which had the Canadian publishing rights to the highly popular *TV Guide* magazine. In Canada, there were thirteen different editions each week as they covered all the programming across the country, including editions in the French language for Quebec and New Brunswick. Today, it is even more complicated when one considers all the different cable and satellite companies offering so many different programmes Canada-wide. In addition, *Canadian Living Magazine* was a major product in a group of magazines published, printed, and distributed in Canada by Telemedia. Fred's job was to produce subscriptions (you guessed it!) by Direct Response.

During his time at Telemedia, Audrey worked as an office manager at an auto dealership in Cambridge. It was expedient that they move to a condominium in Milton - halfway between Cambridge and Toronto. Every day, their two cars went - one to the west, and one to the east. Since they used Milton as a bedroom only, they called it their "Milton Hilton." Their family members remained in the Cambridge house while they attended University in Waterloo, in a neighbouring city.

In the early 1990s, a whole new phase of their lives - called retirement - began. They take part in many a ball game, hockey game, and golfing tournament of their three grandchildren. They have time to do it. Fred is a past president of their local Probus Club. Fred has participated in nearly ten years of delivering Meals on Wheels in the community. They take an active part in the local Lawn Bowling Club. In addition, they have bridge-playing friends, computer projects, and tender care of lawn and garden. They have a full life indeed - and love it!

Fred and I grew up in the same community and were classmates at school for a total of twelve years. We played together - usually softball - over the years. In our teen years, we lived across the street from each other. When we attended Continuation School (small High School) in nearby Brownsville for three years, we often rode our bicycles together. Fred attended Radio College during my last year at Aylmer High School. After both of us left home, we did not see each other very often. I stayed overnight once in 1955 when he and Audrey lived in the Toronto area. Fred took me to the CBC studios for the Jim Coleman programme following the fight. I called on them in 1960 when I was living in Alberta and vacationing in Ontario. The next time that we met was on Labour Day weekend in 1995 at the Corinth Public School reunion. Since then, we had been out of contact until I began to research for this book.

15
Hallie Larsen

Petrified Forest N.P., Arizona, United States

Do you believe in ghost stories? After hearing "ghost stories" from some archaeologists who had tried to stay overnight (with a permit) in one of the ruins at Mesa Verde National Park in Colorado, Hallie and some colleagues asked permission to attempt an evening visit to the same ruin. Everything was beautiful, with lightning on the horizon and stars coming out as they hiked down to the ruin. Once inside, they felt comfortable and welcome, keeping their voices down and exploring in the dark with lanterns and flashlights.

Suddenly, a can of beer, which one of the guys should not have brought, accidentally dropped. It rolled into one of the ceremonial rooms! Something was wrong. There seemed to be an abrupt change in the atmosphere of the ruin. The group felt no longer welcome or at ease. They beat a hasty retreat, crawling through the exit tunnel and climbing ladders to the top of the mesa! Unfortunately, the gate refused to open. It had to be pushed up above one's head - a quite awkward move. What will they do? Several of them went back through the ruin and, after a long wait, perched on the ladders. From here, they rescued their friends from above. How much of this adventure was their own imagination and how much was actually "ghosts"? Who knows! They were not about to find out at that point.

Hallie was born in Escondido, California, USA, a city a

little north of San Diego. She began her schooling at Central Elementary, in the same city. She has a Bachelor of Science in Biology degree and is working on a Master of Science in Resource Interpretation degree in 2006.

She recalls two memorable experiences when she was in university. One of her favourite experiences was a field class in geology to Lassen Volcanic National Park, in California. The students camped out for several days, exploring the lava flows and geothermal features.

On another occasion, her archaeology class had an interesting assignment. The students were required to go "dig" in the San Francisco dump. That experience was informative and rather frightening! It was also disgusting, but basically it was what archeologists do – although when it is less fresh. Imagine pulling down mountains of used diapers, rotting food, vast caches of cans, boxes, Styrofoam cups and containers, slithering piles of noodles, and dead pets and other animals. There were also live animals: dogs, seagulls, rats, cats, smaller nastier creatures, and transient people. Surgical gloves and waders were all that protected the students. They were required to gather all of this waste, categorize it, catalogue it, and hypothesize about it.

The main theory of the class regarding this dig was that the society responsible for this was a very disposable culture, one that wasted considerable amounts of resources, and one that did not care about what happened to the waste. The people seemed to think that resources and land would never run out. This was particularly clear from the amount of material that was very recyclable, such items as metal (aluminum and tin cans and scrap), glass, and furniture that could have been refurbished. Why was this experience so scary? This culture was our own. What an indictment this is!

There are so many memorable trips that Hallie has taken, but one that will remain firmly in her mind is part of a summer spent with a group in Algeria, learning about the culture, the region, and the archaeology thereof. They were making an inventory of the Roman ruins in that part of the Maghrib (which includes Algeria, Tunisia, and sometimes Libya), their location, and their condition. They camped out the entire time, traveling in an old refurbished British Army vehicle pulling a trailer, nicknamed Samson and Delilah by the group.

They visited villages throughout the trip, seeking out ruins both on the map and those known only by the local people (which sometimes did not work out the way that they had hoped). One place they visited was a well-known ruin site called Timgad. This very interesting site was a military colony founded by the Emperor Trajan in 100 CE and was where many retired Roman officers went to live as a sort of informal guard on the frontier. The students visited markets every day to purchase food. Bathing was an adventure: one taken in a donkey trough; another in the rubble of a Roman aqueduct, at a broken vineyard pipe; and in a rented one with two other people at a resort in El Djerba. The land was spectacular, even when a sand storm at the edge of the Sahara struck them. The people were beautiful, complex, and fascinating. Hallie loved that region and would like to return there one day.

Hallie has been a National Park Service park ranger in the United States for most of two decades, currently at Petrified Forest National Park in Arizona. She is very pleased to be a recipient of a Certificate for Ten Years of Service in the Government of the United States of America. It was presented to her by Karen Wade, then Director of the Intermountain Region of the National Park Service.

One time, as a ranger, she presented a programme at night at Badlands National Park, in South Dakota. She waited in the dark as a volunteer brought the visitors out to where she was waiting. They never saw Hallie, but listened to Coyote telling stories as fireflies flickered through the grass and stars spread above the natural amphitheatre formed by badlands. It was a night to remember. This is but one experience that she had in about one dozen parks where she worked.

While working at Sequoia National Park, in California, Hallie belonged to a hiking club. All the employees hiked in this park and its neighboring park, Kings Canyon, which were two of the best for trails. Every weekend and even after work, they would walk along the trails and report back on their success. There were several levels: at 100 miles *(161 km)*, a hiker could win a mug; at 200 miles *(322 km)*, he/she received a shirt; at 300 miles *(483 km)*, he/she received something else. There were only two people who completed the 400 miles *(644 km)* that summer - Hallie and her friend Bob. Regrettably, there was nothing for the 400-mile level; perhaps, those in charge never expected that anyone would hike that far in a season.

The places that she explored that summer and into the fall were incredibly beautiful. Sequoia is best known for its world-largest trees, the Giant Sequoia, *Sequoiadendron giganteum*. Walking among these giants is humbling and awe-inspiring as if you were in a natural cathedral. The park also has a vast wilderness of granite peaks - a world of rock, leading up to the highest point in the lower forty-eight states, Mt. Whitney. There were canyons filled with roaring rivers, foothills of oak and wildflowers, glacial lakes the colour of turquoise, and high meadows where black bear fed amidst purple shooting stars and lilies. She felt accomplished for hiking so many miles and fulfilled for discovering so much. Anyone who has enjoyed walking on mountain trails – wherever it be – will agree with her.

Her dear friend Cliff, whom she met at Sequoia National Park nearly twenty years ago, will always be in her heart. He has passed on, but Hallie will remember him for his devotion to friends, his creativity, and his *joie de vivre*.

She feels that her greatest accomplishment in her work has been in helping visitors make personal connections with any of the parks in which she has worked. However, this is what she does practically every day. Another important accomplishment has been going back for her graduate degree and being one of the first in a new Masters programme that will benefit the national parks for many generations to come.

Hallie recommends ways in which park visitors can help to preserve the natural features, geological and/or biological, in her park and in other parks. Learn about both natural and cultural resources and pass on that knowledge to help people care about the park. People protect only those things about which they care. While you are in the park, the best way to protect the natural resources is to leave them where you find them so that others may also enjoy them.

I asked her to tell what staff teaches the general public, inside and outside the park. She notes that this is a huge subject, but she mentions a few ways. In the park, they have free publications that introduce the park and its natural and cultural resources to the public, exhibits along the road (at overlooks and on trails) called waysides, a trail guide, exhibits that are both seasonal and permanent at the three facilities in the park, informal visitor contact along trails, curriculum-based educational programmes for schools, and formal presentations by interpretive rangers and volunteers that give opportunities for learning and making personal connections. Outside the park, they have curriculum-based classroom presentations, special event participation with exhibits, publications, and activities, the park website, information sent through the mail, and articles they write or in which they assist in such publications as *Arizona Highways*.

The region of Arizona which includes Petrified Forest N.P. has had a drought for more than a decade. The staff can really tell the difference in the many plant species in the park. This is a natural cycle of drought that has occurred in the region forever. Two animals that are on the decline are prairie dogs and pronghorn. Prairie dogs are a keystone species, very important to all the other species of the grassland; but people have tried to eradicate them and have done so in many areas. Pronghorn need large open ranges; but the park is a healthy, but small, island amidst an impacted region.

She has always let the care of her health slide as opposed to other parts of her life. However, she is now trying to return to basics with that part of who she is. She is to be commended for this attempt as it can have long-term positive effects on her life.

Her philosophy of life is to try to love what she does, whether it is work or play. If more people would abide by her philosophy, they would be healthier, both physically and mentally. For hobbies, she enjoys writing, gardening, camping, photography, travel, and web pages.

I met Hallie by email when I was preparing a page on the fauna and flora of Petrified Forest N.P. for our website. She was the one who responded to my request. She not only approved my page, but also brought it to the attention of her staff. Although we have not been in contact much, she has been interested in helping. On looking back, as well as considering my invitation to her to participate in this book, I can see her practising her philosophy. She is a good ambassador for the National Park Service in general and for her park in particular.

16

Helena Gazdik

Surrey, British Columbia, Canada

To a child, especially a boy, it usually is much more interesting studying the habits of a *Libellula vibrans* (Great Blue Skimmer Dragonfly) than trying to master one of Chopin's Études on the piano. However, this is a little girl! As her interest developed into knowledge, it eventually became her ticket to Canada.

Helena was born in the Czech city of Zlin. She grew up in the beautiful spa city of Luhacovice. Her father was the chief balneologist (one who studies the therapeutic use of mineral baths), as well as a scientific researcher. His study was mainly in Human Bio-Climatology - the influence of climatological changes on humans. An example would be the influence of elevation, humidity, pollution, and barometric pressures on asthma.

In grade 4, a Russian language study was added to her native Czech language. A year later, a Slovak language course was introduced, in addition. At the high school level, she studied the Latin and German languages.

As mentioned above, Helena was fascinated with living creatures, especially insects and their behaviour. Her father was a fanatical pianist and insisted that all four of his children learn to play the piano. One sister became a music therapist. However, playing the piano was not for Helena. In typical childhood fashion, she found a loophole which she exploited.

She would pretend to go to the piano lessons, but instead would walk to a small dam near their house. Here she would put the music sheets under her so that her clothes would not be soiled. Then, she proceeded to watch frogs and insects and develop her own collection of insects.

Helena grew up in the Cold War era in Czechoslovakia, a satellite state of the Soviet Union. During their high school years, all students, including girls, had to undergo basic military training. They learned to throw grenades, to shoot with rifles, and to run long distances wearing a gas mask. North American students have it easy by these standards. The people of her country were living in the state of fear of a Third World War.

The closest university to Luhacovice was in Bratislava, Slovakia. Therefore, she moved there and began studying to become an entomologist. Being a passionate animal lover, she spent her free time in the equestrian sport. It was through this sport that she met her husband, Anton, who was twice silver champion of Czechoslovakia in equestrian jumping.

August 21, 1968, was a black day in Czechoslovakian history. Armies of Russia and other Warsaw Pact members invaded the country to quell any attempt to move toward democracy. The way of life was inevitably changed. As the country was now under the control of Russia, many people tried to escape. Some succeeded; some were shot while trying to cross the heavily patrolled border (machine gun towers, army dog patrols, electric fences, and occasional mine fields); and some were taken back and imprisoned. What governments will do for the sake of ideology and control!

Anton and Helena escaped, each through a different country, in 1974. They reunited in former Yugoslavia, in the city of Rijeka. Then, they illegally crossed the Alps into Austria, where they were placed in a refugee camp in Traiskirche, near Vienna. The authorities finger-printed and photographed the couple. After a time, they were given working permits.

First, they worked in sweatshops in Traiskirchen. Later, they procured jobs in a factory in Schrack, where Helena worked on an assembly line. Living and working conditions were pathetic! The lack of proper food and the high level of stress adversely affected Anton's health, resulting in his contraction of tuberculosis. After eight months of unsuccessful treatment in a sanatorium near Vienna, surgery was performed in which a part of his lungs was removed.

In the meantime, Helena was given a grant from Professor Dr. Hoffrat Schonman, the director of the Entomology Department in the Naturhistorisches Museum in Vienna. His overwhelming recommendation provided an opportunity for Helena at the Simon Fraser University in Burnaby, British Columbia, Canada, where she was given a grant to work as a technician in the Zoology Department under Professor Brian Beirne.

Helena and her husband arrived in Vancouver soon after Anton was released from the sanatorium. He had great difficulty obtaining a job without Canadian experience. How can someone have Canadian experience without someone in Canada providing employment for an immigrant? It was the old Catch-22 dilemma!

After the expiry of the SFU grant and several months of intensive English language school, Helena obtained her first job. She was hired as a travel agent at Globe Tour Travel Agency, specializing in Eastern Europe, particularly Russia and Ukraine. Being fluent in the Russian, Czech, German, and Slovak languages and being able to converse with people who spoke Polish, Ukrainian, Bulgarian, or Serbo-Croatian was an asset. Several years later, she took a course in the Spanish language.

Later, because of her science background, Helena was offered a position in a medical laboratory as a technician. She held this job for several years, until her first daughter was born. Because she did not like the long commuting to work, she sought a position closer to her home. As a result, she was hired by the Surrey Public Library (known at the time as the Fraser Valley Regional Library) in December 1979. She was improving her English language skills and started to take library science courses. By this time, she had two beautiful daughters. After many years of reference work at the Guildford and the Whalley Branches, she transferred to the newly built Semiahmoo Library Branch of the Surrey Public Library. Currently, she is on the team of Global Librarians answering reference questions electronically. She is also an art coordinator for the library.

Throughout the years, Helena has taken courses in different arts and crafts. On her family's holiday on the island of Murano near Venice, in Italy, they toured a glass blowing factory. They became enamoured with glass in any form. Both she and Anton had taken classes in stained glass. After the trip to Murano, they took classes in lamp worked beads. Just recently, Helena has successfully completed a glass-fusing course. She enjoys art in any form. She paints with pastels, oils, and acrylics. She previously was a member of the Langley (BC) Spinners and Weavers Guild. There are very few crafts that she has not tried.

Pam and I met Helena when she was a reference librarian at the Whalley Branch of Surrey Public Library. She helped us numerous times, and we were always impressed with her work. The Surrey Public Library, in general, and the Semiahmoo Branch, in particular, are indeed fortunate to have on their staff someone as capable as she is and who has as much experience as she has. They can be thankful that one little girl had an interest in insects.

17

John Alexander AND Glenda Mae Toll

Dunnville, Ontario, Canada

Accompanied by Chief Ed McGeachy from nearby Frankford, John was driving a marked Ontario Provincial Police cruiser along #2 Highway into Belleville, Ontario, Canada. Suddenly, on rounding a curve, a car appeared and almost forced the police car off the road. Quick as a flash, John changed directions, and pursued and pulled the offending driver over. The occupants were a couple on the first day of their honeymoon, which commenced in the little community of Hyndford, near Ottawa, Ontario. The driver had been drinking and, as a result, was not in the proper condition to be driving.

When the driver arrived at the Detachment office, he proceeded to involve himself in a fight with other officers. That was not a good way to respond! He was wrestled to the floor. When subdued, the man was taken to the lockup cells at the Belleville police station. Ed and John then delivered the poor bride to the motel room that the couple had booked. This must have been awful for the unfortunate girl, having to spend her honeymoon alone in a strange motel. Feeling sorry for her, John went home and instructed his wife Glenda to go to the motel and bring her back to their home.

In the morning after the bride had been served breakfast, John drove her to the Belleville station. By now, her new husband was in a condition to be released from his cell. Ordinarily, he would have been charged with impaired driving. However, in view of all of the circumstances, the police laid a charge of "careless driving"; and he paid a fine of $25.00 and was set free to continue with his bride on their honeymoon. What an experience this was for beginning a honeymoon! John often wondered if they stayed together, and if any children they might have had were told how they spent their first night of married life.

John was born in Toronto, Ontario, Canada, to Victoria Margret Rogan, an immigrant from Ireland who had been working as a seamstress for T. Eaton Company. It was noted at the time that Timothy Eaton, because of his origins, tried to hire immigrants from Ireland. Named William Burrell Rogan by his mother, the baby was placed in the care of the Children's Aid Society because of a split between his parents. He was adopted at fourteen months of age by Carman and Ada Toll, a farm couple from Blenheim, Ontario.

John and adopted brother Douglas attended school at SS #6 Harwich for their first eight grades, and then Ridgetown High and Vocational School.

In John's days in public school, the students were required to learn 200 lines of memory work and to recite them. One year, he memorized "The Deacon's Masterpiece" with 142 lines and said it for the teacher at recess. She was so impressed that she asked him to recite the poem to the whole school when class resumed. That same year, he learned "The Cane Bottomed Chair" (which he can still recite) with 56 lines. Thus, he accomplished the total year's requirements with two poems. He loved literature, and actually enjoyed memory work.

The reading book for about grade 3 or 4 was *Golden Windows*. Many reading books then included some of Aesop's *Fables*. To show how times have changed, he remembers a poem from one of the books that his mother used in class in the late 1920s that was entitled *"Scotty Dog Mick and Nigger Boy Dick"*. It told about a coloured boy and his dog sitting on a log by a stream. The final lines were "And Oh what a din when the log rolled in with Scotty Dog Mick and Nigger boy Dick." Can you imagine that title in a reading book today? He also notes that the dog was mentioned first.

Another high point for John was discovering some of the classics of literature in several different courses at university. In discussing them in seminar sessions, he learned from another student later that one of the professors had made a note about some of his points on a couple of subjects and used them in other classes. That was an honour!

Glenda was born to Oscar and Della Horn, in Detroit, Michigan, United States. When Glenda was six months old, Oscar went on a hunting trip and was fatally shot by a young hunting companion. Peter Gotelaer, a farmer from the Ridgetown area of Southwestern Ontario visited his sister Gusty, a next door neighbour to the Horns. After Oscar's death, Peter and Della became close friends and eventually married. Thus, Della and Glenda moved to a farm with no running water or indoor plumbing, a new experience for the two from the big city.

Glenda attended S.S. #7 (Rushton's Public School) and Ridgetown High School. Her most memorable experience as a student was her participation and training as a cheerleader at Ridgetown High School. The effort of learning routines and practising them with the other girls formed close bonds of friendship and a sense of accomplishment, which she recalls with pleasure.

She also attended Troy United Church and the Young People's group connected with it. Here is where Glenda and John met.

In 1950, they were married, after which they settled in a $15.00 a week furnished apartment in Windsor, where John worked for Ford Motor Company. They later moved back to the Blenheim area and lived in a small farmhouse with no running water.

In the spring of 1952, John joined the Ontario Provincial Police and attended the Ontario Police College in Toronto. After graduation, John was posted to the Belleville District of Eastern Ontario. He and Glenda lived in a $35.00 a month house on the shore of the Bay of Quinte. Again, there was no running water or indoor plumbing. After three years, John was transferred to the St. Thomas Detachment, in Southwestern Ontario. He also served for three years there. While living in the St. Thomas area, he and Glenda started a Young People's group for teenagers in the Sparta and Union United churches. They still have a Bible given to them in appreciation of their efforts.

In 1958, John transferred to the Department of Lands and Forests as a conservation officer. One year later, he attended the Ontario Forest Technical School (also called Ranger School) at Dorset, Ontario. Glenda and the children moved back to a farmhouse on the Toll farms. When John was posted to Dunnville, Ontario, south of Hamilton, in 1960, they moved there and built a permanent home, where they still live.

In 1967, John registered at Brock University, in St. Catharines, Ontario, as a mature student. He received a

Bachelor of Arts degree in 1972. The next year, he worked for the Ministry of Natural Resources (formerly Lands and Forests) in the Niagara District, as a conservation officer, park superintendent, and then as a public relations officer, doing television and radio news releases. In connection with this service, he published a booklet *MNR in the Classroom*, which outlined methods of delivering conservation ideas to various classes.

John became a member of St. Marks Lodge (Freemasonry) in Port Stanley, a town south of St. Thomas, in 1957 and affiliated with Amity Lodge No. 32 in Dunnville in 1960. He served as Worshipful Master of Amity in 1973 and as District Deputy Grand Master of Niagara District A in 1982–1983. Then, he was known to his Masonic brethren as Right Worshipful Brother John Toll. He has been a member of the Lions Club for more than twenty-five years and has served as president of the Dunnville Lions Club twice.

He also maintained membership in Grace United Church in Dunnville and served as chair of the official board for several years. He is presently on the board of directors of the local Crimestoppers organization.

His main hobby is gardening, delighting in giving vegetables and flowers to friends and neighbours. His large garden area includes a lotus pond.

John is presently a member of the "Citizens Assembly on Electoral Reform." This process, which has already been explored in British Columbia and in the Netherlands, is to review the electoral process in various countries and jurisdictions around the world, and to suggest changes for the Ontario system. One person from each Ontario Riding (John represents Erie-Lincoln) will meet for six weekends in the autumn of 2006 in Toronto to study the several types of process, and then spend six more weekends in late winter and early spring in 2007 to formulate a report, and to present it to the Ontario Government.

In 1951, Glenda gave birth to John David. Then, Dennis Peter was born in 1954. Ruth Ann was born in 1958. As the children grew older, Glenda was able to become involved in the community, and served as Girl Guide leader and later as commissioner of the local guide organization. She also became a Kinnette and served as president of the Dunnville club.

Answering a life-long interest in flowers, she and a friend opened a florist shop under the name "Glen-Ruth". After her partner retired, she became the sole owner. She has some outstanding memories from her years as a florist.

They had a delivery to a house in the country to a married woman. The flowers had been sent by a man who was not her husband. When the girls went to the door, the bill for the flowers was sitting on the seat of the van. Before they could leave the driveway, the husband came running across the lawn, through the snow in his stocking feet, demanding to know who had sent the flowers. Thinking quickly, the girls covered the bill, and then said that the order had come in by wire and they did not know who had sent them. That was close! As a footnote, the "happy" couple soon split up, and the lady and the sender "got together."

In another incident, a man came into the store saying that he was really in trouble and needed some flowers to bail him out. The girls said they would guarantee the flowers. Sure enough - in the next week's local newspaper was an advertisement that simply said, "Glen-Ruth, the flowers worked."

On another occasion, a man came in and ordered an arrangement to take to the hospital where his wife had given birth to a new baby. Thinking to make conversation while she made the arrangement, the florist offered congratulations, to which the man replied, "Well, thanks, but this one isn't mine, but it's okay, we got everything worked out."

Perhaps the incident which incited the most fun for the two florists involved the local undertaker, whom they knew quite well because of their numerous trips to his business when delivering funeral flowers. He was quite a jokester, and they determined to "get even." Therefore, on April 1, they waited until he was out for coffee, and then took the store display dummy, an attractive looking young woman, put an "April Fool" sign on her bare chest, placed her on the work table in the preparation room, and then covered her with a sheet. When the undertaker returned and glanced in, he thought that a funeral delivery service from the city must have brought a body, but did not realize the difference until he removed the sheet. That undertaker must have had a red face when he saw that he was the victim of a practical joke.

Glenda always enjoyed involvement in community organizations and became a member of the Board of Governors of the Haldimand War Memorial Hospital in Dunnville, serving in the various committees and, in 2004 and 2005, as board chair. She is pleased that a long term care facility was added and a 42-unit apartment building was started during her term.

John and Glenda are proud of the successes of their three children and their six grandchildren, and happy that all of them have post-secondary education.

John has a desire to continue learning, from whatever

source is available. He has been a student of nature all his life and continues to marvel at new discoveries. He understands the basics of life in nature, but what exactly is instinct? That is yet to be comprehended. He continues to study.

Glenda says that, although it takes time and effort to be involved in community and service projects, the benefits of forming long-lasting friendships with interesting people and the sense of accomplishment for projects completed make it all worthwhile.

John and Glenda have toured several countries in Europe and have spent parts of many winters in St. Petersburg, Florida, United States. John's most memorable travel experience occurred in the Galapagos Islands, where he swam with sea lions, and of trips into the Amazon jungle by dugout canoe. He claims that he is not really athletic. However, he broke an "Olympic record" when a bull sea lion chased him off the beach in the Galapagos. No one can convince John that sea lions are clumsy on land because they do not have feet like land mammals.

One day after school in Union, Ontario, John stopped by on his way home from work to meet me and to invite me to his house for supper one evening. Although I was shy and not very talkative at the time, I accepted, and enjoyed the visit. Some time later, Glenda stopped by the school to invite me to direct a play with the church Young People's group, of which she and John were leaders. Again, I accepted and acted as a rookie director. Many times since then over the years, I have recalled the practices and the nine Friday nights of performance in area communities and thought about how I might have done it differently. Nevertheless, it was a learning experience for me and I hope that it was enjoyable for the group. The Tolls and I were out of contact since I left Union in 1958 until I contacted them in 2006 in regard to this book. I am pleased to have a copy of John's book *Tornado,* in which he describes the effects of the severe storm that struck Oxford County, Ontario, in 1979.

18

Kathleen Ellen Fagnan Melston

Rockwall, Texas, United States

Someone has done something to help you. You say thank you and ask what you can do in return. The person says that you do not have to do anything. How does that make you feel? Should you want to try to keep the favours even? Is there some other way to show your appreciation? This was the situation that Kathy felt when her good friend and colleague, Jan Williams, at the Library/Media Center in Chofu Elementary School, in Japan, had opened her home to Kathy during her three years of overseas work.

Jan told Kathy to follow the advice that one of her friends, a military wife, gave to her under the same circumstances. This person told Jan to be there for others who were away from home, lonesome, or in need, and not expect anything in return. This meant so much to them that Kathy made the same commitment for herself to follow. What a wonderful way to approach others! For these ladies, lasting friendships resulted. Although many people do follow this approach, there are too many who do not.

Kathy was born in Springville, New York, United States. Her education began at West Valley Central School, in West Valley, New York. She obtained a Bachelor of Science in Education at University College of New York, in Geneseo, and a Master of Library Science at Syracuse University, in Syracuse, New York.

As a high school senior, Kathy had the opportunity to go to Washington, D.C., with her class. What fond memories she has of the event! There was so much to see and to learn. Besides, it was really the last event in which these young people participated as a whole before graduation. Most of them had been together since kindergarten - and now their time together was nearing an end.

When she was in college, she was a member of an all-girls' chorus. It was so thrilling to sing at the New York State Pavilion at the 1964 World's Fair in New York City (Queens). To add to the thrill, Governor Nelson Rockefeller of New York and Cardinal Spellman of the Archdiocese of New York were in the audience when the girls sang.

She worked in New York State as a school librarian at both elementary and secondary levels. For three years, she was an elementary school librarian working for the U.S. Department of Defense Dependent Schools in Japan. She lived at Fuchu Air Base and taught at Chofu Elementary School. That was a wonderful experience for this teacher-librarian. Then, for the last eighteen years, to date, she has been director of the Rockwall County Library in Rockwall, Texas, near Dallas.

She has taken many trips that were memorable for what she learned, but probably the three years of living in Japan had the biggest impact on her life. While in Japan, she had the opportunity to travel to the Soviet Union, India, the Philippines, Thailand, Taiwan, Hong Kong, South Korea, and many places in Japan. She really took advantage of her time in the Orient to come into contact with various cultures.

One never knows how many lives may be affected by something that one does or says. Kathy was very pleased to receive a note from a former student telling her that she had never been much of a reader until Kathy was her librarian in elementary school. A little message like that means so much.

As director of the Rockwall County Library, she has been involved in building not one, but two, libraries. The first time was a renovation of the former post office in Rockwall in 1991. The library moved from a 2,800 sq ft *(260 m^2)* old church to a 7,000 sq ft *(650 m^2)* former post office. Now, she is involved in the building of a 52,000 sq ft *(4,831 m^2)* library facility. The library has come a long way!

She feels that working toward the building of the new library for Rockwall will result in her greatest accomplishment. However, she does not take all of the credit. She sees the final step as being an accomplishment for all the library supporters who have wanted this for more years than Kathy has been the director. For all of her eighteen years as director, she has wanted to help them realize the completion of their dream. Two bond issues were passed - one for land and one for the building. The grand opening is scheduled for the summer of 2008.

Rockwall County is the smallest county in Texas, but it is the fastest growing one. It has five small cities. Some people feel that their cities are not being served by the County Library since it is so small. However, the new library will serve them better, at least for the following ten to fifteen years. Then branches will be needed, but the County may not be able to afford them. This is a future goal for Kathy, even if it currently seems to be impossible. Her dream is to see a Rockwall County Library Association and an agreement with the other cities that they would provide the library, the staff, and the money for materials and the County Library would provide central cataloguing and processing along with rotating collections, training, and consulting services. A strong written agreement that would cover this sort of cooperation in the future would be needed, but it has not happened yet.

The greatest change in the operation of libraries during her time is the use of computers for library operations and accessing information. When she was at Syracuse University for her MLS, one course was on data processing and programming. She will always remember the instructor taking the class into a room where there was a huge computer processing data that was on punch cards. Now, the same amount of information can be placed into a personal computer. Computers have made the old card catalogue obsolete. The amount of information available on the Internet has changed the way libraries conduct business. Computers have not made books obsolete, but they have broadened the capabilities of the library and librarian to provide needed information. Searching the web can be overwhelming because of all the information through which to sift. However, a good reference librarian can help patrons learn how to use this tool better to locate that for which they are searching.

The function of the library has not really changed with the advent of the computer age. Rather, librarians have had to adapt to the impact and to learn to harness the web. Kathy tells people who wonder if the planners have included sufficient shelving in the new library that information is delivered in many different ways today, and room has to be made for all of them. Rockwall County Library now has ten public access computers. In the new library there will be five times that number, including a technology lab to teach people how to use computers and software. What an opportunity for the citizens of the county that will be!

The staff is now looking at subscribing to downloadable audio books. Patrons will be able to download them to their computers at home for a checkout period of three weeks. This service will be offered in addition to the continuance of purchasing audio books on CD and cassette. One day, the library will subscribe to a service through which patrons can download movies. However, those will not replace the DVDs collection.

It is an exciting time to be working in libraries. Usage of the library is steadily increasing and will probably more than triple after the move. Kathy does not see the demise of libraries as some doomsday persons have predicted.

Kathy feels that, as in society as a whole, some patrons are ruder, more impatient, and more demanding than in the past. The cell phone has not helped that situation. Many parents still expect the library to be a safe place. However, it is not so any longer. They continue to drop their children off and leave, even though the policy says that children under a certain age need to be accompanied by an adult. The library is a noisier place than it used to be. It has become a community gathering centre. People want to be able to talk – perhaps have a cup of coffee. These concerns are not unique to Rockwall County. They occur everywhere. New libraries now have quiet reading areas or rooms. The new library here will have a quiet reading room and group study rooms on the second floor. The first floor will be a busier place with the children's and teens' areas.

Kathy tries to treat everyone as she would like to be treated. Every day she prays about that. If everyone would hold such a philosophy and would live by it, can you imagine what this world would be like? Her philosophy is always evolving. She mentions reading a quote from Albert Einstein for which she would like to aim: "There are two ways to live your life. One is as though nothing is a miracle. The other is as though everything is a miracle." Life is a gift from God to be lived to the fullest.

Her hobbies are reading and traveling. Is that any surprise, given what her experiences have been?

One day in the spring of 1991, I stopped by the first library mentioned above to see if I might be a volunteer. Our family had recently moved from Missouri to Rockwall. I recall being taken into a small office to present my case to the head librarian with the friendly smile. Kathy accepted my offer, even though all that she knew of my past was what I told her. She set me to work at a table cataloguing books.

When the move was made to the new building, I went, too. I was able to find a quiet spot to perform my assignment. Occasionally, I did some personal research. On two occasions, I acted as a representative of the volunteers in making a presentation to the Commissioner's Court, the body responsible for the library. Numerous times, I have heard Kathy speak of the importance of the volunteers to the library. I enjoyed working with Kathy and her staff of librarians.

Even though I have not been in Rockwall since we moved away in 1995, I still have fond memories of the staff and the library. I commend Kathy for her leadership and the staff for their efforts to provide service to the citizens of the county.

19

Maria Luísa Viana de Paiva Boléo

Lisbon, Portugal

You never know what will result from a little kindness. A mother with an eight-year-old girl came into the store where Luísa was working. They wanted to purchase two clasps for the child's hair. They searched and searched for a long time through everything, but they liked nothing. Then the mother looked towards the clerk and said, "My daughter would like some clasps like the ones that are in your hair." Luísa immediately took those and offered them to the little girl. This made her very happy. The mother insisted on paying for them, but Luísa said, "I offered them to the child, and will not accept anything for them." The mother still insisted, but the clerk would not accept. On the following day, the mother and her daughter returned to the store and handed Luísa a beautiful bouquet of flowers. What a surprise and kind gesture that was on their part! This act touched the clerk deeply.

Luísa was born in the city of Coimbra, Portugal, and was the fourth of nine children. Her father's family was from the Castelo Branco area, and her mother's family was from Santarém. They had known each other for some time, dating for five years because he was studying in Germany. They were also known in Catholic cultural circles. Their wedding took place in Coimbra, the city where the oldest Portuguese university is located.

He returned to Coimbra in 1935 and began to prepare for a doctorate. Eventually, he became a renowned researcher in the disciplines of dialectology, philology, and Roman linguistics and a professor of Letters in the local university. He had many works published; and, as a result, his name - Manuel de Paiva Boléo (1904-1992) - was listed in the National Library of Portugal (http://www.bn.pt).

He received the collar of the Grand Master of the Santiago da Espada Order (the highest non-military decoration) at eighty years of age, for a life devoted to teaching and research. Many friends of the family and of the university attended his installation ceremony. Suddenly, at the age of eighty-eight years, he died.

Luísa's mother was from a middle-class family, and had two grandfathers who were doctors. Maria Eugénia Anacoreta Viana de Paiva Boléo (1910-) first studied in an English home for four years, and completed her studies in a school in Coimbra with the equivalent of secondary school. She knew French and English and even took a course in elementary pediatrics, which was then used by women who expected to be mothers and homemakers. In her education, she also learned to embroider with admirable perfection. Her children's first baby clothes were made by her with the greatest affection.

When they were married in September 1938, they had employment because they were selected from among the families of the villages where they were known and had stayed for many years in their homes. They left only to be married.

Luísa's childhood was very happy. Today, as an adult, she considers that it was exceptional. Her parents had many profoundly Catholic friends. All in her family were practising, not nominal, Catholics. Christmas and Holy Week were the most celebrated religious days. However, in adulthood, only two of the nine children today are Catholic. Luísa took her first communion at seven years of age in the Doroteias Chapel, which had a students' home on the street - Rue Filipe Simões - in Coimba, where she lived.

All nine of the children were born at home because that was the practice at the time. Their mother did not have any problems during pregnancy and delivery. There are only six of the children still living. Jorge died from ulcerated colitis; Pedro, in the war in Angola; and Isabel, from cancer.

Luísa's primary instruction was given in the home of one of her father's sisters, who was a teacher at a primary school. In the morning, she would teach in the official school; and in the afternoon, in her home. It was maintained by two sisters who helped with the housework. The school was a type of private college, and visited by the children of the upper class families of Coimbra. Luísa, although not from an upper class family, came into contact with doctors, entrepreneurs, lawyers, and judges. Today, there are several important persons in Portuguese society who studied with her in this school, notably the author Teolinda Gersão and such university chemistry professors as Luísa Planas Leitão.

She was a good student, especially in some areas. Ever since she was a little girl, she had drawing skills. She wanted to follow the history of art, but she was unable to do it. Instead, she studied history.

The school environment had tenderness, with neither great punishments nor the smallest violence. The children felt like laureates when they received little books or coloured pencils as prizes for having good notes.

She studied at Infanta de Maria High School, today the equivalent of secondary school. It provided seven years of study, with three levels of examinations. These were in the second; in the fifth, when the course of study was chosen; and in the seventh, which gave access to higher education - university.

Luísa chose the Architecture/Painting course which, at the time, had seven subjects of Letters/Humanities and Pure Science/Drawing or Descriptive Geometry: Literature, History, Portuguese, French, Mathematics, Drawing, and Physics/Chemistry. She did not finish the seventh year because she lacked the study of Mathematics that she had already completed as a working student in 1974. She studied seven years of French and three of English at the Infanta de Maria High School. In addition, she also understands Spanish well. For many years now, she has used only Portuguese from day to day because her work in the Finance Ministry and her current work do not demand another language.

She often visited the Belas-Artes in Porto, a city which is typically middle-class and very popular. The festivals of St. John at this time were so enjoyable and lively that she has never forgotten them. She made friends with several families of this city, with whom she still is a friend and goes from time to time to visit.

During the years 1970-1974, she began to take an interest in politics and to be aware of the dictatorship of António de Oliveira Salazar and of the leadership of Marcelo Caetano. Later, she became affiliated with the Socialist Party, of which she is still a member today.

She began to write for newspapers and magazines on the

subject of the history of women in the last ninety years. Then, she turned to writing about customs and historical figures, both Portuguese and foreign.

Her first job was in the Federation of Labour Guild of the Province of Beira Litoral, of which Coimbra is the capital. In 1971-1972, she was an art teacher in Figueira da Foz Secondary School.

In 1973, she moved to Lisbon, where three of her brothers lived. She worked first as a secretary in the large architecture studio of the highly-regarded Francisco de Conceição Silva, who created such tourist projects as the Torralta and the Balaia Hotel in Algarve.

She began traveling when she was twenty-two years old. She enjoyed spending vacations in the Canary Islands and on a cruise to Madeira while she was still single.

On April 25, 1974, there were great changes in Portuguese attitudes toward the family, customs, and teaching, in addition to the regained liberty. At this time, she experienced a great political feeling within herself. The dictatorship had terminated, and the overseas colonies were striving for their independence.

At this time, being married and having children did not seem to be important. She had been married only six years and had one son. She is divorced at the moment, but she shares her house with the father of her son. Her housekeeper works sixteen hours a week to clean and to iron, and has worked in her house for more than twenty-five years. This lady has become a good friend with Luísa.

For ten years (1981-1991), she worked in the Office of European Law (Ministry of Justice) at the time of the preparation and the entry of Portugal into the European

Economic Community - now known as the European Union. The work involved the translation of directives and the research of community documents.

For a year and a half, she was in the office of the Attorney-General of Portugal. She worked in the library and in the Documentation Services, in a work involving the law sector. This placed her in contact with judicial subjects.

She lived on a street near the Largo do Rato in Lisbon. While she worked, her son was cared for in the Attorney-General day care centre (old Palace Palmela). Since this was five minutes from her house, it permitted her to spend more time with him.

Luísa began to study diligently as a night student at the Universidade Autónoma de Lisboa. She finished the course and decided to move to an activity related to Women's Rights. After public competition, she was accepted by the Commission for the Equality and the Rights of Women (CIDM), which still exists under that name today.

She found this to be a very interesting work. She worked first in the editorial centre of the published research for the Commission, and then she directed the research, coordinating with several others. It was an important time in the founding of the equality of opportunities for women. The International Year of the Woman in 1975 gave an enormous boost to this work because, in Portugal, where there was - and still is - much discrimination of women.

Women are already in many professions in which they had been forbidden for centuries; but, in politics and in places of management, there are yet very few. Luísa has begun organizing the migrant women in France, near Paris and Lyon. She has been invited to present conferences regarding this topic in Madeira Island and at the University of São Paulo, in Brazil.

As a freelance journalist, she has been in Spain. However, she has never worked continually in foreign countries. She has worked on a Master's Degree in the History and Culture of Brazil at the Universidade Clássica de Lisboa, but she not been able to do the final work. Since 1999, she has worked in an administrative position in the General Tax Office of the Portugal Ministry of Finances.

She lives in Lisbon about twenty minutes by bus or Metro (subway) from her work at the Praça do Comércio, the main square in Lisbon, which is located near the Tagus River. She has walked many times to work because it takes her only thirty minutes, and she does not like to drive in the city. In 1986, she purchased a rundown house near Ericeira Beach and restored it. This is where she likes to spend weekends and summer vacations when she is not traveling. Her travels have taken her to such countries as Spain, France, Denmark, Germany, Austria, Bulgaria, Greece, Belgium, Italy, and Brazil (Rio de Janeiro and São Paulo).

Luísa does not consider reading as a hobby because she writes so that she will read more. The pastimes that she really likes are cultural - visiting museums, participating in conferences, and attending book releases, concerts, and ballet. It is also pleasurable to go on cruises, to garden, and to cook - what she rarely does because her companion does it better.

Working in a perfume store in the past created some amusing experiences because it was in a Commercial Centre that was open twenty-four hours a day. During 1970-1980, there were not many Commercial Centres in Lisbon. However, boys and men would come to her store wanting to give perfume to a lady friend, a wife, or a mother. As they had no idea what they wanted to buy, they would ask Luísa to make a suggestion. Her response to such a request was, "How am I the person who knows which perfume to recommend?"

Her greatest fulfillment in life has been the writing of a book which took three years to complete because she was able to spend time on it only after work and on weekends. Published in December 2004, it is entitled *Casa Havaneza - 140 anos à esquina do Chiado* (Havaneza House - 140 years at the corner of the Chiado). She is currently researching for a book which will be the biography of a Portuguese queen.

For four years, Luísa has been President of the Assembly of the Parish of the Sacrament (near the Chiado in Lisbon) and has developed activities for the improvement of the living conditions of older people in the three old quarters of Lisbon, with rundown homes and with stairs, which they now can ascend and descend with canes. In Lisbon, people do not work with the local authorities, but they use them only for complaining.

She feels that the Portuguese are not civic-minded, showing little interest in their city or their country. They are pessimists and suspect all politicians. The forty-eight years of the dictator Salazar removed persons from the government agencies. Besides, the older people have received very little instruction.

Luísa is a member of the ruling body in the São Mamede Parish, the parish where she lives, but she does not have an office position.

She lives in an old neighbourhood, where the more affluent and better known families of Lisbon live. There are mansions and very beautiful houses. The city is like those in nearly all of the capitalist countries. In her residential neighbourhood, there are adequate traditional commercial stores, and people spend much time in conversation over coffee. The environment is almost like a village.

Her son does copy work for an international publicity company, is single, has a girl friend, and has bought a house in December 2005, for which he will pay in seventy-five years. There are no houses to rent in central Lisbon, and none that young people can afford to buy.

One time, I received an email message from Luísa with an amendment to my website page that lists Portuguese royalty. After doing more research, she sent me additional information for the page. Since her knowledge of English and my knowledge of Portuguese are limited, we use French as a medium of communication, with which both of us have some knowledge. This has worked well.

20

Martha Elena Arévalo de Duff

Arteaga, Coahuila, México

Your neighbours are watching! Martha found this out one day when a neighbour confided that her husband was very jealous of Martha's lifestyle. Whenever he saw Martha's family doing something with their children, he exclaimed to his wife, "Look at them, they are playing! I ought to be doing the same with our children." Sometimes, he saw the family enjoying gardening, and said, "I have always wanted to do that with my children." Or worse, when he was seated in front of his television and did not find a programme that he liked, even then he exclaimed, "What must our neighbours be doing? Surely they are playing!"

Martha has often wondered why people deprive themselves of their dreams. It appears that they do so only because they prefer to have a very expensive lifestyle. That happened with those neighbours - owners of a car and the current year's model of a light truck; but with the excessive workload, they were devoid of time and energy to enjoy their children.

When she looks around her and listens to other families talk about their lifestyles, it grieves her to realize that this world consists of so much avarice and egotism. She asks, "Is no one interested in helping others unselfishly anymore? Does no one have feelings anymore? Have people become money machines?" Even after all their efforts, they are never satisfied:

first a car, then a truck, or a house, furniture, decoration, the latest fashion in clothes, meals in restaurants, pets, celebrations, and the list goes on.

Martha was born in Monterrey, Nuevo León, México. She began her schooling in a kindergarten in San Nicolás de los Garza, a suburb of Monterrey. After attending pre-school for a year and not wanting to continue for another year as required, she pressured her parents to register her for grade 1. "It is the same boring thing," she explained to them. Therefore, she entered the primary school at age five.

Martha completed her studies with a bachelor's degree in the Faculty of Psychology at Universidad Autónoma de Nuevo León (UANL), and later obtained a master's degree in the Faculty of Education. Each semester during her university studies, she received a congratulatory letter from the director of the university for being the most outstanding student. Even this did not make a difference at graduation time.

In her early school years, her best experiences were in receiving recognition each year as the student of the year. However, in spite of being a girl with "academic success," she was always rejected by her peers. As a result, she did not have real friends - only school companions. They looked to her occasionally when they needed assistance with their assignments. Others met in different homes, went for walks, and played together; but Martha was never included.

Later, as a young college student, she found refuge in her studies - research and the practicum - in the second semester, although the educational rule stated that they were to be taken in the seventh semester. She felt better by being the friend of three great teachers: Lupita Villarreal, Natalia Carlos, and the latter's husband Jorge. From them, she learned much;

and they provided the opportunity for her to enter as an observer at the Clinic of Rehabilitation, even though it required more time to be spent on studies.

Her hardest experience in the university was at the conclusion of her studies, since, in Mexico, degrees are not awarded with the passing of all the examinations. Several options existed; and she chose to have a general examination, which is oral and individual. In order to present it, she had to make many trips because of paperwork, with a substantial cost each time.

When the date arrived for her professional examination, she felt calm and secure, so much so that she decided not to study anything. She thought, "My life has prepared everything for me and I have studied hard so there is nothing else to study. They are going to ask only on the last five years of studies."

Regrettably, Martha did not realize that this confidence would be held against her. The examiners reprimanded her, not only for saying that she did not study for this examination, but also because, when asked her opinion on the education, she responded that it was mediocre. She presented many examples of young professionals who faced the sad reality of not knowing how to do anything. For that reason, they had to settle for such employment as salesmen, receptionists, or secretaries.

After the teachers had deliberated, they told her that they could not authorize her degree because she was not prepared. Obviously, she felt terrible; but she was able to keep herself from crying. She bid farewell to each one, saying, "Indeed, you have verified it once again. You have accepted those students who are not prepared and rejected the ones who are. Thank you very much."

She did not know how she could resist crying or shouting. When she left the office, there were many of her companions there to congratulate to her. But they were shocked when Martha said that she had not been approved! They soon realized that if she could not obtain her credit, how could they? When she arrived at her house, she exploded into weeping. She did not understand why one must be dishonest and lie to accomplish something. The school was bad! Why not accept it? Why bother looking for alternatives to improve the system? She managed to recover and received good offers for work. The potential employers did not require a degree. They knew her path as a student was not only theoretical but also practical.

Six months later, she decided to take the examination again; and returned to respond in the same way as before. Once again, the authorities failed her. This time, she did not cry. Now, she was determined to fight.

She returned for the examination the third time, maintaining her points of view. Finally, they passed her, because they knew that, in two weeks time, she would be representing the State of Nuevo León in a national congress. How was it possible that one who had been reprimanded could represent the state? After the examination, the director approached her and said, "We are going to pass you, but keep your mouth shut. All of us know that there are problems in the education system, but we cannot say anything. If we make it public, students will attend no longer, we will not have work, and you will affect many." Since that time, she has decided to fight; for no longer is she alone. She now has a "wonderful husband" who supports her.

When she was single, Martha worked in several institutions and government departments, among them the Clinic of Rehabilitation of the Faculty of Psychology (UANL), where she began as a volunteer and later as a student adviser. In the Research Center (UANL), she had the opportunity to work as an informational researcher and analyst. In the Community Development Centre of the DIF (Integral Development of the Family) in San Nicólas, she worked as a psychological therapist and coordinator.

Finally, she worked in the programme *Women in Solidarity* in southern Nuevo León with women farmers who were in extreme poverty. It was her first experience in working in the rural area, where the mentality, the interests, and the necessities were not comparable to those of the city. There, people strive to have something to eat; whereas, in the city, people strive to gain more possessions. There, she could live with the people and discover and feel what the people experienced - indispensable tools in performing good work as a social promoter and programme designer.

Martha enjoyed her work experience very much. Her two main areas have been as a psychologist in the rehabilitation of children with learning problems and guidance to the parents in Nuevo León and Coahuila and as a social promoter in the rural area of Nuevo León.

During her professional life, she has worked with different ages of people, including babies, children, young people, and women farmers. One of her greater satisfactions is that, of all the people with whom she has worked, individual or outside group, most of them have managed to achieve a great advance in life, becoming analytical, critical, and reflective, with a desire to learn. Martha maintains pleasant memories of each one of them and her experience has caused her to advance equally.

It was very rewarding to have the whole group of those women attend each meeting without the promise of receiving something in return. Those were women who had to rise at 3:00 a.m. to make long walks to carry water and then to be punctual in arriving at the meetings. The objective was to have women participate who could learn to manage their own affairs and make their own decisions and this was being fulfilled. But suddenly, overnight, the government decided to cancel the programme without giving a convincing explanation.

Martha continues to "shake her head" at governmental proposals for programmes that are supposedly going to prepare people. Even now, local politicians do not like people to learn. They prefer to keep a town ignorant and, therefore, controllable. If someone offers culture, the government says that there are no resources. If someone offers education, the government says that schools already exist. If someone offers ideas for people to develop their own resources, the government says that they cannot because they will ask for many resources; and they think that the people are lazy and do not want to work anyway. If someone offers something on health, the government says that it is good enough but will give a medical centre even though there are no resources for electricity or for a doctor.

Still, Martha believes that if the government cannot or does not want to support true growth or education, somebody must do it and she and her family must try. Others, too, must not close their eyes or cover their ears because everyone has something to offer, if they would only do so.

When Martha was twenty-eight years old, she took a trip to Texas, in the United States, in order to learn how to survive in a country in which she did not know the language, the culture, or the religion. Her desire was to be economically independent, not using credit cards or receiving aid from her parents. She learned much about the life of illegal immigrants, including how Americans harass young Latino women. It was difficult to be single in such a world. The best part about her experience in Texas, she says, was meeting Sean - a Canadian, cultured, full of love, values, and manner of serving others. Today, they have two sons: Alejandro (born 1995) and Josué (born 1998), both of whom are being educated at home.

When single, Martha worked for government offices in Monterrey; but three months after her marriage, she presented an idea to her husband; she would resign from her position because their schedules did not coincide and it was very difficult to coexist as a couple. She wanted more available time to be with him! How could he argue and he readily approved the suggestion. They did not want to become a conventional couple who would have little time for each other, to integrate, and to love. Nor did they want to be a couple who could only worry about work and an income.

Since then, she has dedicated herself to the home, which she considers to be a great school. She is continually learning about family health, nutrition, ecology, and home schooling. Sometimes, she and Sean offer courses at schools, in churches, or in groups interested in different subjects, mainly in the basics - "how to teach mathematics" and "how to teach reading and writing," but she offers private classes in any academic subject. Sometimes, Sean or their children advise her, mainly in respect to English.

Martha is frugal and supports her husband. They buy under a rule: "Things are purchased only because they are needed, not because they are wanted or because others have them." Her first language is Spanish. However, she takes advantage of her knowledge of basic English to offer private language classes to primary and secondary level students.

In 1992, she met a great friend - María de Jesús González Puente, a social worker by vocation, an honest and simple woman. From her, Martha learned much about group activities, political management, administration, and economy in the home.

After fourteen years of having known her, she has not met another person of her quality, straight-forwardness, and love of giving to others. María was a living example showing that it is better to live with simplicity than to corrupt oneself with the glitter of money. She was a woman who did not fight to have a house, in spite of being orphaned, who did not seek to have a car, or to shine always in the latest fashion - a woman against consumerism. Her great wealth was being the possessor of many happy hearts. Since then, that beautiful example has been shared by Martha with her family; and they also continue the struggle, not only for themselves but also for others.

Martha maintains that her greatest achievement during her career has been to be able to give up the pleasures of materialism and comforts. Had she not rejected these great work opportunities that would have provided economic wellbeing, she knows she would have lost something greater - her principles and her ideas of community programmes. Besides, working independently in the home gives her the opportunity to take care of and to enjoy her family and to educate from the home. What greater achievement is there?

To others, it may appear that Martha does not have anything; she is poor. They cannot understand why she feels happy and very fortunate. They do not realize that it is because she really has a family - one that shares dreams, goals, hopes, ideas, frustrations - everything.

In order to be more successful in their lives, people need only to fulfill the accomplishment of a dream. The dream of Sean and Martha is to live in the country and from the earth, and also to share with people their knowledge in health, ecology, English, Spanish, computers, astronomy, administration, and education. Their dream is to advance the hand of farmers; and, if something exists that this couple does not know, they will seek, research, and learn together.

For many years, they have fought to obtain this dream. They have continued to struggle and will continue to fight. It does not matter that their feet are tired from much walking, their hands are full of calluses from hard work, or their skin is burned by the rays of the sun. It does not matter that many think that they are crazy. However, there are others that admire their determination even though they themselves would not dare do what Sean and Martha are trying to do without the support of government or of churches.

She does not seek any honour or monument; but she says, if a monument were considered, she would raise two: one for her parents-in-law, Duane and Pamela Duff, and one for her parents, Luis Arévalo and Maria Olvera. Each one of them supports the family in his/her own way and she is very grateful. Thanks to their support, Martha and her family are now able to travel down their chosen path.

For fun, Martha likes to do many things; but the main

one is living with her family, sharing at meals, playing badminton, filling balloons with water, or reliving Sean's childhood through slides. However, she believes that her family thinks that her favorite pastime is "talking". Sometimes, they would like to terminate her conversations so that they would be able to say something. She also loves their teasing!

Martha loves to cook and is an excellent cook. She has developed many vegetarian Mexican dishes that even non-vegetarians enjoy. She particularly likes to watch Sean and their two sons savour each dish, with their faces reflecting their delight in tasting it.

Martha's philosophy is "Firmly maintain your goal. Do not abandon it, and you will obtain it." She knows that it is difficult; but, whenever they visit a farming community, she can see hope in the faces of those old men, curiosity in the glances of the children, tranquility in the mothers, and enthusiasm and energy in the young people. She sees all that and more, simply because Sean and Martha valued them enough to want live with them and work with them to help each one advance. At the same time, she sees total happiness in her family because they are working together doing what they love with people about whom they care. Martha, Sean, Alejandro, and Josué now live in Mesa de las Tablas, Coahuila, México, where they are working with the community in developing a learning centre.

We first met Martha when Sean brought her to our home in suburban Dallas, Texas. Martha could not speak English, while Pam and I could not speak Spanish. It was an awkward few minutes while Sean was in his bedroom changing clothes. Since then, all of us have honed our skills in charades when

"Span-glish" could not convey a meaning. After she and Sean had been married nearly a year, Pam and I, with our other son, Cameron, moved to Mexico. Our families shared a home for six years in Nuevo León, in Chiapas, and in British Columbia, Canada. From the first day of meeting, we knew Martha was going to be a part of the family. Both Pam and I are very happy to have Martha as a cherished daughter-in-law.

21
Norman Edward Olson

Victoria, British Columbia, Canada

Happy birthday, Mr. Principal! The older boys of the country school in Alberta, Canada, devised a unique way of honouring this man. They borrowed - without the owner's knowledge - a local farmer's wagon, took it to school, dismantled it, hoisted it piece by piece to the roof of the school, and reassembled it there. This was accomplished under the cover of the darkness of night. Everyone who witnessed the wagon on the roof the next day thought it was hilarious. When little Norman arrived at school, he joined in the marveling of this exciting trick. It was reported that, after the honouring of the principal, the wagon was returned to its rightful owner. The affair was considered a big joke in town and was the topic of discussion for a few days.

Norman was born in Entwistle, Alberta, a small community west of Edmonton. He has written an account of his experiences of living in rural Alberta and has given me permission to draw from it for this chapter. His father, a farmer of the northern United States, heard that there was free land in Canada. Thus, a few years before Norman was born, he decided to homestead there, despite his wife's disapproval.

When Norman was a small child, he and his family moved to nearby Evansburg. One day, Norman had a great scare. A loud noise was approaching. He looked into the sky and saw a big object that had wings that did not flap. He dashed for the house, hoping to outrun this strange thing. Norman had seen an airplane for the first time!

Another scary experience occurred one day when his brother was sitting in the kitchen playing with a shotgun. He disobeyed his mother when told to put it away. Boom! The lamp on the table went out. Norman threw himself to the floor, screaming. He had not been hurt, but was greatly frightened. There was a hole in the wall. His dad's suit in the closet on the other side of the wall was ruined. The far wall of the bedroom was peppered with buckshot. His brother was much more careful after that incident.

Eventually, the family moved to the homestead in the bush 18 miles *(29 km)* north of Evansburg. There were no roads as such, no schools, and no close neighbours. Norman and his younger sister thought nothing of their extreme poverty. It was a way of life, but, to Norman in later years, a valuable experience. Their first home, though temporary, was a make-shift log shack on the edge of the only clearing in the area. He relished the experience of making a bed in a wagon one windy night and sleeping in the open.

They traveled on the surveyed road allowances. The wagon ruts created mud holes. If the trail were too bad, traffic would detour through the bush on its way to town. The nearest neighbour was two and one-half miles *(4 km)* away, while the next one was six miles *(10 km)* away. Whenever there were visits, they would be joyous occasions.

One joyful event was the attendance at a school Christmas concert several miles away. It was a pleasant sleigh ride on a moonlit night to the school. Norman was so overwhelmed to see so many excited children and all the beautiful decorations. Much to his surprise, he heard his name called to receive a present from Santa Claus.

There was plenty of wildlife in the bush - moose, deer, ducks, prairie chickens, and partridge. This meant an amply supply of wild meat. During the winter, the meat could be kept frozen. His father also occasionally butchered a hog or beef. The smell of frying pork chops on entering the humble house after being outside playing in the cold was a joy.

Driving to town by horses and wagon about once a month for supplies was an all-day job. The children would wait for their dad to bring back such items as Rogers golden syrup, and tins of peanut butter and strawberry jam. These meant more to them than such staples as flour, sugar, and coffee. In addition, their mother would provide such homemade items as bread, buns, and cranberry jelly to eat. There were times of scrimping - and even of going without. The sacks in which one hundred pounds *(37 kg)* of flour came were used to make a shirt for Norman, a skirt for his sister, or some other necessary item. Their mother did have a Singer sewing machine - now an heirloom in his sister's family.

For Norman, it was a thrill to see his father and a friend prepare logs that they had cut and skidded. The logs were peeled, cut precisely in length, notched, and placed into position to form their new house. The walls became higher; and then the roof, door, and windows were put into place. The materials smelled rich to him. It was, to the boy, a huge mansion. Such a beautiful home this was! He did not comprehend the worries that his parents probably had.

One time, Norman was intrigued with listening to a gramophone at the home of a neighbour. He did not understand what the source of the voice coming from the box was. When a record was changed, it would be dusted by a large feather. He has never experienced the same thrill from seeing any record equipment since that day.

Winters were long – and so were the evenings. The long, cold snaps kept the children inside much of the time. The house was heated by the kitchen stove, day and night. The tea kettle was constantly singing. Since wood was the only fuel, Norman's dad would stay up at night to keep the fires going when the weather was cold. Since there were no storm windows, frost patterns would appear on the glass. These were fascinating.

This gives a glimpse of life as Norman and others experienced it in bygone days before we had all the conveniences of today. Difficult as it was, people survived, and are probably better for it.

He attended Evansburg School in Evansburg from grades 1-9. It was early summer of 1933, in the height of the Great Depression (later dubbed the Hungry Thirties); and Norman had recently left school. Because his mother had been widowed three years prior and the family was living from hand to mouth, he decided to go to work to help support the home. His adventure in trying to be the breadwinner when no jobs were available is told below.

Norman has also written an account of his one and only experience as a hobo and has granted permission that it, too, can be used here. Some of the highlights of the adventure are included in this account. For those who lived in the 1930s, seeing hobos was common. This was a period of history in numerous countries that is unique and important.

A friend with severely impaired vision suggested that they – both teenagers – set out for British Columbia in search of work. Although Norman did not really think that they would find anything, he was excited with the idea. Like hundreds of others at the time, they would use freight trains as their mode of transportation. They would be hoboes! He had a difficult time convincing his mother. He felt that life on the road would not be any worse than that at home in those depression years.

They rigged up a gunny sack with a stout rope tied to each end so that they could sling it over the shoulder and have free hands for grasping moving ladders or climbing into open boxcars. Each of their bags contained a light make-shift sleeping bag and some food for the start of the trip, at least. Oh, yes, they had cash in their pockets. Norman had a one-dollar bill.

Late one dark night, they waited at the coal dock a couple of miles *(3 km)* away for a scheduled freight train. When it arrived, they climbed aboard an empty boxcar. Soon, they were on their way to a new adventure. Although there were a few misgivings about this trip, they continued to Vancouver without incident.

It was necessary to purchase two one-way ferry tickets, costing twenty cents each, in order to proceed to West Vancouver, where his friend's sister lived. They stayed here for a couple of days, enjoying the opportunity for good meals and baths. When they left, the hostess gave her brother a dollar and some food to carry. After buying two ferry tickets, they were on their way to the home of Norman's sister and family, who lived in Trail, British Columbia. The boys hoped to obtain work at the large smelter in that city.

They traveled on the Kettle Valley line on trains that stopped every night. On arrival in any town, they located the local hobo jungle. It would be near the railroad at the edge of a town. Besides water, if possible, there were usually make-shift shelters, fire pits, and wind breaks.

Each night on arrival, they would pick their spot, roast a couple of potatoes in the open fire, warm up a can of beans or stew, and have a slice of dry bread and always a pot of coffee made over the open fire in a blackened tin. This continued for several nights, but the food ran out. Norman decided to go to the back door of a house on the edge of town. He knocked. A lady answered and asked what he wanted. He explained that he was out of money and food and asked for a little food. The woman left for a few minutes while Norman wondered what she might do. She returned with a couple of slices of homemade bread and a large slab of cheese. The hungry teenager was so thankful! That was the only time in his life that he ever begged for food.

At last, after a brief run-in with police, the boys reached Trail. Following a couple of days at the home of Norman's sister, they went to the smelter. Alas! They were just two more persons applying for jobs that did not exist. After a few more days, it was time to head for home. They went west, and then cross-country toward Kelowna, stopping overnight once. A farmer gave them a lift over the last few miles. On arrival, they discovered that the train to Kamloops was not a daily one. Thus, there was some waiting at a jungle area. From a local cherry-packing plant, they obtained culled cherries to eat.

In Kamloops, they caught a ride on a freight train headed for Jasper, Alberta. Probably, their most frightening incident happened there. As the train approached this town, known for its tough police, all the hoboes jumped off. As they headed for the right-of-way fence, an RCMP officer approached and ordered them to stop. They ran! After they had an opportunity to rest, they started for the highway. Whom should they meet but the same officer. With drawn gun, he ordered them to raise their hands. They froze! Then the officer advised them that, the next time when they are ordered to stop, they should do so. The police are looking for a particular person. If they should see someone fitting the description, they are likely to shoot first and ask questions afterwards. Then, he offered them a small job to earn some food. When no one accepted the offer, the officer ordered them out of town. There was no hesitation!

The hoboes boarded the same train just east of the town. This took them toward Edmonton. On arrival back home, Norman and his mother were happy to see each other again. The experience was over!

About the mid-thirties, Norman was able to buy his very first radio. The price was $55.00, being paid at $5.00 per month for eleven weary months. It was a mantle radio powered by a wet cell battery and two dry cell batteries. It also required an outside aerial that was a chore to accomplish because height was essential for reception. Nevertheless, it was well worth the price and effort for the pleasure that he derived from it. Those long winters, with frigid evenings to match, were so pleasurably offset by those delightful programmes that they could tune in and enjoy.

In spite of some erratic reception, the best part of it all was the fact that, as one listened to voice and sound effects, one's mind filled in all the settings and scenery. Imagination could keep everything as squeaky clean as the listener desired. In that sense, he/she was in full control of the programmes' offerings.

He worked underground in coal mines until he had

eighteen months of experience and then applied for his mining ticket, which he was granted without any difficulty.

One job was in Hinton, west of Edmonton, for a few months where steam coal, which was used for firing stream boilers, was mined. A couple of months after he left, there was an explosion underground, killing five men and severely injuring five others. Norman had worked with each one and knew them well.

He also worked in a coalmine in Carbon, Alberta, northeast of Calgary. It was a four-foot *(1.2 m)* seam, quite restricting, making it necessary to walk bent over all the time. Shetland ponies, very job-smart animals, were used for power. Norman worked with them, hauling the loaded coal buggies from the coal face to the base of the incline where they were towed to the tipple by cable.

On one occasion, Norman's lamp went out, leaving him in the dark and in a panic. However, his smart little pony did not let up and trotted through the pitch blackness to the proper destination.

The last job in which he worked before the Second World War started was in a local coal mine that catered to local trade only. There was one harrowing experience, in which he was about one minute from being in an explosion. He was looking for a track tool and asked the man that worked in the next room about it. He was told that it was lying at the edge of the track just a few paces in. Norman kept walking in and looking, but did not see it. When he noticed a faint smoky haze hanging in the air (from a fuse that had been lit), he realized immediately that a blast was pending. He exited on the double. He was very upset with the man for not telling him about it. Had Norman reported the incident, the man would have lost his job.

A few days after Canada entered World War II, Norman joined the army, remaining in it until about one month after the war in the Pacific area had ceased. Thus, he spent a total of six years in the infantry, serving overseas in England, North Africa, and Italy. Norman was among the first of the Canadian Army to be shipped overseas at the beginning of World War II. He describes the trip on the Atlantic Ocean.

On arrival at Halifax, the soldiers immediately boarded a large ocean liner, a Polish ship named the *MS Batory*. Since it had not yet been converted to a troop ship, they had cabins with white linen sheets on the comfortable beds and stewards to look after their needs. What a break that was for early volunteers!

At the outset, the sailing was smooth; but the further that they moved into open water, the rougher it became. About two days into the crossing time, the wind began to blow and gradually increased with time, causing the mighty ship to begin to heave – really heave.

There was no rain or snow, only a gale force wind with nothing to check its velocity. The whole expanse of the ocean was transformed into gigantic waves on one hand and bottomless pits on the other. Norman remembers standing on the upper deck (the main deck was constantly flooded) and watching as the bow of the ship nosed down at what seemed like a forty-five degree angle into a swallowing depression and thinking it could not possibly survive the dip. However, at the extremity of the downward plunge, it would begin its upward heave and finally point to the sky at an opposite mind-boggling angle. This went on for two or three days. He began to adjust and his inner panic subsided, especially as he noticed the crew members taking it in stride as though all was normal.

He was happy when the ship sailed into Glasgow harbour. This ordeal was over and a new adventure was about to begin.

After the war, he worked for thirty-six years as a locomotive engineer on the Canadian National Railways in Canada, mainly Alberta. Do you suppose that he ever thought in 1933 that he would someday be riding in the cabs of locomotives instead of in empty box-cars?

There is one experience that is dreaded by men in a railway locomotive - seeing someone or something on the tracks, too close to allow the train to stop. It happened to Norman! It was a very sad and upsetting experience.

One bright, sunny Sunday morning, the crew was on a run from Edmonton to Whitecourt, to the northwest. As the train rounded a curve traveling briskly along, the crew noticed something on the tracks lying between the rails - a common experience. As they drew closer, it looked so much like some old rags which had been left there. When the train was close enough, the men were horrified. Two young people were asleep on the road bed! Norman instantly applied the brakes in emergency, but there was no way in which the crew could stop the train in time. When it did screech to a stop, the men ran back - and oh, what a sad mess! Both young people were shattered and dead. When a train is stopped under such circumstances, by law, it must not be moved until the police, who are immediately informed, have completed their careful investigation and issued its release.

At the official investigation, it was determined that both native teenagers, a girl fifteen and a boy eighteen, had been partying the day before and, on the way home, likely very early in the morning, had decided to take a nap which, of course, was a foolish thing to do.

After stopping and checking out the results, Norman performed his own bit of investigating. His locomotive consist was made up of three diesel engines operated by one set of controls. When he checked the first unit, there was not the slightest sign of any marks; but the undercarriage of the second unit bore much evidence of hair and blood. This meant that, if the teenagers had had the presence of mind to lie flat, they would have survived. The first unit passed over them while they were still sleeping; but, likely, it had wakened them with a start. The rest is sad history. Norman was literally sick for weeks.

He probably has many other more pleasant stories of railroading. Norman worked in no other line of work except that he has served continuously as a self-educated and self-supported minister since 1949.

He has found any holiday trip to be interesting and memorable. These include visits to England, Wales, Spain, France, Holland, continental United States, Hawaii, and Mexico. He holds great memories of them all!

In his younger days, he loved to fish, and to play golf and snooker. He still likes to play snooker regularly in his retirement home. When he was 85, he tried oil painting for the first time. He feels more comfortable with it after learning how to do it. For two years he has been a member of a writing group. It was a struggle at first, but the notes provided for this chapter indicate that he is becoming more comfortable with it.

Norman recognizes that many people have had a great influence on him. However, the one who had the most effect on his life, his thinking, his values, and his thirst for knowledge was Roy A. Cheville, Presiding Evangelist of his church. When Norman was ordained to the office of Evangelist, Dr. Cheville came and spent a glorious two weeks to help with his orientation. To Norman, he was the epitome of a few lines of Kipling's *If*:

> "If you can talk with crowds and keep your virtue,
> Or walk with Kings – nor lose the common touch.
> If neither foes nor loving friends can hurt you,
> If all men count with you but none too much."

He will always be indebted to his mentor for the example set for him.

He feels that his greatest accomplishment was realizing the goal that he had set for himself at the beginning of his life's work – which was to be able to retire with an adequate pension. He has realized more than twenty-five years of enjoyable retirement. Everything else was icing on the cake!

There is one regret, although he states that he is not "crying the blues." He has limited formal education, but that has not hindered him from educating himself. He has found this process to be even delightful and profitable. He is most thankful for what his church has done for him. It created the major turning point in his life.

Norman believes that he has something important to which he holds – open-mindedness. He has only one thing which he will chisel in stone: "I will never chisel anything in stone!" Many people look for final answers, and build up a comfort zone which, over a period of time, becomes a rut. A rut has been defined as a grave with both ends kicked out. He holds to his conclusions lightly because answers may be timely, but are seldom timeless. He will not play the role of an immovable object in the path of irresistible forces. That, to him, is his philosophy of life.

I met Norman one Sunday morning in 1958 at church in Edmonton, Alberta. Before moving from Ontario to attend summer school at the University of Alberta, I had written to him. He invited me to his home for dinner with his family and a family friend. It was about twenty years later when he was at our house for a meal. On that occasion, I was happy to show him my collection of railroad books. On the cover of one of the books was the picture of a locomotive that he had driven. Most of our relationship with Norman involved our church work. It has been a pleasant relationship. I would like to thank Norman for the use of his autobiography notes in preparing part of this chapter.

22

Oakley Duff

Spencerville, Ontario, Canada

What a difference one hour and one-half can make in a volatile city! It was peaceful when Oakley, Vonne, and Skylar set out from their home in Islamabad, Pakistan, on their way to do some shopping. It was so different when they were returning home. A violent demonstration had broken out, but now the mob had been dispersed by the authorities. On the street were tear gas, fires, and rocks. Some streets were blocked by barbed wire. It was so unnerving, unlike what the family had ever seen! Oakley was quite concerned that his family could be caught in a violent confrontation as they tried to make their way home. It was necessary to detour through side streets, not knowing whether or when they might encounter the demonstrators and authorities - dodging fires and rocks in the street much of the way. Fortunately, they avoided direct confrontation and eventually reached home safely and without incident. What a relief it was to be home!

Oakley was born in Tillsonburg, Ontario, Canada, a town southeast of London and southwest of Hamilton, and a short distance north of Lake Erie.

He began his formal education at Corinth Public School, a two-room rural school located near the hamlet of Corinth, a few miles from Tillsonburg. From Aylmer, he has his clearest high school memory. On November 22, 1963, at the end of the school day during extra curricular activities, the news of the announcement of President Kennedy's assassination passed quickly from one student to another. Oakley remembers hearing the news from a friend as he left a meeting of the school's United Nations Club. Many students gathered around a radio to listen to the reports. Everyone was shocked and saddened by the news.

Oakley earned a Bachelor of Arts in Political Science degree from the University of Toronto. While a student, he had his most memorable experience in university. It was a near death experience that a group of four students had while driving to Boston University from Toronto in the winter of 1967 for a student exchange week. Somewhere on the expressway in Massachusetts, the driver was forced to brake suddenly, resulting in the car spinning out of control. It turned a full 360 degrees, somehow missing traffic behind it, veered across the median and over the lanes going the other way, skittered through the oncoming traffic, and then careened down a steep embankment into a field, where it spun around again before coming to a stop. It was a miracle that the car avoided a collision and did not upset. None of the group was hurt, but all were in a state of shock. Amazingly, the students managed to push/drive the car back up to the highway and to continue their trip to Boston unscathed.

The trip home was no joy either. Near Buffalo, New York, they encountered a fierce snow storm that slowed them down considerably. With great relief, they finally returned safely to the university in Toronto. Their guardian angels certainly protected them on that trip!

Oakley speaks English, but can read French fairly well. He has managed well in the numerous countries where he has lived and visited.

He worked as an immigration officer for the Canadian Government and self-employed as a migration management consultant as follows.

He lived and worked for two years or more while employed with the Canadian Government in Canada, Hong Kong, South Africa, Poland, Netherlands, and Pakistan. He worked for periods of one week to three months while employed with the Canadian Government in Trinidad, Guyana, Barbados, Macau, Swaziland, Lesotho, Botswana, United States, Eire, Sweden, Finland, Latvia, China, and India. He was diplomatically accredited to Denmark, Norway, and Iceland; but he did not visit these countries. He worked on projects for periods of one to three months in Canada and of one week to one month each while self-employed in Russia, Azerbaijan, Armenia, Georgia, Turkmenistan, Tajikistan, Uzbekistan, Kazakhstan, Indonesia, Australia, East Timor, and Sri Lanka.

While he was an immigration officer, he had numerous memorable experiences, in Canada and abroad.

Very early in his immigration career, in 1972, in White Rock, British Columbia, on the United States - Canada border, he met an interesting personality. In addition to inspecting travelers entering Canada by car at the Douglas/Blaine (Peace Arch) border crossing and at the adjacent Pacific Highway truck/bus/car crossing, the officers also inspected train passengers traveling from Seattle to Vancouver. The train stopped in the nearby city of White Rock, where Canada Customs and Immigration officers boarded it to conduct inspections.

One evening during the train inspection, Oakley had occasion to check a dear, little, old lady. She was in her seventies, white-haired, and looked very fragile. More than thirty years later, he still can see and hear her clearly and remember her name. Although she likely has passed on by now, for privacy reasons, he refers to her here only as Edith W. or Mrs. W.

The standard first questions during immigration inspections are, "Where do you live?", "What is your citizenship?" and (if a foreigner) "Where are you going?" and "What is the purpose of your trip?" In reply to these questions, Mrs. W. exclaimed, "Edith W. I am an American citizen and I am going to Westminster to be canonized. I stand upon the legal law, the legal law, the constitution of the United States!"

Now the stated purpose was rather unusual, as was the vigour with which it was stated, particularly coming from a frail-looking senior citizen. His subsequent questions seeking clarification and requesting identity documents received the same response. It rapidly became clear that the poor lady was demented and that she could neither be inspected properly on the train, nor be allowed to continue on to Vancouver.

Oakley politely asked her to accompany him off the train to sort out her plans in the office in the train station. However, she shrilly refused to move from her seat. Of course, he wanted to treat this fragile-looking (but quite balmy) elderly lady with dignity and respect, but he had to remove her from the train. Wishing to avoid the application of physical force (especially against a little old lady), he disembarked and telephoned from the train station for a female officer to come over from the Douglas office in the hope that she might be able to persuade poor Mrs. W. to disembark. A few minutes later, his female colleague, Rose, arrived; but she could not get sweet Mrs. W. to move either.

By this time, all the other inspections were finished and

the train was ready to leave. Somehow, they had to take Edith W. off the train. But she was adamant that she was going to Westminster to be canonized and stood "upon the legal law, the legal law, the Constitution of the United States!" She was also attracting the curious attention of the other passengers in the railway coach.

Finally, Oakley took her bag from the overhead rack and started to walk off the train with it. At this, she jumped up, seized the other end of the bag and tried to snatch it away from him. Surprised at how spry she really was, he instinctively backed up, still holding the bag. She followed, still hanging on to her bag, chanting "The legal law, the legal law, the Constitution of the United States!" He kept on backing up, pulling the bag with her attached, followed by his intrepid colleague, Rose, who ensured that Mrs. W. could not return to her seat. He backed all the way to the train door, climbed down the steps backward, and retreated backwards into the station, with the bag in his hands and Edith W. clutching the other end, while Rose followed behind her.

Eventually, they placed Mrs. W. and her bag (fortunately she would not be parted from it) into a car and took her back to the United States immigration office. The U.S. authorities subsequently put her on a bus to Seattle. Later, Oakley learned that she had tried to enter Canada the night before on a bus at Pacific Highway and one of his immigration colleagues there also had a terrible time in sending her back to the U.S. side. Altogether, for such a sweet-appearing, little old lady, she presented one of the most bizarre experiences that Oakley had in his career.

One experience that he had in China in 1987 probably contributed indirectly to his decision a few years later to become a vegetarian. At that time, he was managing the immigration office at Vancouver International Airport. Along with Mark, a former Foreign Service colleague who was then posted in Hong Kong, the department selected Oakley to represent Canada in an exchange visit with immigration officials from China. The immigration managers from Beijing and Shanghai Airports first came to Vancouver to observe the Canadian operations and then Mark and Oakley visited Shanghai and Beijing. Included in the exchange were the inevitable official dinners and tours. No doubt their Chinese counterparts found some of their experiences in Vancouver as remarkable as the two Canadians did in China.

Shanghai was memorable particularly for a dinner that their Chinese counterparts hosted in honour of their guests. The Chinese are very hospitable and offer an amazing variety of delicacies, some of which are unusual to Western tastes. The host will also select specialties and place them onto the plate of their guests. Good manners require that the guests not only eat them, but also give convincing evidence of having enjoyed them. The latter, of course, results in more treats being added to the plates. Mark and Oakley, though both Foreign Service veterans and familiar with Chinese customs and culinary experience, were not culinary adventurers; and the latter did not even like sea food.

The Shanghai specialties turned out to be river eel and sea cucumber. The river eels resembled (and maybe were) a mess of worms. The sea cucumber - no vegetable - was a close imitation of a six-inch *(15 cm)* grey slug. Fortunately, neither the eels nor cucumbers were moving. The Canadians looked at each and studiously avoided helping themselves to either of the exotic dishes, concentrating on the noodles and more familiar Chinese dishes. However, they were not going to avoid the issue that easily!

Noticing that their guests had not sampled Shanghai's best, the host carefully selected appetizing morsels from each of the dreaded dishes. With great ceremony, he deposited them onto the plates, urging them to enjoy the esteemed local specialties. Looking at each other with resignation and not a little trepidation, Mark and Oakley sampled the fare. Trying to avoid the texture and taste, Oakley swallowed the eel portions unchewed, washing them down with copious drinks. With considerable effort, he managed to keep them down. As they were quite crispy, the sea cucumbers were more of a challenge. Oakley still distinctly remembers the crunch as he had to chew them somewhat before again washing them down with a drink. How unsavoury they must have been!

They managed to survive the dinner by sampling a couple rounds of the host's gracious offerings. However, Oakley doubts that the host was convinced that they really liked those local specialties. Afterwards, the two Canadians agreed that dinner was one of their most challenging experiences in representing Canada abroad. Comparing that with street riots, it must have been a horrendous experience!

Oakley has had occasion to meet heads of state and heads of government.

- Mrs. Leger (acting as Governor-General during her husband's illness) at a 1974 reception for Canadian Foreign Service Officers;
- Pierre Trudeau, during his visit to Trinidad in 1975;
- Jean Chrétien, during his visits to Netherlands and Pakistan in the 1990s.

He and his wife Vonne were invited to meet the Dutch Queen

in 1995, but instead they had to return to Ottawa to attend a necessary meeting.

He noted that the single most common reason for immigrants wanting to come to Canada was to achieve a better life for themselves and their family (opportunities for employment, education, safety/security, social mobility, and quality of life).

The Netherlands was the country in which he felt most comfortable. He enjoyed the people (Dutch and ex-patriots) and the work. He found the European life style very pleasant. Availability of vegetarian foods and ease of travel to nearby European countries were other positive factors.

On the negative side, he felt concern for the safety of his family on at least two occasions in Pakistan. One is related above. The other one was the bombing of the Egyptian Embassy in Islamabad early in their posting in Pakistan. At the time, Oakley was on business in Karachi. When he heard about the bombings during a meeting with Pakistani government officials, he was worried that family and colleagues may have been injured. As it turned out, many at the Egyptian Embassy were killed. Fortunately, no one at the Canadian mission was killed or injured. However, the Canadian mission's windows were blown out; and a large pane of glass hit his assistant's desk, which fortuitously he had vacated just moments before. For months until they left Pakistan, the bombed-out shell of the Egyptian Embassy reminded them every time that they passed it (which was frequent) of the vulnerability of life.

Oakley has encountered many impressive and helpful people throughout the years. Probably, the one who had the most positive effect on his career and life path was Lorne

Hanson, the BC/Yukon regional Director of Immigration for whom he worked in Vancouver, British Columbia, from 1983 to 1988. A former RCMP officer, he exerted strong leadership in the regional immigration department by example, encouragement, and stimulation of excellence and imagination in his staff.

Given his policing and Security Service background, Lorne took keen interest in the Immigration Intelligence Section, which Oakley then headed. He knew that his section always had to be on top of any person, issue, or event that might affect immigration in the region, as Lorne expected it and was extremely well-informed. As Lorne personally knew all the senior officials of every law enforcement agency in his region and the neighbouring United States, he expected that Oakley's section would be similarly plugged in. His support and expectations of the highest performance contributed significantly to Oakley's professional growth in this role and to the reputation their section gained throughout the department and other law enforcement agencies.

After leaving Oakley in that position for a few years until a potential successor was groomed, Lorne told him that it was time to expand his horizons and accept other assignments. Although Oakley had a wide range of experience, Lorne told him that he could do more - in fact, anything to which he put his mind.

Therefore, Oakley accepted a series of assignments over the next few years that considerably expanded his horizons and changed the course of his life. Those assignments gave him experience in operational management, project development, and coordination. Those experiences proved invaluable when he eventually left government service and went into migration management consulting in his own company. As well, one of those assignments that Lorne arranged took Oakley to Ottawa, where he met his wife, Vonne. He will always remember and appreciate Lorne Hanson as a positive force in his life.

He takes satisfaction in contributing to a number of accomplishments during his work career. Some of these involved the successful resolution of complex or high-profile cases or the completion of challenging projects and programmes in his immigration career. However, he feels that the most meaningful and enduring accomplishments relate to the selection, training, and development of personnel whom he had the opportunity to help grow and advance professionally.

At the Canadian mission in Hong Kong, he worked with one secretary who had a previous record of performance problems. Over time, the two established a good working relationship and her performance improved. She later immigrated to Canada and became a productive Canadian citizen, eventually working as an immigration officer in Toronto. Another clerk in the Canadian Embassy in The Hague, Netherlands, whom he hired for a new anti-fraud and liaison position, rose to its challenges and grew in the job. Later, he joined the Dutch immigration service to help establish and supervise a similar function.

In Vancouver, he hired three intelligence analysts who developed into the most highly respected immigration intelligence unit in Canada - with a worldwide reputation. Over the years, they have advanced through successful immigration careers in senior assignments in Vancouver, Ottawa, and Canadian embassies around the world. Another officer who had some performance issues while Oakley was managing the immigration office at Vancouver Airport responded positively to his suggestions for performance improvements in succeeding appraisal reports. He overcame the identified issues and later was promoted to a senior adviser position in the region.

These and other people with whom he has worked over the years all had innate talent that only needed encouragement, some guidance, and the opportunity to learn and grow. Their contributions over the years are far greater than anything that Oakley could have accomplished by himself. He is grateful that he had the opportunity to work with them and to contribute in a small way to their successes.

On a personal level, Oakley would like to have been (and to be) a better husband, parent, sibling, friend, neighbour, community worker, and citizen. On a professional level, he would like to have been a better immigration officer and consultant. His life is still a work in progress and he intends to continue to work with and for purpose in his life. Professionally, too, he can effect more success.

An example of one professional area is in his overseas consulting in capacity building in third world immigration services. This work has involved assessing the current capacity of those services (institutions, legislation, procedures, systems, resources, facilities, equipment, and national documents) and recommending improvements. While these assessments have resulted in projects being launched to introduce the suggested improvements, his involvement has usually ended after submission of the report. He believes that more could have been accomplished in the implementation of those projects through ongoing involvement and will try to negotiate such participation in future work.

Oakley's philosophy of life has evolved through various stages and influences into a growing awareness of the spiritual nature of being. He believes that all of us emanate from and are part of a universal Source (God) to Whom there are many paths of enlightenment. Starting with a fundamentalist Christian upbringing, he later reacted against its ritual, but still retains many of its tenets. In university, he was exposed to the readings of philosophy, particularly existentialism, and drifted to agnosticism. As he matured, he continued to feel uncomfortable with the rituals of established churches, but found common elements in the various world religions - Hindu, Buddhist, Judaic, Christian, Islamic - and New Age writings. Those elements, along with life's experiences, have contributed to his current philosophy of life, which continues to evolve as he tries to expand his understanding.

He has taken many trips that have been memorable through meeting people of different cultures and nationalities, learning something of foreign countries and seeing new and interesting sights. Included are the postings and business trips to the above-mentioned countries, plus tourism in Canada, USA, Philippines, Spain, Gibraltar, France, Belgium, Luxembourg, Germany, Czech Republic, Slovakia, Hungary, Austria, Tunisia, Switzerland, Greece, Italy, Antigua, St. Lucia, Mexico, Bahrain, United Arab Emirates, Scotland, England, and Wales. Travel in the following countries was especially memorable:

- Canada - for the expanse and natural grandeur experienced on several cross-country trips - hitch-hiking and by train as a youth; and by driving and by air as an adult, particularly the British Columbia mountains and

Yukon (Gold Rush Trail of 98);

- Greece (the Parthenon, Olympia, Delphi, Meteora) - for the history and spectacular scenery of Classical Greece;
- Eastern Europe (Berlin, Prague, Budapest, Vienna, and the routes from one to another) - for the beauty and history of the cities and the considerable political/economic/social changes from first visits in the early 1980s (characterized by a repressive atmosphere and scarcity of consumer goods) to subsequent visits in mid 1990s (finding more openness and spread of consumerism symbolized by proliferation of McDonalds restaurants);
- United Kingdom - for its history and natural beauty, especially in Scotland (Highlands, Edinburgh/Stirling castles), but as in Europe generally, characterized by a noticeable attitude of reserve, compared with North America.

Oakley enjoys hockey, football (participation when young, watching when older); hiking and camping (when young); making/maintaining a skating rink in the front yard for their son (each winter recently); travel (including associated research and planning); reading (all his life); and crossword/Sudoku puzzles.

Oakley would like to express his feelings about an experience that was very difficult for him and his family. Possibly this experience will be of help to someone who reads it.

The experience which has had the greatest impact in his life is the suicide in 2005 of his step-daughter, Tristen Janaya Solís. Though not his biological daughter, Janaya was part of his immediate family and his daughter in fact for fifteen of her twenty-two years on this earth.

The death of any loved one is difficult for the survivors to deal with, and the associated grief is not to be minimized. However, the loss of a child, whether infant or adult, is especially crushing and life-changing. Nothing is ever the same again! What happened in life before loses importance and relevance. An unanticipated suicide by a young, talented person with so much potential is even more painful - at once bewildering and guilt-inducing.

Nothing prepares a person for this experience. Once into it, books and counselors are of limited or no helpfulness. While the support of family and friends is a positive factor, no one except other grieving parents can fully understand what parents feel and experience following the death of their child. As he and his wife have discovered through peer group meetings, the grieving never ends. Time may bring changes in the nature and intensity of one's grief, but the wound never completely heals.

Everyone experiences grief differently. His wife's experience is different from his. Their experiences are different from those of other people. But there are some common elements in grief that people may share.

The loss of a child can shake one's confidence in all aspects of life and challenge one's philosophy and faith to the core. Nothing seems secure any more. Purpose and meaning can disappear. Life itself can seem unimportant. The future can be perceived as remote and of little importance. Painful thoughts and memories can intrude unexpectedly at any time. Fears may abound - possible loss of another loved one, how to cope with the external world, how to relate to other people, and other fears. Joy and happiness seem to have fled, with little prospect of ever returning. Despair may prevail over hope.

In his experience, coming to terms with the loss of Janaya is a proverbial work in progress. Coping with grief over time entails acknowledging the pain. Anger has to be expressed. Feelings of guilt need to be acknowledged and expunged. The loss of both the loved one and one's previous way of life has to be accepted. The need for some purpose in one's life has to be recognized. A start has to be made towards rebuilding a new self - or rediscovering the true self. Despair must be dissipated. Faith and hope must be nurtured and eventually re-emerge and prevail.

This seems to be a long process, with the steps recurring out of sequence, in a series of setbacks and progress. The path may be winding; but there are signposts along the way, and it need not be traveled alone.

Oakley is my "little" brother. He was only three years old when I left home in Southern Ontario to become a school teacher in Manitoba. I would see him on trips home. When he was twenty years old, he spent a week with me in Edmonton, Alberta, when I was attending summer school. When he was an immigration officer and my family and I were living in Alberta, we saw him and his family between his foreign tours of duty or when he was assigned in British Columbia.

"Join the Navy and see the world." Oakley joined Canada Immigration and saw the world.

23
Pamela Nadine Land Duff

Surrey, British Columbia, Canada

It was supposed to have been a routine visit for a home health agency nurse to a housing project in a poor area of Dallas, Texas. She had been here a number of times previously to see her patient. She drove into the parking area and was about to leave her car. Suddenly, a vehicle drove up behind her car and hemmed it in! The nurse politely asked the driver to move so that she could visit other patients after finishing here. He was intoxicated and flatly refused. What should she do? People in the houses heard the commotion and promptly evacuated to witness the proceedings. Totally surrounded by African-Americans, she had mixed feelings. "So this is what it feels like to be in a minority." She thought "I'm dead meat!"

One of the men approached her. What will he do? Firmly, he said to Pam, "You go help Mama. We'll take care of him!" She obeyed without hesitation. She rushed into the unit, hurriedly changed "Mama's" dressing - barely meeting the sterile technique. It may have taken ten minutes at the most. She rushed to her car. Where were the hordes of people? There was only one woman remaining. Pam thanked her, and the lady nodded. The threatening storm had suddenly dissipated. Gratefully, the nurse proceeded to the home of her next patient.

Although there were other times when her safety might have been in question, she was never hurt. In fact, neighborhood lookouts would sometimes warn her to stay clear as something was about to happen. She always heeded their advice. She feels that they extended this courtesy to her because she treated everyone with respect, regardless of their circumstances.

Pam was born in Saskatoon, Saskatchewan, Canada. Although she began her public school education in Watrous, Saskatchewan, she attended several schools in the first two years because her mother was in a hospital during that time.

Although she later became a nurse, her first and foremost profession was all that entailed in being in the home. She fed the children the standard diet until one day she realized her oldest child just might be malnourished. She reached that conclusion while she was watching a documentary on Africa in 1968 when her oldest son was about three years old. It was a shock when she saw symptoms of malnourishment attributed to the children in Africa. Her well-fed (so she thought) son looked just like them. How puzzling it was! This set her on a path to determine why his appearance suggested underfeeding when he ate very well. His overactive behaviour was also a concern because it was the main reason his younger sister did not walk at an early age. She was afraid to venture out for fear that this human "tornado" would blow her over.

Pam began to read books by Adelle Davis, since this was before the time of Dr. Feingold and his research into the link between food and behaviour. Thus began the long path of trial and error. For three months, her child was on Ritalin, prescribed by the doctor. As she could not bear to see him acting like a zombie, she terminated the medication, opting instead to focus on his diet.

She read and studied, learning much about food and supplements. As a result, the whole family embarked on a more nutritious path. She and her husband purchased a mill, ground their own grains, and baked their own breads, cakes, and pancakes. Everything which Pam made was "from scratch" because she wanted to know every ingredient that went into her family's bodies. In time, she became known for her homemade goods, including eight flavours of ice cream, and sold many items at the local Farmers' Market, which she and her husband helped to establish in their community.

Prevention Magazine wrote an article about her in April 1977. She had had some success with "taming" the hyperactive nature of some children who attended the camps for which she cooked. The parents were pleasantly surprised with their quieter, more focused, children at the end of the week's camp; but, when they found out that it meant a change in diet, almost all said that it was not worth the effort. That kind of attitude always saddened Pam - almost as much as when she later met a father who divorced his wife instead of stopping smoking when he found that it was causing his son's asthma attacks.

A number of years later when her husband retired, Pam worked for the Canadian Red Cross in Ontario before she entered nurse training. She remembers a special patient whom she had during that time. The lady was 100 years old and told stories about living near Toronto prior to its becoming a city. She still relished in the thought that her father would allow only her, and not her sister, to drive the horses to town to sell their freshly churned butter. The thing that Pam remembers most about her is the first day when she went to give the lady a bath. She made it quite clear that there was to be no soap used on her face – because it would cause wrinkles.

After Pam's three children finished high school, she went back to school in Missouri and obtained her degree in nursing. For a few years prior, she had been working as a nurse aide in homes, nursing homes, and hospitals, which she continued to do as she obtained her degree. For a time after graduating, she was one of only a handful of nurses in the United States who was certified in Gerontology.

Pam classifies her professions as housewife, mother, and registered nurse. She worked away from the home some in Alberta and Ontario, Canada, but mostly in Missouri and Texas, United States.

When she began to work full-time, she succumbed to shortcuts, causing her health to suffer as a result. It was not until she had suffered several bouts of heart failure when she was virtually near death, that she revived her interest and knowledge to try to heal herself through proper nutrition. By this time, severe digestive problems had also developed, complete with internal bleeding. In time, through strict diet changes and supplements, she regained her health totally and completely to the point where she could once again return to working part-time. What a turn-around this was! This time, she has the best of both worlds. She combines her nursing knowledge with her nutritional experience and understanding to help others find a formula that might work for them in regaining their health. As she has discovered, what works for one may not work for another; but the key is to keep looking for that unique formula.

There were two major turning points in her life. The first one occurred when she and some other young mothers would meet for "coffee". They soon recognized that gossip sessions were emerging and decided that this should be avoided. To counter the tendency, they met to learn new crafts. They made many interesting items. This group helped to found the local Farmers' Market, which became an outlet for the sale of some of their work and other products that they could supply. The whole community benefited from this organization.

Another turning point came early in her nursing career. In what area would she specialize? She had no idea except that she did not like hospitals! Fairly regularly, one particular Alzheimer patient would come in to the hospital where she was working because of an infection. Invariably, the woman would climb out of bed and wander out to the nurses' station. As this was a nuisance, the nurse in charge of her care would tie her into bed. Pam always despised that practice.

One day, she asked if she could be the patient's charge nurse for that shift. To prepare, she read her history and found that she had been a nurse. It did not take a "rocket scientist" to figure out why she was continually going out to the nurses' desk and heading straight for the charts! On that particular day, Pam took her to the nurses' station in a wheelchair - untethered. She supplied the lady with some empty papers and charts, along with an assortment of pencils and pens. For the entire morning, she sat quietly scribbling, shuffling papers, and opening and closing the empty charts. She even resisted going back to her room and wanted to stay and eat her lunch at the nurses' desk - "obviously remembering something every nurse has to do at one time or another." When the other nurses asked Pam why the patient was there, she stated the situation - and then added, "That might be you or I someday."

All too often nurses become so absorbed in the mechanics of the job that they forget the person behind a diagnosis. It was not long after this incident that Pam left the hospital and started to work in nursing homes, rapidly reaching the administrative level. Later, she went into home health care, where she dealt with the elderly in their own homes. But, no matter where she went, what she did, or how many patients she had since, Pam never forgot that one patient who forever changed the course of her career and her focus for compassion.

Three other patients are credited with teaching her understanding and the need for respecting others. One was "Bill", an alcoholic who was periodically brought into the psychiatric ward to stabilize. Everyone had trouble with Bill. One night, Pam was called from another floor to see what she could do with him. When she entered his room, he was in a screaming fit and medical staff was trying to tie him down. She sat down beside his bed and watched. Very soon, he calmed down and the others left the room. Pam quietly started to chat with him, mainly because she did not know what else to do. After her 12-hour shift was finished and it was time for her to leave, Bill stunned her by saying, "Thank you." When she asked him for what, he replied, "For treating me like a person." Point taken!

The second patient was a young mother who had just given birth. She had had three abortions previously; but, for some reason, she had decided to keep this baby. Pam was told to give her a sheet of instructions and then to leave. When she entered the patient's room, she saw that the mother was extremely nervous. She asked so many questions that Pam knew that she had to stay for a while. By the time that she had answered all the questions, the mother was much more confident that she could care for this baby whom she had chosen to keep. The lesson learned was that people need help and support to a greater extent than they need judgment.

The third person was a young mother who had just been told that she was being reported for child abuse. The nurses were given instructions that they were not to associate with the mother and were to leave the room immediately after she was told. After all the doctors and nurses, including her, had left the room, this young African-American woman was abandoned to her collapsing world. Pam felt strongly that she must return to the room. She talked with her for a while and encouraged her to accept this as a turning point in her life where she could now obtain the help that she needed. Pam does not know what happened to her, but she does know that the woman helped her to become a more compassionate person instead of a starkly cold "supposed professional".

A different type of experience occurred when the Age of Steam Railroad Museum in Dallas, Texas, booked the Challenger for a vintage train excursion. Pam was asked to be part of the medical team required for the trip. The other person was an EMT. Confident that nothing ever happens on such trips, she sat back to enjoy the free ride. That was her first mistake! The "All aboard!" call had been sounded only ten minutes earlier when the train suddenly ground to a halt. Tourists and volunteer crew alike tried to find out what the cause was. Eventually, the report came back that this huge steam locomotive had hit someone. Pam ran back and discovered that her colleague was discussing whether or not they should be involved. Since she is one who always becomes involved, there was nothing to discuss. She pushed him out the door and said that they would sort out the ramifications later. That was her second mistake! As they performed CPR on the man, news helicopters circled overhead and people were gathering round. By the time that the rescue squad appeared on the scene, they knew it was a lost cause; but they had to keep going. Needless to say, she does not remember much of the rest of the excursion; but, after this traumatic experience, she remained cautious whenever she was asked to "come along for a free ride."

On another occasion, she was scheduled to attend a nursing seminar west of Fort Worth, Texas. As she drove along the back roads with no idea where she might be, the inevitable happened - a very rare flat tire. Who does she call? 911. Of course, the dispatch had to ask for her location - as if she knew. Miraculously, a sheriff deputy appeared some minutes later and repaired the tire. What a pleasant relief that was! He said it was easier for him to do that than to give her directions where she could go for repairs. How DID he know??? She did not say that she had never changed a flat tire. Nor did she say that she had never been in this part of Texas. She thanked the deputy profusely and continued on her way, having another miracle occur when she found where she was supposed to be - even though a little late for the opening of the seminar.

After developing heart problems and having to leave the nursing profession, her digestion deteriorated to the point where she could eat only a few different foods. She could no longer tolerate grains of any kind, milk, and most fruits and vegetables. For about two years, she consistently lost weight to the point where it scared everyone.

Once again, she literally gave up on life; but Duane, as in the past she says, kept encouraging her to find a solution. Here she was, helping others from around the world who wrote to the family's website; but she was unable to find what would help her. One day when she was in a health food store, she lamented the fact that she had tried everything. "Have you tried L-glutamine?" the clerk asked. With a "ho-hum-here-we-go-again" attitude, she decided to try it.

Within two weeks, the bleeding and pain had stopped. For her, this was the turning point. For others, it may take something else. From this experience, she really knew for certain that each person has to find his/her own combination for healing. What works for one may not work for another. Unfortunately, this technique takes time, money, and the will to keep trying.

Today, Pamela is back at work, but in a totally different capacity - working in the health food industry part-time. Using her nursing knowledge of disease and its progression, she is better able to match a specific need with nutrients that should help in the healing process. Since the body is comprised of nutrients, it is obvious that it needs them in order to heal itself. It does not need drugs with one active, foreign ingredient that will only mask symptoms at best and always create side effects. However, there are times when drugs are necessary. During these times, it is crucial that nutrients are also added. Unfortunately, most medical personnel have not been taught about nutrition. They have been taught only about disease processes and related drug therapies.

Pam also volunteers. This activity began with the answering of a call from "People Helping People" for a retired nurse to hold a blood pressure clinic once a month in a low-income housing unit. That quickly escalated to two each month and several mornings in the office counseling residents. However, she is not one to stay in an office. It was the same when she was a nursing director. She made sure that she was out with staff and patients so that she would know what was happening in her facility. That meant that there were no surprises when officials showed up. In her current volunteer role, she soon began to mingle with the people, trying to understand their needs. As a result, she and the project coordinator, Aziza Sleightholm, have been able to develop several ongoing programmes and seminars.

Over the years, traveling throughout Canada and the United States, especially during the summer vacations from school, provided its memorable moments, many of which were created because her family drove and tented along the way. Setting up camp was always a challenge because of weather, terrain, mosquitoes, and three small children.

Since Duane would plan out their route weeks in advance, Pam neglected to update her memory bank on one occasion. He told her that they would be camping in a certain place that had only cold showers. "Fine," she said. Later on, when they arrived at that place, they could not tent there because the grounds were temporarily closed. Thus, they continued on to another place not far away.

She and her daughter Janet went to take their showers – in cold water. When they emerged, Duane and the boys were there looking all refreshed while the other two were shivering and miserable. When Pam asked why they were looking so happy, they said the showers were nice and hot. Wondering why the men had hot showers and not the women, she went back to the shower room; and, sure enough, much to her disgust, right there beside the cold water tap was one labeled "Hot". They had not thought to look after being told there would be only cold showers. Janet was not a happy camper at that point! How could her mother do that to her? However, Pam learned a valuable lesson - if all else fails, look.

A most memorable trip for Pam and Duane was one to Cambridge, England. They flew over as guests of Tyndale House, a Biblical research centre, to deliver five large boxes of books that they donated to its library. The couple was taken on tours of various university libraries and was left speechless by the number of ancient books. The oldest one which they saw was printed in 800 CE. The architecture of the buildings was overwhelming. They were also pleasantly surprised with the politeness of the people everywhere that they went.

Mexico was another place where Pam and her family learned much. Wherever they went, it amazed and humbled them that the people were so eager to share what little they had even though they knew that their visitors had much more. The people give new meaning to "reuse and recycle" - an attitude that puts industrialized nations to shame. The family is much more conscious of waste, whether it be the water they use, the food they eat, or even the furniture in their homes. Now, they have only what is absolutely needed. Knick-knacks no longer clutter their living space. This is a country that is still near and dear to their hearts.

Pam feels that the only person who has had a significant effect on her life is her husband Duane. This is how she describes him.

"I met him when I was eighteen years old. Six months later, in 1964, after seeing him only five times, we married. Because of his infinite patience, I am who I am today. Duane took a head-strong teenager and turned her into a valuable member of society. Even though there is a fifteen-year age difference, and likely because of it, I had, and still maintain, a high respect for him. Through the years, he has helped me learn many things and has encouraged me in whatever challenge I wanted to accept. His kindness, wisdom, and selflessness have, understandably, drawn many to him, including me. I am very honoured by the fact that he chose me to be his wife."

Pam feels that her greatest accomplishment in life has been teaching her children to be independent, although she admits she has very mixed feelings about this. Nevertheless, she would like to have been a better parent. As it stands now, she feels she makes a much better grandmother.

Pam's main philosophy is that too many little things interfere in relationships. People concentrate too much on the negative or the slightest hurt rather than on the positive. As a result, grudges are formed and relationships damaged. Mistakes will always be made by everyone. How these are handled will determine how happy we are or can become. Most things are trivial, but it is often these that can scar people for life.

Another mistake that is often made is placing people into "boxes" and judging them according to our perception of that particular box. We do it with religions, political biases, educational levels, governments, food preferences, and virtually any belief; all the while maintaining our own right to believe and to practise whatever suits us. Yet, we do not extend the same courtesy to others to do likewise. How hypocritical! Only a few people are able to accept another person fully despite differing viewpoints. We need more such people in the world today. It would then be a better, more peaceful place to live.

I met Pamela at a church institute in her home town of

Saskatoon, Saskatchewan, when I was living in Alberta. As she has stated, we married very soon. We experienced a stretched-out honeymoon, including a month in Seattle, Washington, as I studied three courses at the University of Washington. She has done well in living with a husband who was very shy for years and who is very conservative in his ways. Her support in what I and our family have done is much appreciated by everyone involved. Although we sometimes have a friendly debate over who asked whom to marry, I am happy that we met and have stayed together for over forty-two years ... and counting.

24

Peter R. E. Louw

Surrey, British Columbia, Canada

Peter and Millie were on a cruise ship from Cape Town, South Africa, to Southampton, England. At dinner one night, the Captain made an announcement. The ship would be entering notorious Bay of Biscay, off the coast of France, the next day. He asked all of the passengers to have their packing completed because they may not feel very well later.

Well, he was right! That day through the bay will never be forgotten. It is as if it had happened yesterday. The *Edinburgh Castle* was a big ship. However, the sea was so rough that all the hatches were locked down and the passengers were not allowed to be on the deck at all. A freighter was passing in the opposite direction. Its bow would be lifted high out of the water and then it would come down with water rushing right over it. Peter and Millie found walking upstairs delightful because they could hold one foot up and the steps would come up under it.

The dining room was a totally different place now. First of all, the table cloths were all wet. The edge of the table now had a little ledge to protect the plates from sliding off. The ship was being tossed around so badly. One moment, these two passengers were climbing a hill - and the next moment, they were running downhill. Can you imagine the poor waiter with the high loads of plates? There were many fish and barons of beef on the carpet that day.

Peter was born in Welton, a suburb of Cape Town. Cape Town is the legislative capital of the Republic of South Africa. South Africa is located south of the Tropic of Capricorn. It is bordered on the west coast by the cold Atlantic Ocean and on the east coast by the warm Indian Ocean. These two oceans meet at Cape Point, which is the southern tip of the Cape Peninsula, on which the city of Cape Town is situated.

He started attending school in January 1940 at Battswood Primary School. The school was located in the suburb of Wynberg, which was about three miles from Welton. To go to school, he, his sister, and their friends had to walk every day. He received all of his education at Battswood School in Wynberg. This institution was an outreach of the Dutch Reform Church. Battswood had primary and secondary grades and a training college for teachers. Thus, after graduating from Standard Eight (grade 10), he entered the training college to commence his teacher education.

In 1953, Peter graduated as a teacher with a Primary Lower Certificate, which gave him a licence to teach up to grade 7. After ten years of teaching, he began work on his Grades 11 and 12 Certificate. He successfully completed the six subjects. Following this, he began the immigration proceedings to come to Canada.

After he had obtained a teaching position in Chilliwack, British Columbia, Canada, he started work on his Bachelor of Education degree at University of British Columbia, completing it in 1976. A few years later, he completed his fifth year honours programme. Then, in 1988, he completed a Diploma of Psychology Counseling, also from UBC.

In his formative years, his first language was Afrikaans, and English was his second language. The South African education system was so set up that all schools had to teach both official languages. Battswood, therefore, was an English-medium school, which meant that all subjects were taught in English. Afrikaans would be taught as a second language.

The South African government policy allowed only whites to join the army. Blacks and non-whites could not handle guns and, therefore, joined to be lackeys or servants to the white soldiers. One of the first things that the newly-elected Nationalist government did in 1948 was to disenfranchise the non-whites. Therefore, not having a vote, they could not take part in politics.

As stated earlier, Peter trained as a teacher in Cape Town. The last three years there, he was principal of a school. He resigned from his school as he was waiting on his Canadian visa to arrive. During this period, he joined the subsidiary of International Harvester in Cape Town. His work there was in marketing, by which he was able to make contact with IH companies in Canada. He corresponded and sent merchandise pamphlets all across Canada. Little did he know at that time that, later, he would be teaching in Chilliwack for thirty years. Kish Equipment in Chilliwack was on his mailing list.

He remembers going to Hamilton, Ontario, during the week that he and Millie arrived in Canada. If he were unable to obtain a teacher job, he thought that he could perhaps secure a marketing position with one of the Canadian IH companies. Fortunately, he did not have to do any job searches.

When he arrived in Calgary, Alberta, in December 1968, he had an interview with the principal of Currie Junior High School. Within minutes, he started teaching two weeks before Christmas 1968.

Both Peter and Millie enjoy traveling. Ever since they met, they have gone somewhere on holiday. As a teacher in South Africa, he received three furlough months after ten years of teaching. When his first ten years furlough was available, they decided to travel to England. They took their eldest son, Keith, who was five years old, with them.

They sailed from Cape Town on Friday, December 18, 1964. The cruise would take fourteen days. It was a wonderful experience as there were so many new things to learn. Life on the sea was so different. Everything was carried out according to a strict line of commands. The decks were cleaned regularly, and the handrails around the ship were constantly wiped and cleaned.

Dining on board was a dream. They could eat their way through the whole menu. It was so beautiful just to sit there and be waited on for fourteen days - with no tables to clear or decks to wash. There were many deck games in which to take part. There was also an excellent library where one could spend hours.

Having taught his students about the equator, it was a special moment for Peter when it was announced that they would be crossing the line at a certain time. He remembers taking a drink with him and going on deck. There he stood - downing his drink - of course, seeing only the ocean - no line to cross. Nevertheless, the very thought was so inspiring. One reads or learns about certain things; but when one actually experiences them, one is awe-struck. Their son took part in the first crossing of the line ceremony. It was beautiful to see King Neptune and his mermaids.

For Christmas Day, the crew prepared the dining room for Santa's arrival. They built a fireplace with a long chimney in front of the elevator. So, when Santa arrived, the elevator door opened and he came through the chimney.

On this trip, they also saw the island of Madeira. This was another fort. At first, all that they could see was a mountain in the sea. As we came closer, they could see fields, streets, and buildings. They also had the opportunity to taste the Madeira wines and cheeses. After a few hours on land, they boarded their ship again. The next day, they experienced the infamous Bay of Biscay event.

The fourteen days were now at their end. The ship steamed into Southampton harbour on January 1, 1965. Oh, they were so excited! As a child listening to the BBC radio, London was so far from Peter. Ah, here they were on English soil! Now they had three months ahead of them to enjoy. Every day was going to bring a new experience - a new happening. Oh, so exciting it would be!

This was definitely a memorable trip! They traveled about in London using the tube (subway), train, and red buses (double-deckers). Peter had a visitor's guide map that showed all the places of interest. He and Millie walked Oxford Street, Fleet Street, and the Strand, and visited Westminster Abbey, the Parliament House, and the cottage of Samuel Johnson (one of England's greatest literary figures) - and the list can go on.

In 1965, they watched the telly (television) for the first time. Peter had said that it would be interesting to watch if something spectacular should happen. His wish was fulfilled. Sir Winston Churchill died that January. What a learning experience it was to watch the proceedings!

Next, they booked a continental trip - and here Peter really lost it completely. It was so fascinating! They saw the fabled white cliffs of Dover as they left on the ferry crossing.

Then, they set foot on another continent. Europe was waiting for them. They landed in Belgium, and from there they traveled to Germany, Switzerland, Austria, France, Luxembourg, and Liechtenstein. In Austria, they enjoyed playing in the snow.

A few weeks later, they arrived in Paris, where they stayed for three days. This was all a dream from which this family did not want to awaken. From Paris, they traveled on a fast train to Amsterdam. For three days, they toured Holland. The colourful tulip fields were stunning. An interesting tour took them through a very tightly secured building to see, working in action, one of the many diamond-cutting factories. There were no free samples for visitors. Their guide also took them to a large house that served as home, barn, and cheese-making factory.

Peter's days in the classroom were destined to change drastically as a result of the many new things that he learned. This had been a most educational adventure.

As a student, he had many good experiences. He was looked upon as a leader and often was elected to lead one group or another. He was head prefect for three years and was the bell monitor, controlling over 500 students and 48 teachers.

A memorable experience that he had during his life's work was when he became principal of a ten-teacher school. He had been vice-principal for three years when he went on furlough. When he returned from England, the school was in chaos. His principal was tired and washed out. After the first three days, Peter embarked on an inspection of the school, after which he warned his principal that, if an official school inspection were held, heads would roll. At week's end the inevitable took place. The local inspector arrived to announce that he would be in on Monday morning for a general inspection of the school.

To understand the significance, Peter explains what a general inspection in a coloured South African school entailed. The inspector was a "white", usually a Nationalist. He normally treated the staff "like dirt". He inspected all the children's books, checked the teacher's record book to see if the teacher were at the right place in the annual plans, and might even inspect the cupboards. Depending on his mood that day, he could be very demanding and could drive a teacher "up the pole".

On Thursday, the inspection was announced. On Friday, the staff went home for the weekend. On Sunday morning after church, the principal's son brought Peter the school keys. The principal was hospitalized, and Peter had to face the inspector the next day.

Fortunately, he had prepared his work thoroughly. Therefore, when he was questioned by the inspector, he could tell him what to expect. After two grueling weeks, the inspection was completed. Peter pointed out to the staff what was lacking. Together, they studied the suggested guidelines and prepared themselves for future inspections.

Peter had a wonderful time trying new approaches to teaching. All of these things paid off and the school grew.

The one person that Peter really worshiped was Dr. Edgar Maurice. He met this teacher when he was in grade 7. Dr. Maurice taught English and geography and had a terrible reputation for punishment of students.

It was during the same year that Peter changed his hairstyle from a boy's cut to a big man's style. As Cape Town is a very windy place to keep one's hair in place, solid brilliantine was used.

One day during lunch hour, he went to the barber and had a neck trim done. Dr. Maurice was coming to this class after lunch. When he walked in, he came over to Peter's desk and asked if he had had a haircut. Peter replied that he had. The teacher instructed him to return to the barber shop in the afternoon to have a proper haircut. Of course, the young boy refused. The teacher responded that if he did not have it done, he would do it for his student.

The next day, the consultation was on. Dr. Maurice entered the classroom and asked for Peter's comb. He then procured a pair of scissors from another student and proceeded to perform the haircut. At the end of the ordeal, he gave the boy money to buy a bottle of Vitalis. Peter's use of Vitalis continues today. What made Peter more upset was when – as we were walking to school the next day – his sister, who was teaching at the same school, thanked Dr. Maurice for the job he did with the haircut.

In a geography class on another day, this teacher asked how many slices of bread Peter had brought to school. He went through the whole day writing down the numbers on the blackboard. What he was doing was showing how much grain was needed to be grown if one person ate so much bread in one day.

When Peter started to teach, he met with his former teacher and they became greater friends as their interests were coinciding. They were meeting at live theatre performances, and both assisted with the Boys' Choir in Cape Town. When Peter shared his Canadian plans with him, his teacher told him to immerse himself into the Canadian way of living. Peter told him that he would come back to Cape Town only when he obtained his first university degree.

Dr. Maurice was one person who died too young.

As a teacher in South Africa, he was required to stay on line with the record book and plans for the year. The inspector would check each teacher's progress to be certain that no one went off on a tangent. This approach would curtail providing independent thinking on the part of both the teacher and the students.

In Canada, however, teachers are given the freedom to experiment and try innovative ideas. Having had that freedom, Peter's supervisors found him doing things much more differently. He treated his students as equals and stressed consequences for action. He taught a democratic class where students had the right to express their likes and dislikes.

When the Chilliwack School District started its Gifted and Talented Programme, he was very excited. He was invited to be a member of the committee and eventually taught the pilot group at the grade 7 level. This opportunity changed his whole approach to teaching, which became a great success. It was so encouraging when parents asked how he was able to motivate their children. His students would complete their homework and studies before watching television or playing. That, indeed, was an achievement. Fellow teachers came to him trying to find out what he did to motivate students. He thoroughly enjoyed teaching to the fullest.

Having to renounce his South African citizenship was a painful process. This took place as they were preparing to leave for Canada. When they received their Canadian visas, they checked out the procedure to follow. They had their South African passports, but the due date had to be changed.

The Passport Central office told them that the process would take six weeks.

Thus, Peter and Millie planned everything based on a six-weeks period. First, there was the sale of their home. This was followed by the sale of their car and excess furniture. They called the packers in to pack the crates.

When the six weeks had expired, they contacted the passport office, who told them to phone headquarters in Pretoria. The office in Pretoria informed them that they were not renewing their passports. The alternative was to accept an exit permit. They were told that it could take several months to obtain these.

Their home and their car were sold. The crates were on the high seas to Vancouver. Finally, they visited the passport office and were told that they could receive the permit. The catch, however, was that a permit was not a travel document. The official also informed them that they would have to renounce their citizenship. This process would jeopardize their position because renouncing their citizenship made them prohibitors, which could result in their being put into jail for an indefinite period.

Since Peter and Millie wanted to leave, they did what was required. They were scheduled to sail to England on a Wednesday. Hours before the ship was going to leave, the travel agent informed them that their passage had been cancelled. The only Canadian official in Cape Town was the trade commissioner. He helped them by contacting the Canadian and English ambassadors. The couple received letters from both ambassadors and went back to the travel agents. They re-booked them for the next week on a more expensive ship. That week was totally chaotic, but they "committed their way to the Lord" and knew that everything would work out. So it did.

When they arrived in Southampton, they were called to the Immigration desk and given British passports for their nine-days stay in England. In Toronto, they handed the Canadian ambassador's letter to the officials. After they had read it, they welcomed Peter and Millie to Canada. In 1974, five years later, they and their son received their Canadian citizenship. O Canada - our home and chosen land!

In March and April 2007, Peter and Millie celebrated their fiftieth wedding anniversary in Cape Town, South Africa.

One day as I was descending in an elevator in our apartment block, a friendly couple spoke to me. When we learned that the husband and I were former school teachers, we stopped to talk before they went to their car and I continued on my way. This couple was Peter and Millie Louw. On arriving back at our apartment, I told my wife Pam about these people. Several days later, I met Peter again as we picked up our mail and invited him and Millie to our apartment. Their visit was the beginning of an important friendship for us. We are in contact in person or via telephone as frequently as our various schedules permit. Since we no longer drive, they have taken us places. Also, when we can, we do various things to help each other. Pam and I are happy to claim Peter and Millie as good friends.

25

Philip Kynaston Ward

Airdrie, Alberta, Canada

Is there an old school still in operation in your community? Does it have a history prior to 1900? If it does not, consider schools in England that have a rich heritage. One example is Almondbury Grammar School, in Yorkshire. The school was granted a royal charter by James I in 1608, but can trace its history back about a thousand years before that. The original chantry school was closed in 1539 during the reign of Henry VIII when he closed all monastic institutions. A chantry school was operated by the Roman Catholic Church prior to the Reformation in England at the time King Henry VIII. This was where Philip Ward received his early education.

Philip was born in the town of Huddersfield in the West Riding of Yorkshire, United Kingdom. He began his education at the school in Netherton - a village in the Huddersfield corporate boundary. From there, he obtained a scholarship to Almondbury Grammar School.

His higher education was commenced in the United Kingdom at the University of Leeds, where he earned a Bachelor of Arts degree in History and a Graduate Diploma in Education. It was continued after he arrived in Canada. He attended both the Regina College campus and the Saskatoon campus of the University of Saskatchewan, obtaining a Bachelor of Education (Distinguished) degree and a Master of Education degree. His graduate work was in the history of curriculum development. He has studied French and Spanish, but has lost his fluency with them.

Between 1953 and 1955, Philip served as a sergeant in the Royal Army Education Corps, being the education officer with the Royal Engineers, Movement Control, Port of London. As a result of his service, he holds the National Service Medal. Following his discharge, he was appointed Commanding Officer of the Army Cadet Unit in Cannock, Staffordshire.

His profession is teacher and educational administrator, having taught in England and Canada. He also worked as a superintendent in Saskatchewan. In order to cut down on his workload with the latter, he moved to Vauxhall, Alberta, where he was appointed high school principal.

In Saskatchewan, his experience was extensive. In the mid 1960s, he was principal of the Biggar Elementary Schools in Saskatchewan, which included seven buildings housing over six hundred pupils. Technically, the principal was Woodrow Lloyd, who had been Minister of Education in the Tommy Douglas government and who replaced him as premier when Tommy entered federal politics. Woodrow had guided the Saskatchewan Medical Care legislation through the provincial legislature. However, his position had caused great upset in his home constituency of Biggar. This had infected the schools. Philip had the unenviable task of bringing back order there.

When Philip considered applying for the position of superintendent of schools in 1966, he had the support of Woodrow Lloyd and the head of the department of educational administration at the University of Saskatchewan. His first appointment was to Gull Lake, where he spent two years. Then he was appointed Director of Education for the

North Battleford Public School System. At the time, there was one board which was in charge of grades 1 to 8 and another board in charge of grades 9 to 12. Philip became the first person to be appointed as Chief Executive Officer under the two boards. It was hoped that the two boards would merge into one.

After his second year, there was a massive restructuring of the system when a new high school was built. Now, there were eight buildings housing the twelve grades, plus the school for the mentally handicapped. Adding to the logistics of relocating the students to the schools, Philip was faced with his wife Margaret having major heart surgery at the same time. He also was committed to having libraries in each school within one year. If that were not enough, he was a volunteer overseer for the school for the mentally handicapped. A man of lesser stature would have wilted under this stress!

The personal conflicts among the members of the boards were insurmountable. The questionable planning for the new comprehensive high school, which was in place before Philip arrived, created serious problems. The board realized the errors but tended to defend its position rather than admit that something was wrong. Seeing that he could not resolve the situation and seeing the effect that his work had on his family, Philip resigned his position after ten years in favour of a supposedly less arduous position of being a principal in Vauxhall, Alberta. North Battleford had lost a good man.

Just before Philip left, the Minister of Education telephoned him to discuss the situation. Philip suggested that the only solution was an Order-in-Council disbanding the Collegiate Board and creating a single Board of Education. Soon after, the chairman of the Public Board sent him a message saying that, in an upcoming election, members of only one board would be elected since the Collegiate Board was being disbanded and the two were being amalgamated.

He was Vice-President of the Saskatchewan Locally Employed Superintendent's Association and served on the Provincial School Finance Committee of the Saskatchewan Association of School Trustees. Since retirement, he has served on the City of Airdrie Municipal Library Board as member and chairman. He has also worked as Pastoral Relations Convener for the South Alberta Presbytery and was a member of the Ministry and Personnel Division of the Alberta and Northwest Conference of his church. After moving to Airdrie, both he and Margaret were presbyters in the Foothills Presbytery, but most of Margaret's outside commitments had to be dropped when her health seriously began to deteriorate. Philip still remains active with his local church, the members of which helped him through a very difficult period after the death of Margaret.

Philip gives high credit to Margaret for his ability to perform his various responsibilities, especially during the difficult times. Dealing with school boards and some school districts convinced him that he should not enter politics.

He and Margaret did have some time for travel. During their travels through Thailand, Philip was greatly impressed by the people and their culture.

Philosophically, he is a Christian existentialist. His social philosophy is quite conservative although, politically and economically, he is a socialist. This does not mean that he necessarily supports the New Democratic Party (NDP), who, he feels has gone astray from their original purpose. He remains with the United Church of Canada, although he disagrees with a number of stands that they have taken in recent years.

As a hobby, he writes mostly fiction now. He also is a stamp collector and has an extensive collection of British and Canadian stamps with first day of issue cancellation marks. He has been very active in many positions at various levels of the United Church of Canada. He is also a singer - at one time contemplating a career on the operatic stage - and enjoys singing with and directing choirs.

His grammar school career in an ancient school that oozed history has made a lasting impression on his life. Meeting his wife Margaret at the University of Leeds was the best thing that happened to him. When he was a student at the University of Leeds, he was blessed in having Dr. Matthew Black as his extramural tutor. Dr. Black was a top New Testament scholar. Some have claimed that he was the world's leading authority on the Aramaic influence on the New Testament. The two examined the Bible from a historian's perspective. Philip's meeting with him on a one-to-one basis every two weeks for a year profoundly influenced how Philip reads the Bible. Two years later, Dr. Black was appointed President of St. Andrews University, in Scotland, one of Europe's most prestigious schools.

One day, Margaret and Philip were having lunch with a former pupil in Calgary. This lady is a well-known actress and classical singer and was in the city performing the role of Gertrude in Hamlet. In the course of their conversation, she looked at Margaret, leaned over and took Philip's hand and said, "This man changed my life." Philip was very pleased to think that he had been able to help her and that she appreciated it so much.

On another occasion, he was stopped in the street in Swift Current, Saskatchewan, by a former pupil, who had been a major problem in school. This young man was pleased to report that, after several years, he had taken Philip's advice and applied for the School of Art in Calgary and had won a first place scholarship. He wanted to say thank you for Philip's having stood by him, even when he had been so far out of line.

Receiving credit from former students, whether they had been good or difficult in school, is a joy for anyone in the teaching profession. It is easy to remember the difficult times. However, these little sincere comments help to make it all worthwhile.

I met Philip in his office in Vauxhall High School a few days before the new school year commenced in 1978. I would be one of his staff members for the next five years. He inherited a difficult situation, but I feel that he performed an admirable job. He was firm, but fair and helpful to all. I found him to be a good leader of both teachers and students. For a time, my wife Pam served in the United Church choir that was led by Philip. Pam and Margaret were good friends. After we left Vauxhall, we lost contact until I started to research for this book. Regrettably, Margaret was gone by then. We cherish our memories of both Philip and Margaret.

26

Rita Navalinskienė

Vilnius, Lithuania

Being happy in spite of difficult situations can have a profound effect on one's life. This has been true with Rita. She found youth to be an adventure with its ups and downs. Growing up during the Soviet period was probably her greatest experience. Her family was poor. There was the lack of such basic necessities of life as food and clothing. These were very tough times for her and her family. How could they be happy? Yet, she and her family survived - and were happy. She has not lost her ability to be happy in her surroundings. She has made the best of what was available to her and has been successful.

Rita was born in the city of Vilnius, Lithuania. At the time, Lithuania was a republic within the USSR.

She attended 27th Secondary School, in Vilnius. Today, the school is known as Jonas Basanavičius` Secondary School and Gymnasium. Her first post-secondary degree was obtained at the Engineering Construction Institute of Vilnius, known today as Gediminas Technological University. Her graduation year with a master's degree in management from the International Business School in Vilnius is 2006.

Rita is an engineer of construction and territory planning. She has worked for about four years in the Bureau of Planning, a department of the Ministry of Construction Materials. Then, for six years, she worked in the Lithuanian

Department of Tourism. This was followed by her current position of two years in the Detail Planning Chapter of Urban Development Department of Vilnius Municipality. Since women in Lithuania do not serve in armed forces, she has not had experience in that profession.

She does not think that she has made any great accomplishment that merits being special. Actually, she tries to accomplish an assignment that is given to her as well as possible. She can be assured that this attitude is very important in our society as too many people cannot make this claim. Outside of her regular work, she would like to learn more about painting and interior design.

I asked Rita to tell a little about Vilnius, tourism, and urban development.

As the capital of the Republic of Lithuania, Vilnius is an administrative, cultural, political, and business centre. The Old Town is the heart of the capital - the oldest and, architecturally, the richest part of Vilnius. It is one of the largest old town centres in Europe, covering almost one tenth of the city's area. The Old Town is situated in a picturesque valley of two rivers - the Vilnia and the Neris - at the crossroads of trade routes, and next to the ford, which was guarded by Vilnius castle in earlier times.

According to the 2001 census, the population of Vilnius is approximately 580,000 people, which accounts for 17% of the total population of the country. Vilnius is home to people of different ethnic backgrounds: ethnic Lithuanians (57.8%), Poles (18.7%), Russians (14%), Belarusians (4%), Jews (0.5%), and other ethnic backgrounds (5%).

Lithuania and Vilnius, the capital city, have changed greatly during the first fifteen years after the country's independent restoration in 1990. The most remarkable changes are the effect on the tourism industry and the investment development as a result of Lithuania's entry into the European Union and NATO.

Four places of sightseeing in Lithuania have been included into the UNESCO cultural heritage list:

- Vilnius Historic Centre (1994): Despite invasions and partial destruction, it has preserved an impressive complex of Gothic, Renaissance, Baroque, and classical buildings. It has a medieval layout and a natural setting.
- Curonian Spit (2000): This elongated sand dune peninsula, 98 km *(61 mi)* long and 0.4–4 km *(.25–2.5 mi)* wide, dates back to prehistoric times. Throughout this period since then, it has been threatened by the natural forces of wind and waves. Its survival to the present day has been made possible only as a result of ceaseless human efforts to combat its erosion, by continuing stabilisation and reforestation projects.
- Kernavė Archaeological Site (2004): Situated in the valley of the River Neris, the site is a complex ensemble of archaeological properties, encompassing the town of Kernavė, forts, some unfortified settlements, and burial sites. It also includes other archaeological, historical, and cultural monuments from the late Palaeolithic period to the Middle Ages. The site covers 194 hectares *(479 acres)*.
- Struve Geodetic Arc (2005): This is a chain of survey triangulations stretching from Hammerfest, Norway, to the Black Sea, through ten countries and over 2,820 km *(1,752 mi)*. It marks the points of a survey carried out between 1816 and 1855 by the astronomer Friedrich Georg Wilhelm Struve.

There has been considerable urban development undertaken in Vilnius in recent years. Included are the following projects:

- The administration and commercial centre on a right bank of the Neris River is being modernized.
- A tram line connecting the periphery area and the centre of Vilnius is going to be built.
- A project of joining of the two cities of Vilnius and Kaunas is being implemented.
- A commercial and living district is going to be developed near the centre of Vilnius.

Rita enjoys traveling and has experienced memorable trips to such countries as Norway, Croatia, and Russia. Other very memorable experiences that she has had were when she fell in love with Tomas, the man who became her husband, and when their son was born.

Her first language is Lithuanian. She is also fluent in Russian and, by her estimation, medium in English. I have found she can communicate well in English with me.

She finds it quite difficult to determinate one specific person who has influenced her life more than others. She notes that there are many nice, helpful, warm-hearted people whom she has been fortunate in meeting.

As a philosophy of life, she lives by the credo: "Do nothing that you would not want to be done to you." The corollary of this would be: "Do unto others that which you would want them do unto you." Can you image how many disagreements among people and wars among countries would not take place if everyone would follow her credo?

I met Rita via email a few years ago. I was looking for someone to translate a page on our website into the Lithuanian language. Thus, I wrote to the national tourism department in Vilnius. It was Rita who responded and did the translating for me. Because of some diacritical accents in her language that might not be seen on some computers, she anglicized the letters for the page. Since that time, we have been in contact a few times when I asked her some questions about Lithuania. She has graciously provided me the desired information. She has illustrated to me that she is very knowledgeable of her country and has shown that she is also a good ambassador for it.

27

Robin McKenzie Duff

Victoria, British Columbia, Canada

You are making an interprovincial move. Your wife, your little daughter, and your furniture have gone and have arrived at their destination. You had to stay to finish some work at your place of employment. You are informed that your final pay is being held back, but will be mailed to you. You now do not have sufficient financial means to join your family, but you must go. It was late in the year. What do you do? You decide to hitchhike.

When Robin was a university student working as a Customs officer at Fort Erie, Ontario, across the Peace Bridge from Buffalo, New York, he used to hitchhike home, just over 100 miles *(161 km)* to the west, on weekends. On one occasion, a driver who gave him a ride clearly believed that 100 mph *(161 km/h)* was the appropriate speed for him to drive his car. Robin arrived home in record time that day! However, he was never so glad to leave a car as he was on that occasion. Yet, he was willing to risk traveling from Weyburn, Saskatchewan, to Barrie, Ontario, using the same mode of transportation. He had no option!

Everything went well across Saskatchewan and Manitoba! However, in Kenora, just across the Ontario border, they met a blizzard; and the current driver was ending his trip in Dryden. Robin was dressed in summer clothes for it was mild when he set out from Weyburn. He could not find a place to stay overnight in Dryden, and there was nothing on the road except a bus which would be arriving in Dryden within the hour. He phoned someone in Southern Ontario and had money for bus fare wired to Port Arthur (now part of Thunder Bay) for him. He thought that he had enough money with him to reach Port Arthur. Unfortunately, it turned out he had only enough to reach Upsala – 100 miles *(161 km)* short. Therefore, he rode to Upsala and disembarked there.

He was unable to find any shelter in which to stay until morning when there might be some traffic again. All that he could see was a truck idling at roadside while the driver rested. He was aware that truck drivers did not pick up hitchhikers; but, since he was very cold, he decided to ask anyway. When the driver opened the door and looked down to see who was there, Robin asked in a quavering voice if he could be given a ride. The driver looked for a long time at this shaking individual in summer clothes. During the wait, Robin felt that he would freeze to death if he were not given a ride. The shivering young man gave a silent prayer. At long last, the driver told him to go to the other side and climb into the cab. What a relief that was! When they arrived at Port Arthur, Robin thanked him profusely. Then, he went for his money and then boarded the bus to Southern Ontario. His wife Wilma and their daughter Zoe Anne were so happy to see the third member of their family!

Robin was born at Corinth, Ontario, Canada. He started attending school at Corinth Public School and continued with high school at East Elgin High, in Aylmer, Ontario.

One bad experience he remembers vividly from public school days was having his art work held up by the teacher for the entire grades 5-8 classes to see and hearing it ridiculed by the whole group. Because of this traumatic event, it took him years to overcome the feelings of inferiority and fear of trying anything new.

One good experience in high school was his entering an oratorical contest sponsored by the local Optimist Club. Robin won the high school competition and the county competition. He advanced to the Eastern Canada finals in Ottawa and finished second. The judge told him privately afterwards that he had the best speech. However, the first place finisher had the best delivery. Robin was also asked to give his speech over the local radio station, which he did successfully.

After high school graduation, he attended Graceland College, in Lamoni, Iowa, United States, where he earned an Associate in Arts degree. At the University of Toronto, he earned a Bachelor of Arts degree, a Bachelor of Social Work degree, and a Master of Social Work degree.

When he completed his education at University of Toronto, he, his wife Wilma, and their daughter moved to Saskatchewan to commence his first job as a social worker. They decided to drive a school bus to Regina, Saskatchewan, and take what personal effects that they could on the bus, and tow their car. Unfortunately, they were unable to find the appropriate tow bar. Consequently, Wilma drove the bus and Robin drove the car all the way to Saskatchewan. They camped along the way, but found this to be a long and tiring trip. When they arrived in Weyburn, they left Zoe Anne with some church friends there and drove 100 miles *(161 km)* to Regina to turn in the bus. They returned to Weyburn in their car. They had hoped to find an apartment after they arrived at Weyburn. Unfortunately, there was an oil project going on and all available accommodation was taken. They finally managed to locate two rooms in a basement where they could settle temporarily. A few months later, they were able to rent the upstairs of a house.

Robin's language is English, and he is not fluent in any other. His principal profession was social work in Saskatchewan and Ontario. He also taught undergraduate social work at Humber College of Applied Arts and Technology, in Etobicoke, Ontario, for three years.

During his years at a teaching hospital in Toronto, he had occasion to supervise the activities of his social work staff who were seeking to help a young quadriplegic girl adjust to her disability. At the age of sixteen, while inebriated, she dived into the shallow end of a swimming pool and broke her neck, paralyzing her from the neck down. She was not expected to live. She received no support from her parents or from her boyfriend. Despite the odds against her, she continued to survive. Robin's staff outlined a long list of problems which she faced and reported that she just lay in her bed crying all day. They were at a loss as to what they could do for her. His response was, "Teach her to use her head."

He suggested that she could be taught to write with a pen in her mouth and she could orally use a page turner to read a book. Sure enough, their brainstorming resulted in her learning to become adept at the things which Robin had suggested. Further, an art teacher came in and taught her to paint by mouth. These accomplishments gave her hope, and she attacked each new idea eagerly. Someone found a contraption that looked like a dolly with an upright support for her back, and she was pushed around the hospital in an upright position. Someone else located a wheelchair operated by blowing into a mouthpiece, and soon she was barreling down the halls to the cafeteria in her wheelchair. Next, she mastered travel by Handy Dart bus and was touring all the attractions in the big city. After she had painted several Canadian scenes, her pictures were hung on the hospital walls for everyone to enjoy. Next, a gallery showing was held, and all her pictures sold in one day! Much later, she went to live in a chronic care facility, now able to enjoy some meaningful quality of life! By their focusing on the positives of her potential, they were able to assist her in moving from hopelessness to reaching closer to her optimum level of achievement. She taught the staff that, while tragedy can be stunning, the human ability to overcome handicaps is awesome.

Another memorable experience occurred in his work as a palliative care worker near the end of his career. One day, he received a telephone call from the wife of one of his longtime patients. She was frantic, saying that she thought her husband was dying and no one would believe her. She had been in her husband's hospital room all night, and he had had a terrible night. He was struggling for breath and she was convinced that he was hanging on because he wanted to say goodbye to his mother, who was in a nursing home in Eastern Ontario. Robin told the wife that he would be right there. When he arrived, he found the situation was as the wife had described it. Therefore, he asked her for the phone number of the nursing home and called immediately from the patient's bedside. When the staff from the nursing home answered, he quickly explained the situation and asked if they could bring the patient's mother to the telephone to talk to her son. The staff quickly did so, and the patient's wife explained the situation carefully to her mother-in-law. She then gave the phone to her husband, telling him loudly that his mother wanted to talk to him. The man listened intently to whatever his mother was saying; and all that he could do was to make heavy rasping sounds. Finally, his wife took the phone back again and talked briefly to the mother. While she was saying goodbye, the patient took one more breath, sighed, and was still. Robin told the wife that she was right and her husband had just passed away. He hailed a nurse to bring the doctor, who then pronounced the patient deceased. Following this, the rest of the palliative care team was brought in to provide bereavement support to the wife. Often in palliative care work, it is found that dying patients have unfinished business with which they need to deal before death. This experience was one of the more dramatic events!

In 1967, the Ontario government opened community colleges throughout the province. Undergraduate social work courses were offered in most of them, much to the dismay of the Professional Social Work Association. However, Robin felt that the government was going to proceed anyway. Therefore, the staff for these courses ought to be professional social workers.

Robin applied for and was given the job of setting up the course at Humber College in Etobicoke, a suburb of Toronto. He also felt strongly that the mandate of community colleges was to equip the students to obtain a position in their chosen field. Consequently, he concentrated on providing relevant field practice in social work agencies. He conducted seminars which brought his students and the staff of social work agencies together at Humber College. The result was that twenty-eight out of thirty graduating students obtained employment in the field of social work by the end of the summer following graduation. This was by far the best record of all the Ontario Community Colleges. Best of all, it assured his students that they could have a career in social work and that the option of continuing to the postgraduate level was open to them!

One person who had a positive effect on his life's work was Dr Roy Cheville, his faculty adviser at Graceland College. Not only was he a great help in Robin's educational experience at Graceland, but he also influenced his future course of study. He called Robin into his office one day and asked him if he would consider completing his education at the University of Toronto. He stated that Graceland worked to be accredited with other universities, which was accomplished by having their students attend the accrediting universities. At the time, Graceland did not have accreditation with the University of Toronto. As a result of his encouragement, Robin subsequently attended that university, receiving accreditation for the subjects which he had taken at Graceland. However, it resulted in his changing his major from education at Graceland to psychology at the University of Toronto. This, in turn, resulted in his going into a career in social work rather than in teaching. Dr. Cheville continued to be one of his mentors until his death many years later. His encouragement and support meant a great deal to Robin and contributed to the ultimate direction of his life's work.

One of his greatest accomplishments was in developing a drop-in clinic in the emergency department of the regional hospital where he worked for eleven years before retirement. There was no family service agency in the area, and the only counseling service for interpersonal relationship problems was the mental health clinic at the hospital. They had a long waiting list, whereas, many people came into emergency with a crisis situation. As the social worker in emergency, he had been able to see them initially and, upon referral from the doctors in emergency, could continue. He was able to help a large number of people with individual or marital problems and families to work through critical situations at the time of crisis.

Robin would like to have been more successful with a longer career in social work education. He started out well but quit too soon. This was because of a difference in philosophy with the college executive. He believed a college of applied arts had a responsibility to assist its students in finding employment in their chosen field. He also believed this was only possible when the students had adequate field practice as part of their course of study.

On the other hand, the college executive saw the course as a popular one which attracted a large number of applicants. They felt that the course should take as many students as possible in order to help pay for some of the less popular technical courses. Class size and available practicum placements were of no concern.

He might have developed addiction and immigration service programmes within the auspices of the college and staffed them with his students so that they could obtain their necessary practical experience. He had a teaching master instructing an addictions class for his students and another instructor directing an immigrations service class. The three of them had the required training and experience to attempt this. No other college offered either of these courses; thus, it was an undeveloped field. He wonders what might have been if he had stayed.

Robin feels that everyone has a life purpose and one's task in life is to identify that purpose and to fulfill it to the best of one's ability. Based on his professional experience, he operated under the following maxim: "Help all those whom he is called upon to assist to be able to achieve their optimum level of performance." This was accomplished by adhering to the following: "The difficult we do immediately. The impossible takes a while!"

He and his family took a memorable trip to the Canadian east coast in 1972, visiting Quebec City, Gaspé Peninsula, Nova Scotia, and Prince Edward Island. He found that the people were very friendly and the scenery, breathtaking. They took a trip to the Canadian west coast by car and camper trailer in 1976. He learned much about the beauty of the country, particularly the mountains, and the hospitality of Western Canadians.

As a hobby, he enjoys gardening, growing several vegetables and flowers in small available areas. He enjoys photography, having taken pictures of family, church, and travel experiences over the years. Currently, he is learning to master a digital camera, but is not yet adept in transferring pictures to his computer. He likes astronomy, and has a telescope which he is trying to master. He walks six miles *(10 km)* per day six days a week. He writes letters to children in Indonesia, Uganda, Niger, and Ethiopia, sharing information about each other's country. He lobbies on peace and justice issues: debt relief for third world countries, more assistance for Aids victims in Africa and Asia, and peace and security for refugees in Darfur and other areas of the world.

When he was an infant, he suffered from scarlet fever complicated by pneumonia and a severe ear infection. Finally, his family doctor told his parents that their baby would not survive the night. They called in their pastor to have special prayers for him. He was blessed by the prayers and survived the night and many subsequent years.

In the first year of their marriage, Robin and Wilma were involved in a serious car accident. They were driving their Volkswagen on a very snowy February evening. Almost at their destination, their car skidded on the ice and struck an oncoming car head on. Robin was thrown out a locked door onto the highway while both cars went into the ditch somehow missing him. He regained consciousness in hospital and was sent home feeling that he had been in a fight and was thoroughly punched on every inch of my body.

When he was in his forties, he suffered a heart attack. He was working long hours at a teaching hospital, followed by long hours on teaching projects for his church. On the night of the occurrence, he was suffering from excruciating chest pains on his arrival home after work. In the middle of the night, he went upstairs to obtain some medication and collapsed unconscious on the floor. Wilma tried to assist him to the couch. However, he collapsed unconscious a second time. She called an ambulance and they rushed him to hospital. One of the ministers from his church was called and offered prayers for him while the emergency staff was administering tests. He spent five days in hospital. After that, he worked a part-time shift for several months. He had to change his life style radically and was fortunate to have survived that experience.

Robin has served for over fifty years as a minister for his church. For fifteen years, he was a pastor of local congregations. For fourteen years, he served as church administrator at the district level (in charge of a group of churches). He has also developed several unique programmes of ministry. He co-authored a manual for ministry to and with seniors that was used as a reference throughout their world church.

Robin and Wilma had a wonderful trip when they moved from Ontario to Victoria, British Columbia, in 1996. They shipped their belongings by truck, arranging to have them stored for a month in Victoria. They had no idea where they would live, but trusted that they would find a suitable place in a month's time. They drove the Oregon Trail, had an enjoyable experience, and arrived in Victoria just before the Canadian Thanksgiving. They stayed for two weeks in a motel and searched for a suitable apartment. Finally, they found a beautiful duplex in the western suburbs, a short distance from the Strait of Juan de Fuca, with a full view of the strait and the Olympic Mountains of Washington State. They believe that they were directed to this beautiful home.

Their landlords also have a testimony of how they felt directed in finding the right tenants to live next to them. When they had to vacate because of the owners' need for the duplex for their daughter and her family, they were instrumental in helping Robin and Wilma settle into their present quarters in Victoria.

When they moved to Saanich in 1999, they obtained an apartment in a Seniors complex and discovered that, across the road in the mall, there was a Walker's Club. This club has over 500 members, about seventy-five of whom go to the Mall between 7:00 and 7:30 every morning. Each walks at his/her own pace and own decided distance, reporting to a secretary in the food court. She keeps a record on every member. Certificates are awarded to members for milestones accomplished. Beginners receive 50-mile *(80 km)* then 100-mile *(161 km)* certificates. Then members receive additional certificates when they have walked 500 miles *(805 km)*; 1,000 miles *(1,609 km)*; 5,000 miles *(8,047 km)*; and 10,000 miles *(16,093 km)*. Robin received his 10,000-mile certificate and pin at the club's January 2006 meeting.

Robin is my next younger brother. As children, we spent much time together. As a typical "big brother," I often teased him. However, when someone else did not treat him well, I was there to help him the best that I could. We spent a few weeks together on a summer job near Ottawa, Ontario, when we were teenagers. Two years later, we traveled together by train from St. Thomas, Ontario, to Winnipeg, Manitoba, where he attended a summer school and where I was working. After I moved to Alberta, our family would visit him and his family when we were in Ontario.

28

George Robin Hooper

Surrey, British Columbia, Canada

White-out! An automobile driver's nightmare! Add to that condition icy roads and darkness. That could mean collision with other vehicles or coming to a halt in snowy bank off the highway. This is what faced Robin one November night after being called to Montreal from his Ottawa home at 22:00 hours. Why did he ever accept such a crazy occupation after having survived thirty years at sea without serious mishap? A sugar-carrying cargo vessel had run ground on Lac St. Louis in the St. Lawrence Seaway. Robin, being a marine casualty investigator in the Canadian Coast Guard, had to go.

The parking lot at the dockside was glassy with ice beneath powdered snow when he arrived. A biting wind was driving the snow horizontally into his eyes. To make matters worse, on stepping out of the car, his feet shot from under him and he landed on his tailbone. The pain was excruciating, causing him to stagger around for several minutes before regaining his balance. A salvage engineer drove up. Between the two of them, they found and boarded a small tug that took them toward the stranded vessel. They left the dock; but, not having radar, the tug was unable to locate the buoys that marked the channel and had to be steered by compass. The wheelhouse windows were coated with ice from freezing spray as the small tug pitched into the increasingly steep waves that pounded the bow. Oh, to be in Ottawa in the warm apartment that he had reluctantly left in such a hurry!

After fifteen minutes of peering out the wheelhouse door, they saw a channel buoy looming out of the dark and snow; but it was so coated with ice that there was no number or light visible to tell which buoy it was. It was then decided that finding the ship was impossible on such a night. Therefore, without regret, the tug was turned back toward the dock. The engineer found his car engine frozen solid and had to find a taxi. However, Robin's car started; and, despite heavy snow on the roads and a stop to avoid a white-out, Robin arrived home on the following afternoon. What a waste of time that had been!

The ship remained aground for many days until tugs were able to refloat her. The damage suffered did not prevent the ship from continuing to Quebec City where Robin boarded to conduct his inquiry. While approaching a turn in the channel, the captain had been unable to identify the buoy where to turn and ran too far, leaving the channel entirely and grounding on a reef. In his report, Robin found the captain had made an unfortunate error caused by extreme weather conditions and the lack of an available anchorage in which to seek shelter, giving him no option but to continue.

Robin was born near Barrhead, Alberta, Canada. In the early 1930s, his family moved to Hillbank, on Vancouver Island. His first school was Cowichan Station. In 1943, he left high school to start a career at sea as a cadet officer on the Atlantic in the Canadian (wartime) Merchant Marine.

After the war, he served as deck officer on Canadian merchant ships on the Atlantic, Indian, and Pacific Oceans until 1951, when he joined the Canadian Naval Auxiliary vessels as officer and master, staying until 1974. His home base was Esquimalt, British Columbia.

On completing his apprenticeship in 1947, he attended Navigation School in Vancouver. He received his 2nd mates certificate in 1948, and continued sailing until 1951 when he earned his 1st mates certificate. In 1956, he obtained his master home trade, followed by his master foreign-going in 1974.

Later, he became the deputy director of Naval Auxiliary Vessels at National Defence Headquarters in Ottawa, after which he transferred to the Canadian Coast Guard as a casualties investigator. He also spent some years in the Coast Guard Marine Safety Branch in Vancouver, as a marine surveyor, until retiring on a full pension. During his career, he was awarded the 1939-1945 Star, the Atlantic Star, the Volunteer Service Medal with clasp, and the Victory Medal.

Robin tells of some of his experiences in investigating shipwrecks or accidents, in addition to the one told above.

The St. Lawrence Seaway ...

He operated out of Coast Guard headquarters in Ottawa. His introduction to the job was an easy daylight drive to the Seaway, with a senior investigator, to inspect a vessel that had collided with the wall at Beauharnois Locks, resulting in a dent in the bow of the ship near the waterline and some minor damage to the concrete dock. The vessel was light and riding high out of the water approaching the dock when the bow had apparently swung over before it could be checked. Statements from the captain and first officer were recorded and the engine movement book was checked.

A combination of speed and a lapse in judgment were considered to have contributed to the accident. The matter was settled by a letter of reprimand to the master from Transport

Canada. The paperwork required on return to the office was demanding because the report was to be given to the Minister for action. Many revisions were required to meet the required standards; but, with the help of their experienced stenographer, Robin's report was finally accepted.

Interviewing ship's captains and crews was work requiring patience and tact. Their testimony was tape recorded, but could not be used against them in court, and was only used to assess the possibility of charges to be laid. The captains, pilots, and crews were naturally nervous and skeptical. The ship owners were sometimes hostile, particularly if they felt that their officers were being hounded. Sometimes, the director would be called at home to answer to his Member of Parliament for the methods required to obtain evidence by his employees.

The first summer passed with more and more trips to the Seaway, with some accidents being more serious than others, but none of great consequence. Being a rookie in the field, Robin was sent to the lesser ones first. The increasing size of ships and the limited width of the locks in the Seaway was a prescription for a variety of bumps, grinds, and bruises suffered by ships and jetties. Then there were the problems of winter before freeze-up time. One such incident is told above.

B.C. Coastal Casualties ...

His next job was on the west coast where he was required to investigate the loss of two vessels and a barge loaded with equipment in northern British Columbia waters. The crews were saved and had returned home. Robin first interviewed a deckhand from the tug in a Powell River hotel. He was still badly shaken by the experience, but he was able to recall the events that led up to the disaster.

He was employed by a logger who had decided to carry out a risky log salvage operation off the beaches and islands at the North end of Queen Charlotte Sound. In these waters, a permit is not required to salvage logs, whereas, further south, the law is strictly enforced.

The logger had dispatched a tug and a barge loaded with expensive logging equipment to be landed on the beach to gather and stack the logs. He also sent a fish boat along to supply and transport the crews. The personnel were located two on the tug, two and a dog on the fish boat, and two men operating beach equipment. When the logs had been gathered and stacked on a beach, they were to be formed into a boom and towed to a mill far to the south. The operation was scheduled to be completed by the end of September, when they would head south with the logs in tow; but a weather report was received warning of an impending gale.

The logger loaded his equipment onto the barge to be towed by the fish boat, and the tug with the log boom in tow headed south to find shelter until the storm subsided. Unfortunately, they assumed that the storm would be late in arriving, and were caught in open water by an early and violent fall gale. Soon, both the fish boat and tug had to release their tows, which they could no longer control; and they were fighting for survival in the wild seas. The vessels tried to stay in sight of one another; but, eventually, both started taking more water onboard than their pumps could handle. The sea condition reduced visibility so that visual contact was lost.

This situation continued for some time when the fish boat received a distress call to say the tug was sinking and the crew intended to abandon ship. The fish boat then proceeded towards the last location of the tug. On locating her, they made a successful attempt to remove the three crew members.

It was not long before the fish boat started to founder and sent out a distress call that was intercepted by a southbound Alaska ferry a few miles away. The ferry increased speed and was able to locate the fish boat in a sinking condition and removed the six crew members; but, in the ensuing confusion, the dog was overlooked. It was many hours later when a passing vessel observed the half-submerged fish boat and reported seeing a dog on deck, which they were able to rescue, but could find no trace of the crew.

The events as related by the tug master and the logging company owner matched that of the deckhand whom Robin had interviewed, making his job much easier. No trace of the tug, fishing vessel, barge and equipment, or logs was ever found to dispute their story. Thankfully, all hands, including the dog, survived.

Arctic Casualty ...

One summer, he flew to Frobisher Bay, on Baffin Island in the Eastern Arctic, to look into the grounding of a large Arctic supply vessel. Never having been into the Arctic, this was a unique experience for Robin.

He was flown by helicopter to view the stranded vessel that was sitting high and dry on a smooth rock about ten feet *(3 m)* above the water. The helicopter landed on the rock so that he was able to walk around the ship to view the damage. Fortunately, the ship had suffered none, but was delayed on the rock until the next forty-foot *(12 m)* tide would float it off in about ten days. When floated off, the ship then had to unload cargo before proceeding, which caused further delay in supplying remote outposts before winter freeze-up.

After interviewing the captain and checking the leading

lights for entering the harbour, it became apparent that the lights, which were maintained by the Coast Guard, had not functioned properly. Instead of the two lights in line, providing a safe course for the vessel to steer through the harbour entrance dangers, only one 1ight functioned. This did not provide the safe range line, causing the vessel to stray into danger and onto a submerged rock. The master was not found to be at fault because the Coast Guard was responsible for the operation of the navigation marks. Although there were two Coast Guard icebreakers at anchor in the harbour approaches, the faulty leading lights had not been noticed by either.

Frobisher Bay has large tidal ranges that leave long expanses of sandy beaches at low water. Ships position themselves over the sand at high tide and are stranded high and dry at low tide for discharging cargo onto the beach. This saves having to build jetties that are easily damaged by winter ice.

This experience showed Robin the difficulties that can be expected in the Arctic, and how dependent those who work and live in northern latitudes are on southern Canada.

An Atlantic Tragedy ...

The most unusual casualty involved a rush trip to New York harbour to interview the master of an American ship that was arriving in port after salvaging an abandoned vessel off Newfoundland. The salvaged ship was a specialized type of vessel designed to carry heavy railroad engines between North America and Europe. The vessel was equipped with two heavy lift derricks capable of lifting seventy–five tons each. Also, special wing ballast tanks were fitted to take on water for the trips when the vessel ran light to pick up cargo.

In the hold, a portable tank was located to be swung

over the opposite side when the engine was being loaded to compensate for the engine's weight. This tank was filled with an amount of water equal to the weight of the load. When the ship was proceeding between ports, the portable tank was secured in the hold.

The heavy lift ship had been traveling from Europe to Montreal to load engines when it became involved in a major winter gale 200 miles *(322 km)* south of Newfoundland. Being light and running with ballast, the ship rolled heavily in the increasing swells, so much so that the portable tank in the hold broke free and punctured one of the wing ballast tanks. The released water caused the ship to take on a significant list towards the undamaged side. As the storm increased in intensity, the violent motion of the ship caused the list to increase, at times to over forty degrees, thoroughly alarming the captain and crew of twelve. What terror must have been felt by the crew! It can only be imagined.

They had two choices: to remain onboard and drown when the ship would capsize, as it appeared it would, or to leave the security of their ship and possessions and risk their lives climbing off the heaving ship and huddling in a tiny fragile air-inflated float that was totally at the mercy of wind, sea, and freezing cold. The huge waves made it obvious that no outside rescue could be attempted until the arrival of daylight and the dying down of the wind and the sea. By that time the ship would be gone!

The captain was so certain the ship would founder that he sent out a radio distress call and ordered the crew to abandon ship. As the only usable escape equipment was life rafts, one was quickly launched on the downwind side of the ship with eight men onboard. At that moment, the ship lifted on a wave and fell on the raft, catching it under the stern, capsizing it, and drowning the men under the weight of the ship.

What a horrible sight for the remaining five men as they observed this! They, however, managed to launch the other raft well clear on a line astern before donning lifejackets, jumping overboard, and climbing onto the raft. The wind by this time was so strong that it tore off the protective canopy of the raft, exposing all to the icy wind and snow. The distress call had been received by Search and Rescue, in Halifax; and a patrol aircraft was immediately dispatched to find the ship and to report. The ship was located and kept under observation during the night. When the crew was seen in the raft, extra equipment was dropped close by. Unfortunately, the survivors were too cold and sick to be able to recover it.

An American vessel remained close to the distress area during the night, but was unable to assist the raft for fear of capsizing it. The raft remained afloat during the night. The damaged and listing vessel was observed to be afloat in the morning and the seas were diminishing. Two officers were put onboard from the American ship and were able to start the engine and deliver the vessel to safety in St. John's Harbour, Newfoundland. However, by daylight, the American ship was able to rescue only two living persons from it. The other three crew members were missing and presumed to be dead.

This extraordinary feat earned the salvers a five million dollar salvage award by an Admiralty Court. One wonders if they were not haunted by that terrible night for the rest of their lives as would be the master and bosun, who were the only survivors.

The old adage "to never leave a sinking ship until it is

finally gone," might seem appropriate in this case; but with the fearful conditions and awful choices either option was potentially fatal.

B.C. Herring Roe Fishery ...

Robin's last employment in the capacity of investigator was to write a report on the casualties resulting from the spring herring roe fishery in British Columbia.

The fishery is short, often a month or less; but it can be very profitable, depending on the price paid by the Japanese who buy the roe as a delicacy. That year, the price varied from $800 to $1,200 per ton. This means boats, often in exposed locations, must be equipped and ready on the grounds to take advantage of the short openings at a time when weather conditions are unpredictable. During that spring, many boats took part in the fishery, with five lives being lost, four boats being lost, and five boats being damaged. Compared to previous years, the loss of life was high, except for one year when fourteen lives were lost. In each case, the lives were lost when one vessel sank with the entire crew.

Initially, a lack of consideration for stability was a major cause of accidents. However, that year, lack of precautions in navigation resulted in many groundings. The loss of life was caused by one vessel sinking in a storm when weather reports were possibly ignored. The herring roe fishery is always hazardous because of natural conditions, but these are exacerbated by reckless haste to earn large financial returns.

Robin has indeed experienced much in reporting on disasters of the sea. Although these incidents may involve a small percentage of the movement on the water, they do point out the inherit danger which lies with trade on the water. Weather can be a cruel master of seamen!

Robin and his wife have fond memories of an eighteen-day university tour in 1982 to Russia during the days of President Mikhail Gorbachev. The trip included a five-day cruise on the Volga River and a visit to St. Petersburg (then Leningrad).

Following his retirement, Robin continued his learning in other fields. He was not ready to relax his mind and body. He attended Langara College Art School. Having a liking for the fine arts, he entered Emily Carr College in 1985, graduating in 1988 with a diploma in painting. Desiring more, he studied for and received a Bachelor of Fine Arts in 1991. From 1992 to 1995, he studied archaeology at Simon Fraser University, in suburban Vancouver, and received a Post Baccalaureate Diploma in 1996. In addition to his studying, he has a number of hobbies, including historical archaeology, ceramics, genealogy, and singing. English is his only language.

I met Robin when I was contacting members of the Green Timbers Heritage Society by telephone in 2005. A short time later, we met in person at an Arbour Day event at Green Timbers Urban Forest. Robin and Lorene became friends of Pam and me. After Robin returned as a director of the Society, we often travel together to board meetings. He is an avid supporter of the preservation of the Forest.

29

Victor "Robin" Scott

Blue Springs, Missouri, United States

When was the last time that you had the tires on your automobile checked? According to the owner of Blue Springs Service Center, if people would regularly check the air pressure, rotate, balance and align their wheels, they would save much money in tire replacement. Tires that are maintained can last 80,000 miles *(128,748 km)*, but the staff here frequently replaces them within 30,000 *(48,280 km)* because of lack of maintenance.

Now, consider the cost of one tire. That results in more than two and one-half times the expense that can be avoided. Since there are four tires on an automobile, it means four times that cost if the lack of tire care is not remedied. One can only imagine what other areas of a car are not properly maintained. Wherever you live, take the advice of this Goodyear shop owner to keep your tires properly maintained.

If you are in Blue Springs, Missouri, which is along I-70 just east of Kansas City, you will see the Blue Springs Service Center. If you enter the store part of the center and see a tall, smiling man standing behind the counter and hear a friendly greeting from him, you have met Victor Scott - better known as Robin - the owner.

Robin was born in nearby Independence. Like many teenaged boys, he was not one to focus on his studies at school, but was more prone to wasting time than to applying himself. He says that is probably why he is in the tire business instead of being CEO of Enron. Now, everyone knows what happened to the CEO of Enron and the company itself. Think about it! He feels that he could have saved an entire company! Is that far-fetched? Not as much as it might appear to be.

A man with a good business education and background, wisdom in making decisions, and an honest work ethic can do wonders with such a company. Why could not that man have been Robin? Not only might the company have been saved, but Robin would have had the salary to support that which means so much to him. That is not relaxing on the resort beaches of the world or some other luxury for himself, but it is the joy of giving to good Christian causes that help those who are less fortunate than he is. He feels a real sense of obligation to share since he has been granted so much by God.

He remembers the respect for and the fear of discipline from his junior high school principal, Mr. Georgeoff. He realizes that his experience with this administrator resulted only to his own future good. Children today unfortunately do not have the opportunity to learn the same respect as he did. Somehow, "timeouts" just do not command the same attention. He also remembers Mrs. Baker, his junior high English teacher, who set him straight right away and had his complete attention and respect thereafter. Might there be a connection, since the school is now named Georgeoff-Baker Middle School?

Robin played on the basketball and tennis teams until one day during tennis practice the coach, Norm Michelleti, had more than he could take from him and removed him from the team. After retaliating with inappropriate remarks, Robin was suspended from school for three days. This is not a pleasant memory him, but it is something from which today's students can learn. There is a happy outcome to this tumultuous experience. Now, Norm is one of his best customers at the shop; and the two are good friends.

In the mid 1970s, Robin graduated from Blue Springs High School. He distinctly remembers standing with his cap and gown on in the RLDS Auditorium during the graduation ceremony thinking for the first time, "What am I going to do now?" What a terrifying thought for a teenager! He was not prepared for an after high school experience! Since his friends were enrolling into college, he ascertained that this would be the proper avenue for him to take. Thus, he became a student at Southwest Missouri State University. He knew nothing about life or what to do next. Three semesters did not provide the answers in regard to his future. Maybe going to Florida might. After about a year as a SCUBA diving instructor, he decided to return to Missouri.

Although Robin has never had the privilege to serve in the armed forces, he does have a great thankfulness, respect, and appreciation for those who have. As an English-speaker, he claims the extent to which he is bilingual is being able to order from Spanish terms on his favourite restaurant's menu. The thought of running for any public office is not appealing at all. He has not experienced national recognition. However, he has often received domestic recognition as the local ATM by his four daughters. That cannot be all that bad, can it?

His favourite pastimes have evolved from basketball and tennis to fishing and golf; but what he enjoys most is doing things with his wife of twenty-five years and their four beautiful daughters. The Scotts have taken many family trips to different places, the most recent being a road trip to the

Grand Canyon. Robin's family had never been in the southwest and was awestruck by the majesty of God's creation!

For over twenty years, they spent the first week every year at a Christian resort camp called Horn Creek, in Westcliffe, Colorado. These were probably the most influential family times that they had on vacation because they spent time together every day having devotionals at breakfast, playing during the day, sharing fun events in the evenings, followed by Bible study each night with their friends who came the same week each year from all over the country. In the process lasting friendships were developed.

Robin has taken several trips sight-seeing, fishing, and golfing from southern California to Alaska, Hawaii, north-central Saskatchewan, Belize, Jamaica, Bahamas, and Mexico. These trips have included other U.S. states and Canadian provinces.

A Cajun friend said to him after their vehicle had broken down in the wilderness of northern Saskatchewan, "Oh well! Dis time next year you'll never known da difference." Given the situation and the location, that was a calm remark. However, it has meaning for all. People tend to "make mountains from molehills" and do not realize what a waste it is. Robin approaches life from a realistic and positive attitude. However, he often comments when people around him become stressed, "Life is too short to worry or be miserable."

Two of his ten employees have been with him for over twenty-two years each and most of the others have been with him from six to sixteen years. He has always believed in treating his employees in the way that he would want to be treated if "the shoe were on the other foot." He bases the way that he conducts business – whether it be employees, customers, or vendors – from a Biblical standpoint of honesty, fairness, service, and knowing that he will be judged one day for the way that he has conducted his life and treated others. That is a philosophy that everyone should follow.

For someone who had no idea of what to do with his life, Robin Scott has been a success in life. Not everything can be measured on the balance sheet. Enron could have used him!

When our family was living in Independence, Missouri, in the late 1980s, we received a coupon for a free oil change at the Goodyear shop in Blue Springs. At that time, I met Robin. Many times after that, I took our cars to be repaired at the shop. The mechanic who provided the repair work most often was Jack Young. So satisfied was I with the service of the staff at Blue Springs Service Center that, when we moved to Rockwall, Texas, I went immediately to the Goodyear shop there for our many auto repairs.

One time when our son Cameron and I came back to Blue Springs for a couple of days, I stopped at the shop to greet the staff. Cameron chose to remain in the car. Robin, knowing that Cameron had had a physical problem, asked how he was. When I said that Cameron was at the moment sitting in the car, Robin dropped what he was doing and went to the car to talk to Cameron. That act meant much to both of us. Robin not only speaks of good Christian ideals, he also lives them.

30

John Samuel AND Helen Hofman

Holland, Michigan, United States

This was Tojolabal country, in the southern Mexican State of Chiapas. Ironically, the name of the village was Libertad. However, there was no liberty for the evangelical converts who lived there. They were confronted with the tribal persecution. One evening, Sam and Helen parked their vehicle a mile *(1.6 km)* away and slipped into the village for a worship service in a home on the edge of it. During the entire service, the owner of the home stood at the door watching the village to give warning of any evidence of reaction from the other villagers. There was none, and the missionaries were able to return home safely that night.

That was one night. Eventually, the twenty evangelical families had to uproot and begin their lives again at a new location, establishing a village which they named Samaria. Accompanied by the Mexican pastor and other church leaders, Sam and Helen visited them there as they were beginning to rebuild their homes and lives. They fed everyone a chicken dinner. You cannot outgive the poor!

Sam Hofman was born in Lethbridge, Alberta, Canada. His Hofman and Zoeteman grandparents were pioneers, farming prairie land west of Lethbridge. The Hofman family came from North Dakota, and the Zoeteman family came from Northwest Iowa. After eleven years of successful farming, the

Hofmans moved to Lynden, Washington, United States, taking the younger half of the family with them.

Sam's father, Tenis Hofman, remained with one of his brothers on the family farm. A while after his parents were married, they moved to a farm near Pierce, Alberta.

His full name is John Samuel Hofman. His mother's father was named John, and her younger brother was named Samuel (who died from a ruptured appendix at age fourteen). To avoid confusion with his uncle and two of his cousins named John Hofman, Sam was always called by his second name.

After a year, his family left Alberta and moved to Lynden. There they attended the First Reformed Church. After Sam graduated from Lynden Public High School, he began his college education with one year at Western Washington College, in Bellingham. Feeling called into the Christian ministry, he transferred to Hope College, in Holland, Michigan, United States. Three years later, he entered Western Theological Seminary – just across the street from the college – from which he graduated.

As a student, one area of good memories is his participation in student government. He was elected Student Body President in his senior year in High School and also Student Council President of Hope College four years later.

The other area of special memories is in vocal music. As a teenager in Lynden, he sang in the church choir and a church quartet. In college, he sang in a fraternity quartet and in the college choir. That included a memorable choir tour to California in 1955.

This background in music was very valuable in their mission work, as they spent countless hours teaching the

Indians to sing their hymns in four-part harmony. Helen also taught a class in piano, and both of them were involved in the editing and producing of their hymnals.

One day while he was at Western Seminary, he went on a blind date with Helen Taylor, a student in the Hope College. It was love at first sight! A steady courtship followed for the next three years. Helen squeezed four years of college into three years so that they could graduate the same summer of 1958.

Helen was born in the northern part of the lower peninsula of Michigan State in her parents' home on a dairy farm near the village of Lucas, in Missaukee County. The nearest city of any size is Cadillac, which is 7 miles *(11 km)* to the northwest of Lucas. She has four sisters and one brother.

She started school at age four in the country Lucas school just an eighth of a mile *(200 m)* south of her parents' home. The teacher was a distant relative and, when Helen begged to accompany her sisters to school, the teacher said that she was no trouble and told Helen's parents to let her attend, despite her young age. The following year she was placed into the first grade, being the only girl with a class of ten boys. When her class entered the fifth grade, all were bussed to the consolidated school in McBain, Michigan, 5 miles *(8 km)* to the southeast of her home.

As a shy 13-year-old high school freshman, she was hired to clerk at the local grocery store in Lucas, and worked there Wednesday evenings from 4:00 p.m. until 10:00 p.m., all day on Saturdays, and full time in the summers during her four years of high school. She knows this developed an ability in her to meet strangers and helped give her some much needed self-confidence.

Helen loved her high school years at McBain. She and a few other students were allowed to write and mimeograph a school paper - which was great fun. She always loved to write. She also enjoyed being a majorette, being in the Junior and Senior class plays, playing on the girls' high school basketball team, and singing in the girls' choir. She was proud to be one of the "Taylor (her maiden name) girls", and proud to be the daughter of Weller and Clara Taylor. She graduated from the McBain Rural Agricultural High School in 1954.

Her dad had the only registered Holstein dairy herd in the area, the only one who raised certified seed potatoes to sell, the President of the School Board for many years, an elder in their church, and was on many other prominent boards in the county. He made it possible for all of his children to attend college, and was always willing to sell a dairy cow when the college bills arrived. All graduated from college debt-free. What a gift to his children that was! How many families of today's college graduates can make that claim?

In the fall of 1957, at a Sunday morning service, Sam and Helen heard a missionary tell of the need for an additional missionary couple in southern Mexico. They immediately felt called to this work, arranged for an interview, applied for the position, and were accepted. Following their marriage in August 1958, they drove to Mexico City to begin Spanish language and Mexican cultural studies.

In 1959, they were assigned to the Tzeltal indigenous area in the southern state of Chiapas. They joined Paul and Dorothy Meyerink with the tribe. The initial evangelistic and translation work had been done by two Wycliffe Bible Translator missionaries. The two couples were given the responsibility of providing a training programme for the indigenous church leaders. The first converts had been won in 1948; and, ten years later, there were about 7,000 converts worshipping in thirty locations.

Two years later, they purchased the Buenos Aires Ranch in the Jatate River valley as a location for the Tzeltal Bible School. Beginning in 1963, the two couples spent the next twenty-three years constructing homes and school buildings, teaching classes, writing textbooks, preparing audio-visuals, and administrating the Bible School and the medical work. The Tzeltal church continued to grow as the Tzeltals shared the Good News with their people. They did extensive traveling among the people, including much filmstrip and movie evangelism.

In 1988, Sam and Helen moved to Las Margaritas to begin their ministry among the Tojolabal people. Living in a Mexican town also gave them the opportunity to improve on their Spanish language fluency. With the help of bilingual Tojolabals, they produced literature in the Tojolabal language. They arranged for the reprint of the Tojolabal New Testament, which had been translated by a Wycliffe Bible Translator missionary. They also prepared a larger edition of the hymnal. They were involved in the resettlement of Tojolabal believers who had been expelled from their villages and the care of the large number of refugees resulting from the Zapatista uprising in January 1994.

In 1994, they moved to San Cristobal de Las Casas in response to an invitation to help the highland Tzeltals in the revision of their Bible. This was a six-year task, with Helen doing all the keyboarding and both of them being involved in the translation and editing process. During this time, Helen also produced a three-year series of Sunday school lessons for two age levels for the Tzeltal children.

The move also made Sam and Helen more available to the Amatenango Tzeltal Christians, where they assisted the Tzeltal missionary Roberto Santis and his wife Micaela. They assisted this persecuted group of Christians in the translation and printing of a hymnal and a New Testament in their dialect of Tzeltal.

One vivid memory is their first visit to the notorious village of Cancuc. The first converts had had their homes burned about five years before and had rebuilt a quarter of a mile *(400 m)* from the village. When they neared the village, the Tzeltal church leaders with whom they were traveling were able to rescue a young girl from two men who were trying to kidnap her. She was the sister of one of the believers who were travelling with Sam and Helen. That night, they held a service in a partially completed chapel. Helen was playing the portable organ and both were teaching them a new hymn, which said:

"Firmly give yourself to Christ;
Don't be afraid, He will help you.
Consider the salvation you receive from Christ;
Don't be double hearted."

The chorus then says:

"Don't be afraid of sickness; don't be afraid of death.
You are in the hands of Christ.
He will protect you everywhere;
Don't be at all afraid."

After the practice, one of the men said, "Here we are singing about not being afraid, but meanwhile I am afraid that they are hearing the sound of the organ and our singing in the village and that they will come and burn down our houses again."

After serving for over forty years as Reformed Church missionaries in Chiapas, Mexico, Sam and Helen retired from missionary service in 2000, and moved to Holland, Michigan, where their daughter and their married son and his wife and two daughters are living. Their older son lives in Chicago and teaches at the University of Illinois.

Their final visit to Chiapas in 2002 is a cherished memory. They returned to the Tzeltal Bible School for the dedication of the highland Tzeltal Bible, which had claimed so much of the last six years of their ministry there. There were between 3,000 and 5,000 Tzeltals gathered there for the celebration, and they took all 15,000 Bibles home that day. With over 60,000 Tzeltals worshipping in over 400 Presbyterian churches, they have become one of the largest tribal churches of Latin America. Their fervency and courage have always been an inspiration for Sam and Helen.

In addition to their writing in the Tzeltal and Tojolabal languages, their publications include a textbook on church history in Spanish and a devotional booklet, *Light from Tzeltal Lamps,* published by Words of Hope in 2001. Sam wrote articles regularly for the *Missionary Monthly* and the *Church Herald,* a collection of which was published in 1993 as the book *Mission Work in Today's World.* In 2004, he wrote an article for the Reformed Review of Western Theological Seminary titled "The History of the Chiapas Mission."

Sam does have one regret: "I wish I had another lifetime to help the Tzeltals in developing their agriculture. We tried to do agricultural work at the Tzeltal Bible School and to teach them better farming methods, but we lacked time and expertise. Especially in the highlands, someone needs to help them develop their fruit and vegetable farming."

Despite their distance from Michigan, their ties to Hope College remained strong through the years, partly because four of Helen[1]s siblings are also alumni. Their three children, David, Jonathan, and Lisa are all Hope graduates, as is Jonathan's wife. Six of Helen's nieces and nephews are also graduates of Hope College. That is a good roster of alumni for their family.

Helen cherishes the closeness of her siblings. In 2006, the six of them, with their spouses enjoyed a wonderful Labour Day weekend shared in a bed and breakfast facility in Pentwater, Michigan. Four of them live in Michigan; but one had to drive from Ithaca, New York; and the youngest flew from California so that they could spend this time together. The highlight of the weekend was the impromptu Sunday morning service that they shared in the living room, singing hymns, reading scripture, and praying together. What a wonderful experience it was!

Our son Sean met Helen Hofman in a business establishment in San Cristóbal de Las Casas, Chiapas, México, when we all were living in that city. Helen invited Pam and me to her home to visit her and Sam. That was the beginning of a long friendship. They invited us to accompany them when they went to some of the villages for church services. A few times, Sam and I went alone. Our family found it very educational to enter the Mayan culture – even though we did not understand the language of the people and their services. We have many good memories of these people who would give of what they had to their Canadian visitors and their missionary friends. We thank Sam and Helen for the opportunity.

31

Stanley D. AND Yvonne Smith

Duncanville, Texas, United States

Many people have had their names listed in a local newspaper. Some have seen their names in a non-local newspaper. When that newspaper is the *Wall Street Journal*, there must be good reason. However, being quoted on the front page of that publication is an honour. This happened to Stanley Smith when he was vice-president and chief accounting officer of Southern Union Company, of Dallas, Texas. This is a vertically integrated natural gas company with over 900,000 retail gas customers. In the 1980s, the price of gas was removed from federal regulation. A reporter of the *Wall Street Journal* called to ask how deregulation was going to affect his company's business - and then quoted him.

Stanley was born in Clifton, Bosque County, Texas, United States, a small town to the northwest of Waco. He attended school in nearby Whitney. His sixth grade teacher, Etha Wilson, had a significant impact on his life. She was an academically tough, nurturing professional who would not accept less than her students' best efforts at learning. She had an unspoken way of making them want to learn and want to please her. Stanley credits her with helping instill in him the desire to do his best. He was blessed in having such a teacher!

He graduated from the Hankamer School of Business, at Baylor University, Waco, Texas, with a Bachelor of Business

Administration degree, ranking sixth in his class. He holds the distinction of having been the first in his family to have graduated from college.

Stanley would like to have developed a more extensive vocabulary and become more comfortable at public speaking. The importance of those skills was not fully realized until he entered into the professional business world.

Between 1967 and 1969, he served in the U.S. Army where he earned the Certificate of Achievement. All his time was spent in the United States. His professional work was in accounting and finance within the United States. He has also been much involved in the management of a not-for-profit corporation, the Southwest Railroad Historical Society, in Dallas, Texas.

His philosophy is to follow the Golden Rule. There are several ways to word this since it is common to many religions. One is: "Therefore all things whatsoever ye would that men should do to you, do ye even so to them."

He treasures his visit to the Smithsonian Institute in Washington, DC, as the one that is most memorable for what he learned. As a hobby, Stanley enjoys listening to western swing music.

Stanley has been deeply involved with the activities of the Southwest Railroad Historical Society in Dallas, Texas. This is the body that operates the Age of Steam Railroad Museum in Fair Park in that city. For numerous years, there has been planning for a physical move because of limited available space within the park. As more equipment becomes available, finding a suitable spot in the museum becomes a major problem. Since I was at one time involved with the process, I asked Stanley to provide some information about it.

Space had become available in the west end of downtown Dallas, not far from where President John Kennedy was shot. In the 1990s, many meetings had taken place to try to make a feasible deal. Stanley was president of the society for a few years of this period. Eventually, the idea faded away primarily because of the staggering environmental issues with the property and the Society's inability to raise the ten million dollars asked for the property. A land speculator has purchased the land since.

The potential new home that is under consideration lies across Washington Avenue from the current site. It involves four tracts of land totaling about 7 acres *(2.8 ha)*.

The first site is owned by the State Fair of Texas and is used currently only during the twenty-four days of the fair and on the day of the annual Cotton Bowl football game. The Fair board is interested in trading that property for the current property of the museum on the fair grounds. Both parties would probably benefit from such a deal.

The second one involves an unimproved right-of-way 50 feet *(15 m)* wide owned by Dallas Area Rapid Transit. It is understood that DART no longer plans on using it. The Society hopes to acquire this by donation or long-term nominal lease.

The third one is an unimproved plot of the same width that is owned by the City of Dallas. It is platted for Pacific Avenue, but has not been developed for that. The same approach would be taken as for the second one.

The fourth plot is currently owned and operated by Triple S Dynamics. This would have to be purchased for about $5.5 million.

Negotiations are underway to acquire the first three

tracts discussed above. The museum does not have the money required to purchase the fourth tract. The City of Dallas prepared a massive Capital Bond programme to be submitted to the voters in early November 2006 for their approval. As a result of hard work, intensive lobbying efforts, and some good luck, the proposed bond package includes $2.75 million for the Age of Steam Museum to purchase the Triple S Dynamics property. AOS will be required to match the City's $2.75 million. They are optimistic that they can do it. The bond passed.

The collection has grown to the point that there is no room for even one more piece of equipment in the Museum. More space is urgently required, and this property is the best and most realistic opportunity available at this time.

To facilitate the efforts to raise funds, M. Goodwin and Associates, a professional museum planning group, has been retained to develop a long-range strategic plan for the new museum.

The name of the corporation will be changed from "Southwest Railroad Historical Society" to "Museum of the American Railroad." The name "Age of Steam" will still be used to refer to the exhibit within the Museum of the American Railroad. The expert states that it is essential to have a name that carries a "national in scope" connotation.

All hope for the best in the acquisition of this property. The museum receives visitors from many countries throughout the world. For the railroad enthusiast, it is one of many railroad museums worth seeing. Much credit can be given to staff and volunteers for the achievements seen at the museum over the years.

Knowing that Stanley's wife Yvonne is a teacher in the

lower grades and had a few students whose parents had come from Russia for specific work projects during my time in Texas, I asked her to tell a little of her experience.

Yvonne was teaching second grade when the first Russian student came into her class. The child's father was a scientist working with the Supercollider Project. She did not speak English, but her parents spoke some. Although her name was Alexandra, she insisted on being called Alice because she wanted to be American. She became "Americanized" quickly; and, by the end of third grade, it was difficult to distinguish her from any other girl in the school.

The next girl, Olga, arrived three years later. Her mother, Tanya, had married an older man who traveled to Russia as a Bible translator. He married Tanya in Russia and brought her to Duncanville, Texas, and into the house with his "real" wife! Needless to say, that caused a big problem. Some church members took pity on Tanya and found a place for her to live. Olga was an extremely shy child. She would not attempt to talk in class nor speak English. When it came time for the State Fair of Texas, Yvonne made arrangements to take Tanya and Olga to the Fair, hoping that this might create a bond between student and teacher. Students must bond with teachers in order to feel free enough to speak if they are really shy or scared.

Seeing the Fair through the eyes of the university graduate from Russia was one of the most interesting experiences in all the years that Stan and Yvonne visited the fair. Tanya had never touched a farm animal before. She was fascinated with the wool on the sheep. The delight as she showed her daughter the different animals made her giggle. When they arrived at the automobile building, she kept asking if the cars were really for sale. She was fascinated with all the food. When asked what she would like to eat, she replied, "I eat anything, because in Russia, we eat whatever is in the store." Then they walked by the Russian exhibit. When shown a miniature doll of the Czar, she did not know who it was.

Stanley took her on a tour of the Age of Steam Museum. When he mentioned the engine that had been made for the Czar, she stepped back and put her hand of her hips and asked, "Who is this Czar?" Then it was assumed that all references to Czar Nicholas have been erased from their history books. Tanya told Stanley and Yvonne that it was important for her to come to the United States and bring Olga because, in her country, she would work hard all her life and have nothing; but here she could work hard and could have something.

Yvonne won Olga's heart that day. She told her mother that night that Yvonne was her next favourite person after her grandmother. On Monday, Olga began to speak and smile. The State Fair ends in late October, and Olga was proficient in English by the time school ended in May. She passed the important state assessment in third grade with the highest rating possible.

Tanya was an architect in Russia. After living with and caring for an elderly couple for about two years, she worked for a dentist in Duncanville, hometown of the Smiths. There she met a good man, married him, and moved to Plano – another suburb of Dallas. Olga is now in college.

This shows the effect of a little concern by a teacher on a student. These were good experiences for Yvonne. This also shows that we who live in the "First World" should not take our blessings for granted.

Stanley and Yvonne have been blessed with two wonderful children who grew up to be great adults. They believe that their guidance, their setting examples, and their love for their children had a very positive impact on their development.

I met Stanley at a Historical Society meeting in a railroad car at the museum in 1992. As was the custom, he asked all who were there for the first time to stand and introduce ourselves. From that time on, I enjoyed working with Stanley. He supported me with my programme of making railroad presentations in schools and public libraries. He participated in my first two library presentations. He invited me to serve on the Society board and to chair one ad hoc committee. I always felt that his leadership was an asset to the Society.

Yvonne was at the museum occasionally. She and I had a common professional background as school teachers. Once, she brought one of the Russian mothers to see the museum. I had the honour of showing the two ladies some of the equipment despite our language barrier. It was a good experience for me.

32

Susan P. Land

Arvada, Colorado, United States

Would you be willing to climb down into a well? Why would it be necessary? What if it were to retrieve a corpse? That is what faced Jerry and Susan, of the forensics department of the Oklahoma State Bureau of Investigation. They were on call when they were requested to travel to a remote spot in Oklahoma to "process" a scene where the body was in a well. Some guy killed his girlfriend and "hid" her body in a cistern. All the way to the site, the two investigators were saying, "I am not going into that well! They will have to put a gun to my head. Even then I won't go!" Neither one likes spiders or snakes! Eventually, they arrived at the remote site with the OSBI agents and the Sheriff's Deputies.

Someone finally decided that the Coroner should be called to pronounce the body "dead"! Mind you, the body had been there for several months! Therefore, they waited for the coroner to come upon the scene. Keep in mind that not only was it a hot day, but the investigators were being sandblasted by the wind! Finally, he arrived with his wife. What a pleasant place for romance! The coroner was a rather large man. The well had a concrete block on top, with a small opening. Do you see where this is leading? To everyone's surprise, the coroner squeezed through the opening - shirtless and with an oxygen tank, but he succeeded. Fortunately for Susan, he would not follow his wife's instructions to remove his pants, too!

The body was declared "dead", the concrete block was removed to make it easier to remove the body, and several officers volunteered to bring it up. In addition, no one put a gun to their heads to force them to go into the well! It was just an ordinary day in Oklahoma.

Susan was born in Watrous, Saskatchewan, Canada, a town southeast of Saskatoon. She began her education in grade school in Sutherland, a suburb of Saskatoon. She has one particularly unpleasant memory of her early schooling.

Her fifth grade teacher scarred her for life! In art class, the students were supposed to use some abstract type of drawing technique, but Susan was unable to understand it. Therefore, the teacher took the little girl's drawing (which looked like something identifiable instead of abstract), along with someone else's drawing (which showed what she wanted), and held both up in front of the class and said, "This is what your drawing should look like (the other person's), not like this (Susan's)." Needless to say, Susan did not attempt much drawing for many years, when she finally took a class called "Drawing For People Who Think They Can't." Guess what? She says that her drawings still look like something identifiable instead of abstract.

She obtained a Bachelor of Science degree from Missouri Western State College, a Master of Science degree in Forensic Science from George Washington University, and a Doctor of Philosophy degree in Adult and Continuing Education with emphasis in Continuing Professional Education from University of Oklahoma.

Dr. Russell Smith, one of her chemistry professors in college, pushed her toward forensic science and graduate school in forensic science. She feels that her teaching style in college was based on his. That is a compliment to her mentor.

Many teachers will probably say that the best part of teaching is when one sees the light bulb come on. When Susan started teaching in college, she was amazed at how little thinking students did and how bad their writing was. As she expected, many of her students were traumatized when she required that they think and be able to write. She kept trying to cause them to understand that her approach was to prepare them for the real world of being a forensic scientist or crime scene investigator.

One student, Denise, was extremely introverted. It was necessary to work with her on another level to help her to interact more with the class and to prepare herself for such presentations as testifying in court. When she did her internship, Susan suggested that her research was fit for formal presentation at a forensic science conference. It took some work, but Denise agreed to do it – and lived to tell about it! That in itself was an accomplishment.

A couple of years after Susan had left the college, Denise called. She wanted Susan to know that she was in a master's programme. On the first day of orientation, the twenty students in the programme were told they would have to write several 20–page papers and make several formal presentations to the class. Denise said that she had a smile on her face and that she exhibited the attitude of "No problem! I know how to do this!" The other students were "sweating bullets" thinking about the papers and presentations. Denise wanted her former teacher to know that she could not have done it without Susan's help. Susan really appreciated being told this. Her teaching did make a difference for at least one person. That light came on!

Her current work is that of a crime analyst, which involves analysis of crime patterns and statistical analysis in a suburb of Denver, Colorado. Previously, she was an assistant professor for six years at Metropolitan State College in Denver. For the first fifteen years after obtaining her master's degree, she worked in forensic science with the state bureaus of investigation in Missouri and Oklahoma.

Have you ever wondered what it would be like to appear on a national television show? Susan had the experience – and describes how it affected her. The producers of *Unsolved Mysteries* decided to film one of the cold cases of the Oklahoma State Bureau of Investigation. They wanted all of the people who processed the scene to be part of it. It was Susan's lucky day!

The filming took place at a rest stop along an Oklahoma Turnpike. OSBI bought its participating staff new windbreakers with the OSBI name and logo prominently displayed. Also, they had magnetic signs made to put on the side of the crime scene van. The filming took place in the wee hours of the morning.

The staff watched the Highway Patrol cars drive up to the scene and ad lib some dialogue – over and over and over. There was no script for any of this. Then, the others had the privilege to watch as Jerry, the fingerprint expert, and Susan drove up to the scene in the OSBI van – over and over and over. Jerry was very good at placing the van in the exact same spot each time. Susan knew this because every time that she disembarked from the van, she stepped into the same hole and had to avoid the same used tampon!

They had to pretend that they were processing the scene, taking notes, and conferring. Susan kept writing on her pad of paper, "Get me out of here!!" Maybe it was a good thing that this did not show up on the finished product. Another thing that did not show up on the finished product was anything that referred to OSBI. They edited it so that the OSBI name and logo on the new signs and windbreakers did not show. That was rather funny considering the lengths the bosses went to procure them. Apparently, the producers did not want to show any advertising. My wife and I saw the film on television and noted how bored and left out of the action that Susan was!

It took place somewhere in Oklahoma. Susan and her colleagues were called to a homicide scene out in the middle of nowhere (naturally!) in the middle of the night (of course). The house was shotgun style: long, narrow, living room in front, then kitchen, hallway, bathroom, and bedroom at the back. The body was in the bedroom on a waterbed. The bed had a wood frame, posts, and a mirrored canopy. The scene was processed from front to back.

At one point, the other investigators were in the front of the house while Susan was in the bedroom collecting evidence. She braced her legs against the wood frame in order to reach across the body for the top sheet. As she took hold of the sheet, out of the corner of her eye, she saw the body move! She "vapour locked" and jumped back, only to realize what had actually happened. She had pushed down when grabbing the sheet, thus making the waterbed move - and, in turn, the body had moved! Then, out of the corner of my eye, she saw movement a second time! She jumped again, only to realize that an investigator was coming down the hall. Of course, she laughed at herself and had to explain to the others that she scared herself out of ten years so they could laugh too! The case of the moving corpse was solved.

Many of us in our younger years have had the experience of hitchhiking along the highways when we were traveling. When Susan worked at OSBI, she would give some advice to prospective hitchhikers. "If you hitchhike, we will probably see you later under a bridge or in the bushes where your body was dumped!" Although we had no problem in the past, it takes only one bad lift. Is it worth it?

She recalls one trip which was memorable in that she learned something the hard way. She learned that, when participating in a daylong boat outing at Puerto Vallarta, Mexico, one should not be without a suitable hat, should not rely on soda drinks instead of water for hydration, and should not eat unfamiliar food sold on the beach. This combination had the usual results. From having lived in Mexico, I would recommend that one should choose only reputable restaurants when eating out and should avoid street and beach vendors. On the positive side, she did acquire a good tan.

For her leisure moments, she likes to read and to nap. She is definitely familiar with books as she has provided and recommended books for her sister and her grand-nephews.

People have different ways of saying what Susan states as her philosophy of life. Unless someone is bleeding, most problems are not as bad as we think they are! Heeding this would probably reduce the number of stress-related illnesses in the population.

She describes her first language as being Americanized English, spoken with a very slight Canadian accent. She does not speak or read any other language. The one area where Susan feels that she could be better is in personal relationships.

I met Susan in 1963 when I was attending a church conference in Saskatoon, Saskatchewan. I had been billeted to her parents' home. I may not have known her in future years had I not become interested in her older sister and married her. A year after Pamela and I were married, Susan spent the summer in our home with her sister while I was attending university. We would see her whenever our family would visit her parents when we were on vacation. We also visited her at George Washington University when she completed her studies there. When we visited her in Oklahoma City, she gave us a conducted tour of the crime lab at OSBI. We have not seen each other in several years.

33

Timo Cernohorsky

Crailsheim, Baden-Württemberg, Germany

Many people buy do-it-yourself kits. Most of them can save themselves money in constructing the item. When buying a kit, one should always know what is being purchased and follow the directions. However, there is always an exception. Someone came into Timo's shop. He saw some laminate flooring that he liked and purchased it. He carefully laid it on the exterior balcony of his house. After the first rain shower, the man returned to the shop to register a complaint about the product. If the customer had read the directions carefully, he could have saved himself the cost of purchase and the time for laying the flooring and pulling it up. He did not realize that this product was for indoor use only.

Timo was born in Ilshofen, Baden-Württemberg, Germany. He commenced his education at Leonhard-Sachs-Schule, later at the Albert-Schweitzer-Gymnasium, both in Crailsheim, in Baden-Württemberg. His first language is German, but he also has a working knowledge of English.

Reaching the A-Level GCE (in Germany, *Abitur*) was a memorable moment for Timo. Only with *Abitur* can a student be admitted to a university. *Abitur* is a diploma from a German secondary school after thirteen years. In Germany, there are three types of school after the first four years: *Hauptschule* (grades 5-9), the higher school *Realschule* (grades 5-10), and the highest school *Gymnasium* (grades 5-13).

His state, Baden-Württemberg, has beautiful rivers, valleys, and woods – including the Black Forest. Near Stuttgart, the capital, some famous car manufacturers have their homes: Mercedes-Benz, Porsche, and Maybach. In Ulm is the highest church-tower in the world. Schwäbisch Hall, Heidelberg, and other cities are famous for their historical sections from the Middle Ages. At the Schwäbische Alb, a range of hills, are many castles. They include the famous Castle of Hohenzollern, the home of the Prussian emperors. This is an area of Germany that a visitor will not want to miss seeing.

Timo spent ten months in military service in the paramedic branch of the army, *Bundeswehr*. He was posted to a little hospital outside the normal barracks. The staff members were provided with their own private rooms. There were only fifteen to twenty beds, but all were not in use at any one time. Therefore, he enjoyed a very pleasant assignment with few injured people. The paramedics learned bloodletting, the giving of injections, and much about medications.

Timo's profession is that of a sanitary installer in his state. He has some pleasant memories in this work. His most amusing experience occurred when a man called to say that his bathtub was plugged so that the water would not drain. Timo answered the call. After some work was done, little green leaves emerged. They were tea leaves. Why were there tea leaves in the bathtub drain? It was discovered that the man was an owner of a Chinese restaurant in this town and was using his bathtub as a medium for growing tea plants. Now, he had to find another place for his garden.

Timo is serving also as a department head in a do-it-yourself shop for sanitation, tiles, and wood. One of his experiences in this field is described above.

A very traumatic time of his life occurred during the period when his parents, in their early fifties, died two years apart. His mother succumbed to a tumor. Then, his father, a victim of muscular dystrophy, died from liver failure. His four grandparents are still living, being in their eighties and in good health. Timo is unmarried and is living in the apartment where his parents had lived for thirty years. Timo's brother lives in a nearby town.

Horseback riding, flags, and computers comprise his hobby activities. Because of his knowledge of flags, I have asked him to tell about the history of the flags of his homeland and of one other country. Do you know as much about the history of the flag of your country as Timo does of his?

History of the German National Flag ... *(© Timo Cernohorsky)*

After the overthrow of Napoleon, Germany consisted of many single states. From 1815 until 1866, a state called Germany did not exist. In 1866, the so-called "Norddeutsche Bund" was founded, comprising most of the German states. This union accepted the national flag with the colours black, white, and red. Black and white are the colours of Prussia; white and red, the colours of the Hanseatic cities. This flag continued to be national flag during the German Empire until 1918.

In 1918, the so-called *Weimarer Republik* (Weimar Republic) was proclaimed, and a new national flag was accepted. It had horizontal stripes in black, red, and golden. The colours refer to an old flag which was black and red with a golden seam. This flag was the national flag until 1933.

In 1933, the *Dritte Reich* (Third Reich) was founded with Adolf Hitler as *Reichskanzler* or Chancellor. The "new" national flag was the old one of the German Empire. This flag was the national flag until 1935.

Additional to the empire flag, there was another national flag from 1933: the *Hakenkreuz-Flagge* (Swastika flag), consisting of the same black, white, and red colours of the empire flag. From 1933 until the end of World War II in 1945, this was the German national flag.

After 1945, there was no national flag, as there was no Germany. The country was divided into West Germany and East Germany. East Germany and West Germany accepted this flag (black, red, golden) as their national flag. From 1949 until 1959, the two German states had the same national flag,

In 1959, East Germany changed its national flag by adding the coat-of-arms. From 1959 until 1990, this was the national flag of the German Democratic Republic (East Germany). In 1990, after the overthrow of the socialist regime, East Germany accepted again the "old" national flag - black, red, golden, without arms. This flag existed only for months, because of the unification which took place in the same year.

West-Germany accepted the flag of the *Weimarer Republik* as their national flag in 1949. It remained unchanged after the unification in 1990.

History of the National Flag of South Africa ... © *Timo Cernohorsky*

In 1910, four British colonies (Cape Colony, Transvaal, Orange Free State, and Natal) merged to form the Union of South Africa. Therefore, a national flag was needed. The British red ensign was chosen, with the coat-of-arms of the four former colonies. From 1910 until 1912, this was the national flag.

In 1912, the national flag changed lightly – a white disc was added. From 1912 until 1928, this was the national flag of South Africa.

In 1928, a new national flag was accepted. It had horizontal stripes in orange-white-blue, with three little flags in the white stripe. It is the old flag of Holland, which founded the first colonies in South Africa. The three little flags are: the Union Jack, the flag of the Orange Free State vertically, and the flag of Transvaal. From 1928 until 1994, this was the national flag of South Africa. It remained unchanged when South Africa became a republic in 1961.

After the overthrow of the apartheid regime, a new national flag was accepted. Since 1994, this is the national flag of South Africa. The different colours – red, white, blue, green, yellow, black – stand for the different peoples in South Africa.

One day I received an email from Timo telling me that a page about the Holy Roman Empire on our website needed to be updated. I added the information and then I suggested that another page on the Holy Roman Empire may also be incomplete. He did some research and provided the missing information. Now, both pages are up-to-date.

When I need something translated from English to German or from German to English, I call on Timo. He graciously assists. Anything that is on our website in German has been translated by him. I really appreciate his willingness to help in this matter.

34

Márián Zoltán

Debrecen, Hungary

Are you interested in visiting such attractions as religious art, a Bible collection, archaeology, a protected nature conservation area, a university, or a medicinal and bath centre? If so, the place to go is Debrecen, a city of county rank in Hungary. With a population of over 205,000, it is the second largest city in the country. It is also the centre of the region, the scientific and cultural centre of the eastern part of the country, and a festival city. In the town centre, the main square has been converted into a large promenade with friendly terraces and the biggest ceramic fountain in Europe, with a Mediterranean atmosphere.

During its history, it was the capital of Hungary twice - in 1849 and in 1945. In its main square, Kossuth Square, can be seen the symbol of the town, the Calvinist Great Church, where Lajos Kossuth read out the Declaration of Independence on April 14, 1849. From the tower of the church is a beautiful view of the city. Behind the Great Church is the Calvinist College, where prominent figures of Hungarian culture studied and have been working continuously since 1538. The Calvinist Theological Academy, the Calvinist Secondary School, the Archives of the Calvinist Church, and the Museum of the History of Education and Religious Art are all housed here.

The museum has rare books which are considered to be unique not only in Europe but also throughout the world. The

Bible collection includes the volumes of the Holy Book in more than 250 languages. Next to the college is the oldest square of the town, the renewed Déri Square, which has become an intimate place in the town with its pleasant splashing water and comfortable benches. The Déri Museum, built between 1926 and 1928, presents rich collections of archaeology, ethnography, culture, local history, and historical relics. The greatest attraction of the museum is the world-famous Munkácsy-Trilogy, which includes Ecce Homo, Christ before Pilate, and the Golgotha. These can be seen in one exhibition hall.

In the most beautiful part of the city, in the Great Forest, the University of Debrecen, founded in 1912, is located. Debrecen offers various high-standard programmes all year round. These include festivals, concerts, and other events, making the life of the city colourful. The programmes attract several hundred visitors to the city every year.

The first protected nature conservation area of Hungary is the 1,082 ha *(2,674 acres)* Great Forest of Debrecen. Within its territory are the Aquaticum Medicinal and Bath Centre with its new indoor Mediterranean Pleasure Bath, which opened in 2003; the Fun Fair; and the Zoo. There have been, in recent years, several developments in the civic city. These include the multi-functional coliseum seating 8,000 spectators, where national and international sports events are held one after the other. The seating area of 1,150 persons was opened in February 2006. The largest conference centre of eastern Hungary also includes a four-star hotel with 100 rooms and the Museum of Modern Arts. In the autumn of 2006, an indoor swimming pool was built.

This is the city where Márián Zoltán (here surnames

precede given names, as opposed to the custom in North America) and his family live. Zoltán is the head of the Public Prosecutor Office (since 1989) and a lecturer at the University of Debrecen (since 1997). He has been in the Prosecutor Office since 1973. His wife, Mária Molnár, Doctor of Jurisprudence, is also a prosecutor. Zoltán and Mária have two daughters. Dorina is an English-Spanish teacher and a journalist. Agnes is a candidate for prosecutor.

Zoltán was born in Csenger, Hungary. Following elementary and secondary school, he attended Jószef Attila University, in Szeged, Hungary, between 1968 and 1973, where he earned a Master of Science degree in law science. Between 1973 and 1975, he took post-graduate work in judicial-prosecution and obtained a special degree. In 1977, he wrote the state language examination in English. This was followed in 2002 with the writing of the one in Russian. He holds a Doctor of Jurisprudence degree.

In 1965, as a grammar school student, Zoltán lived in a student hostel with about one hundred other young boys. Their hostel was a very strict one, similar to an army camp. In the afternoons, they had only one hour for resting. The hostel had an old record player and only two Hungarian bakelite records! The boys listened to these two records every afternoon.

His grandmother's sister had left Hungary sometime in the 1930s and, until her death, she lived in Windsor, Ontario, Canada. She returned to Hungary only once, and Zoltán met her then. As a present, his aunt brought him a mini-record of the Rolling Stones "Paint it Black". At that time, Hungary was a communist country behind the Iron Curtain. No "western beat" music was available. It was a great matter that he had a Rolling Stones record.

By that time, he had received a letter from the Grand Duke of Luxembourg, who had sent it to Zoltán's address in the hostel. This included his signed photo and also a lovely present in the envelope. It was a record, the Eurovision Grand Prix song by France Gall, "Wax Doll". Now, he had two very famous and well known "western" songs on record! In the hostel, he gave his two records to the teacher, who played them every afternoon - many times! The happy owner became so popular among the boys because he was the only one who had any record from the West! Every day, they were waiting for the afternoon in order to play the records.

During the Hungarian Revolution in 1956, his father's cousin - Ferenc Márián - left the country for England. He married an English girl named Grace. They had two children. Grace had a sister named Mary. In 1965, the Hungarian officials allowed Ferenc and his family to visit home for the first time. However, Mary, her husband Alex, and their two children also came to Hungary. It was Mary's first trip to Zoltán's home, and it was the beginning of a very long friendship between her family and his.

At that time, he was living in his birth-place village, Csenger, with his parents. As a young teenager, he was interested in people coming from the West! He had recently begun studying English in school. It was a useful experience for him to talk with native English people. When they returned home, he commenced to correspond with Mary.

Two years later, Mary and her family visited again and spent their holiday with his family. The following year, they sent an invitation letter for him to go to England and spend his school holiday with them. In 1960, the Hungarian Communist System did not let its citizens - except for old persons - visit western countries. His request for a passport was refused. How disappointed he was! Thereafter, their English friends visited every second year.

Finally in 1972, he obtained his passport and permission to travel to England. Everybody was wondering how this young boy was able to receive the passport! (Zoltán's father knew somebody who helped in this matter.) With great excitement, he set out by train on his first visit to the West! It was a very pleasant, long journey in which he traveled through Austria, West Germany, and Belgium. On the boat crossing the English Channel, he met a lady from Peru and had a long conversation. Later, they became pen pals.

Mary and her family were waiting for him in London's Victoria Station. During his two months in England, Zoltán was able to practise the language and to visit many famous places - Wales, London, Coventry, Birmingham, Blenheim, Oxford, Cambridge, Warwick, Stratford, among others. He even saw the Queen! This holiday was a wonderful experience for him and an important point in his life!

The next year, he and Mária Molnár were married. Mary and her family visited Hungary again as guests at the wedding. During the past forty years, he has welcomed her more than twenty times!

Zoltán, his mother, his wife, and daughter Dorina also paid several visits to Mary's home. During the hard political years, it was a special event for them to visit a capitalist country and to see the great difference between life in Hungary and in England. It made an important impression for them. The long correspondence and the frequent visits meant great help to develop their English language knowledge as well. This connection has also determined Dorina's studies to become an English teacher.

Mary and Zoltán had become very good friends. She often remembers their first visit in 1965 when Hungarian soldiers with guns were watching their steps at the Austrian-Hungarian border. Zoltán thinks that she followed with attention all the Hungarian political changes from the very strict "Iron Curtain" to the free, democratic Hungary.

In August 2006, daughter Dorina was married. Of course, old friend Mary attended the wedding. Although she was eighty-two years old, she will probably visit her friends in Hungary again. What a wonderful friendship this has been!

Zoltán's duty is the supervision of police investigation of crimes, making bill of indictment and acting as public prosecutor during judicial proceedings. At his office, any crime that is committed by policemen and special crimes committed against policemen are investigated. In 1989-1990, Zoltán was assigned by the Council of Ministers of Hungary to a committee to consider the unlawful judgment against political opponents from 1945 to 1962. The decision at the end of the investigation was that the majority of the cases were unlawful. The recommendation of the committee that rehabilitation of the persons concerned be carried out was approved by the Hungarian Parliament.

In 1996, he represented Hungary on the International Seminar on Organized Crime in Minsk, Belarus, which was arranged by the Council of Europe. His specialized subject was a lecture in English on organized crime in Hungary.

Since 1997, he has been lecturing criminal law at the University of Debrecen's Law faculty and at the high school level. He examines students at the end of each semester.

With the help of his eldest daughter, he has a publication

in the historical magazine *Historia*. It tells the story of a Hungarian-born countess who became the wife of Khedive Abbas Hilmi II of Egypt.

For the benefit of readers interested in the function of the prosecution system in his country, I asked Zoltán for an outline. The organizational structure of the Prosecution Service of the Republic of Hungary is as follows:

a) Office of the Prosecutor General of the Republic;
b) Regional Chief Prosecution Offices;
c) County Chief Prosecution Offices and the Metropolitan Chief Prosecution Office;
d) Local prosecution offices (district offices in Budapest, town offices in the counties);
e) Military Chief Prosecution Office;
f) Regional Military Prosecution Office;
g) Territorial military prosecution offices.

In many aspects, the Office of the Prosecutor General functions as a central public administrative organ. It has the right to initiate the issue of laws or regulations, the right to form opinion about pieces of draft legislation, and the right to issue inner decrees. However, the activities of the Office of the Prosecutor General in the fields of criminal, civil, and administrative law are more characteristic features of its work.

In the course of its activities, the Office of the Prosecutor General:

- investigates cases specified by law (cases belonging to the exclusive investigative competence of the Prosecution Service);
- exercises supervision of legality over the investigations of criminal cases (supervision of the legality of investigations);

- exercises other rights specified by law relating to the investigation;
- as the representative of state power, exercises the right to indict, and represents the prosecution in court proceedings;
- exercises the right to legal remedies stipulated by the Code on Criminal Procedure;
- exercises supervision of the legality of execution of punishments and corrective measures, and takes part in judicial procedures related to the execution of punishments (supervision of the legality of the execution of punishments);
- contributes to the correct application of laws in the course of court procedures (participation of the prosecutor in contentious or non-contentious court procedures of civil, labour, and administrative law or law of economy);
- contributes to the observance of the provisions of laws by state organs, law enforcement organs other than courts, all organizations of the society, as well as citizens (prosecutorial supervision of legality);
- fulfills its tasks arising from international treaties, especially when it provides and requests legal assistance.

The duties of the Prosecution Service can be divided into two main groups. On the one hand, they involve the tasks related to the criminal justice. This is by far the greatest part. In this domain, the Prosecution Service enforces the punitive power of the state. The prosecutor investigates cases specified by law, exercises supervision over the legality investigations, represents the prosecution in court proceedings, and exercises supervision of legality of the execution of punishments.

The other group of the prosecutor's tasks is very

divergent. This means all the duties accomplished by the prosecutor in the fields of civil law, administrative law, labour law, or the law of economy. In the course of his civil law activities, the prosecutor shall initiate contentious or non-contentious legal proceedings in cases provided by law. In his civil law activity, the prosecutor pays special attention to the initiation of legal actions for the prohibition of pollution, for the compensation of damages caused by pollution, for the restoration of the lawful functioning of foundations and associations, and for the winding-up of non-functioning organizations.

I also asked Zoltán to tell a little about the University of Debrecen, where he is a lecturer. The University of Debrecen, like other integrated institutions of higher education in the country, was formed on January 1, 2000, by reuniting formerly independent institutions. Its historical roots reach back to the foundation of the Reformed College of Debrecen (1538), whose three academic sections later served as the base for the Hungarian Royal University of Sciences, created by Statute Number 36 in 1912. With this past of more than 450 years, the University of Debrecen is the oldest institution of higher education in continuous operation in Hungary based in the same city. Higher education in agriculture began in 1868, when the National Higher School of Agriculture was formed in Debrecen.

In 2006, the University of Debrecen had a student body of 26,000, out of which 16,000 were full-time students. More than 1,700 instructors teach at the University, making it one of the largest higher education institutions in Hungary. Its thirteen faculties, including law, two independent institutions, and twenty doctoral schools undoubtedly offer the widest choice of majors and other forms of training.

The quality of teaching, and especially research, is indicated by the fact that more than half of the instructors have academic degrees, and twenty-three professors are members of the Hungarian Academy of Sciences.

Zoltán has time for personal interests beyond his work. A hobby which began in the early 1960s, when he was a young teenager, has given him much satisfaction. At that time, he received an autographed photograph of President Archbishop Makarios of Cyprus. Today, he has about 1,200 original signed autographs of royalty, presidents, prime ministers, and other dignitaries from around the world. When it is difficult to obtain specific photographs, he will work through embassies. Sometimes, it has taken much persistence as in the case with Alexander Dubcek of Czechoslovakia - even when he was warned not to keep asking. He eventually received a personal letter from Mr. Dubcek.

Among royalty from whom he has obtained original signatures on photographs are the following: Emperor Hirohito, Queen Elizabeth II and Prince Philip, Prince Charles and Princess Diana, Queens Margaret II, Beatrice, and Juliana, Emperor Haile Selassie, Kings Baudouin and Albert II, King Juan Carlos, King Olav IV, Kings Hassan II and Mohammed VI, King Hussein, King Faisal, King Simeon II, Grand Duchess Charlotte, and Shah Reza Pahlavi.

Presidents of United States include Harry Truman, Dwight Eisenhower, Jimmy Carter, George Bush, and Bill Clinton. Prime ministers and other presidents include Tony Blair, Harold Macmillan, Margaret Thatcher, General Charles DeGaulle, Chancellor Konrad Adenauer, Pierre Trudeau, Robert Menzies, Presidents François Mitterrand and Jacques

Chirac, Aldo Moro, Indira and Rajiv Gandhi, Deng Xiaoping, Fidel Castro, Leonid Brezhnev, Juan Peron, Salvador Allende, Colonel Kadhafi, Ahmed Ben Bella, Jean-Claude "Baby Doc" Duvalier, Kim II Sung, and Nicolai Ceausescu.

Other people include Pope Jean Paul II, Pope Benedict XVI, and Mother Theresa.

An exhibition of his collection, opened by the former President of Hungary, was held from June 2, 2006, to June 4, 2006, at the Grand Hotel Aranybika, in Debrecen.

I met Zoltán through an email inquiry in which he asked if I knew how to contact a lady with an Egyptian royal background. Regrettably, I could not help him. However, we kept in contact from time to time. His hobby is interesting to me. I have appreciated his friendship since the beginning a few years ago.

Afterword

Thank you for reading this book. I hope that you have found it both interesting and informative. This is the first in a series of books on stories of experiences by adults and stories by school children. If you would like to suggest ideas or contacts with unusual stories for these upcoming books, you can reach me via the **Contact Us** page on our website http://www.innvista.com/. All of my books will be listed on the website.

Printed in the United States
147699LV00001B/25/P

9 780981 078458